ADVANCE PRAISE FOR *BANKRUPTCY • A LOVE STORY*

"In her beautifully written debut memoir, Janet Lombardi captivates us with her personal triumph over deceit and financial infidelity. Lombardi truly gives meaning to perseverance in the face of adversity. This is one book that will leave you feeling inspired and able to overcome whatever life throws at you."
—Lori Bizzoco, Executive Editor of CupidsPulse.com

"Set between the terrorist attacks on 9/11 and the collapse of the mortgage market seven years later, *Bankruptcy: A Love Story* tells the harrowing, true story of a marriage careening between devotion and desperation. Offering an intimate view of the corrosive effects of addiction and codependence, Lombardi's memoir is more than the saga of one woman's stunning descent into financial and emotional ruin. It's a story of discovering that the one true love is love of yourself."
—Desiree Cooper, author, *Know the Mother*

"A fast-paced story about love, sexual identity and the power of money. *Bankruptcy: A Love Story* tells the tale of how our lives careen around unexpected corners and the courage it takes to go along for the ride. You won't want to put it down."
—Carole Zimmer, award-winning journalist and host of the podcast "Now What?"

"What happens when you learn your great love has betrayed you, that the life you've created together is half-built on lies? Janet Lombardi's fierce, perfectly timed memoir about learning to live anew as the illusion of the American Dream dissolves from within will leave you shaken, aware, and enlightened. Bringing her journalist's eye for details and a keen sense of story, Lombardi offers a guide to survival after losing everything, and an empathetic mirror for anyone who has been broken by a devastating secret."
—Liza Monroy, author, *The Marriage Act* ~~d ~~~~~ ~~~ *Your Shoes Are Soon To Be On Fire*

BANKRUPTCY

A Love Story

To Anna and Joe, with love and affection

ACKNOWLEDGMENTS

"Writing is like driving at night in the fog. You can only see as far as your headlight, but you can make the whole trip that way." E.L. Doctorow

So many good people helped me drive in the fog at night. And I am so grateful.

Thank you to Heliotrope Books and Naomi Rosenblatt for believing in this book and making it come to life. It could never have arrived without your enthusiasm and support.

Thank you to the Ragdale Foundation for supporting me in my writing with four artist residencies so I could work uninterrupted for weeks in a magical setting. Special thank you to Jack Danch for your friendship and always making it comfortable.

Miles of gratitude and affection to my "writerlies" Lisa Freedman and Jennifer Wortham for your patience at hearing every word and endless hours of side-by-side writing. Your advice to "go deeper" held itself in good stead as I took the dive to unchartered emotional territory. Couldn't have done it without you both holding the net!

Thanks to Susan Shapiro, mentor and guru, for introducing me to Heliotrope Books and for your generous support. Thank you too to my developmental editor Elaine Silver, copyeditor Michael Bottomley, and writing instructor Andrew Craft. Appreciation to my publicists Sandra Poirier Smith and Mallory Campoli of Smith Publicity. And sincere thanks to my lawyer Sheila Levine for your truthworthy guidance.

Gratitude to my astute editorial advisory group: Lori Vadala Bizzoco, Kristen Elde, Julie Murphy, Lynn Obee, Arlene Schindler, Ana Ureña, and Alyssa Zahler. Additional shout-out to Ana Ureña for helping me build a beautiful web site, and to Lynn, Julie, and Alison Granito for first reads. Thanks Jeff Rutzky for the awesome cover design. Appreciate the help of Rochelle Sumner and Amerigo Biscotti for design ideas and input. Thanks so much to Beth Marchello and Kaelin Bohl for photography.

Thank you as well to the women of the International Women's Writing Guild, especially Dixie King, Jan Phillips, Susan Tiberghien, Maureen Murdock, Lynne Barrett, Dorothy Randall Gray, Suzi Banks Baum, and Betty Fanelli who have been super supportive in steering me in my path as a writer. Thanks to my writing comrades who may have listened, read, or given good advice: Wendy Karasin and Gloria Feldt, among others. Special thanks to Heidi Ledet and Marty Schneider for inviting me to stay in your Woodstock home to finish this book!

To my sisters and their spouses/significant others, I love you and heartfelt thanks for always being there: Lucille DiGiacomo, Stan Yoel, and MaryAnn Alessi, and Joe Alessi. Love to my nieces and nephews, too!

I could not have written the book without the support and love of Michael Post, Max Post, and Joel Post for understanding and encouraging the writing of this book. Thanks, too, to Rochelle Sumner. This is our story.

Lastly, thank you to Ray McGahan—you make every day a delight and adventure with your beautiful love.

Beyond our ideas of right-doing and wrong-doing,
there is a field. I'll meet you there.

—Rumi

Her

CHAPTER 1

I scrambled the quarter mile from the train station to the Little League game at Hickey field on a hot September night in 2001. The sun in the west baked the asphalt parking lot and found my back like a bullseye, sticking my silk blouse to my shoulder blades. I'd exchanged the sandals of summer for office pumps and wished I'd had time to go home to change. I was anxious, as always, to get there. Time was not on my side when it came to my sons, Adam, eleven, and Matthew, fourteen, already in middle and high school. I'd soon be handing down Adam's baseball shirt with the local sponsor's name, like McDonough Electric or Greektown restaurant, and wanted to soak up every at-bat.

I waved to Adam in the outfield. He didn't acknowledge me. I scurried to find a place on the metal bleacher near someone I knew and not a clique of women who whispered about their intimate lives and would ignore me. Though I found chattering during a game rude, I was still jealous of their "popular girl" status. I was an outsider, grateful to head off to work every day so I didn't have to care so much about the goings-on in town. At forty-seven, I had a business life, even though I was constantly rushing, remembering, listing, preparing, organizing, attending, and worrying about what my family needed.

As we were leaving the game, one of the coaches, Jim, stopped to chat with Adam and me.

"I'll take this kid on my team anytime," Jim said squeezing Adam's shoulder and flashing a toothy smile.

Adam's eyes shone in gratitude for the sentiment. I knew how much Adam needed to hear about his strengths and I was grateful for Jim's consistent reminder. It was as if Jim was in on some secret we shared about Adam's charm that the rest of the world hadn't noticed.

Adam had been diagnosed five years earlier with ADHD. His teacher recommended we have a neurologist examine him.

"He's got a sweet nature," she said, "but can't sit for long, is distracted by nearly everything, and talks too much. Sometimes he clamps his fingers around his lips to keep from blurting out." She pinched her lips together to show us, then offered me a tissue for my tears.

I wondered how the world would see my beautiful son: would it love his Elvis Presley imitation, his speed and grace on the soccer field, his insightful questions that revealed a crooked curiosity that led us to nickname him "Curious Adam," after the little monkey in the children's book.

Jim's slicked-back hair fell in his eyes; he pushed it back. The slight space in his front teeth gave his face character and his cheekbones lent him a handsome, Irish altar boy look—angelic yet mischievous. I imagined him as a child with freckles and hair black as tar. He had a pretty wife and three kids, including a son on Adam's team.

"Thanks," I said a bit flirtatiously.

"I mean it. Adam here's a natural. Good athlete. He'll go anywhere I put 'im. And he's smart."

We talked as we ambled to the parking lot. Jim lugged a duffel bag of equipment while his son, Sean, and Adam tossed a baseball as they followed.

"So long," we said as we got into our cars, ready to face dinner, homework, showers, and the stalling before bed.

Twenty-four hours later, Jim was dead along with the other 650 Cantor Fitzgerald staff and the over 2,500 victims piled in the pit of the World Trade Center.

✦

By the time my husband Josh arrived at my midtown office at two p.m. on September 11th, most co-workers, except for a small group, had rushed home to their families. I paced the mauve carpeted hallway, walking my anxiety like a thoroughbred, afraid my husband wouldn't make it to me, that the Empire State Building, only three blocks away, would be detonated and debris would choke us, that the railroad would derail, that friends wouldn't make it home that day. Even though I dispatched my best friend and neighbor Amanda to get a message to my boys that we were okay, I felt an urgency to get home.

When Josh stepped through the doorway my body relaxed. Then I noticed a plodding,tentative gait had replaced his usual sturdy pace. Gray soot covered his oxblood loafers and he left ash footprints on the carpeting wherever he stepped. He shouldered his brown leather brief-case with the thick flat strap. It weighed twenty pounds and he wore it messenger-style. He'd had shoulder surgery three months prior, and I was sure he ached as he lumbered up Broadway from lower Manhattan.

The group I was waiting with at the office eyed him eagerly like he'd just returned from the other side of the moon. No one said any-thing. I hugged him with restraint not only because I was surrounded by officemates but because I didn't want to disturb the ash feathering his body. I already regarded him as a living tribute to the event. My lower body gingerly leaned away rather than into him. I didn't want to touch the ash, which felt infected with death and frightening as if its power could harm us in some way, which it later did. I squeezed his hand.

Josh, forty-nine, sported a white Yankees cap, dusted with fine ash, a camel-colored sport jacket and cuffed khaki pants. He was caked in what was later identified as plastics, PVC, office furniture, carpet, Freon, natural gas, jet fuel, metals, asbestos, glass, fiberglass, paper, and other components of the office buildings. He looked sheepish, as if he wanted to apologize.

His sunglasses peeked out of his shirt pocket and the tip of his nose was red from crying. Later I understood that hapless look, but then I didn't know the guilt he felt about saving himself, not going into the towers, coming to my office instead so we could ride home together safely to Long Island.

As the days followed, my husband crumbled like the collapsing towers we'd viewed over and over on TV. We couldn't keep our eyes off the looping image of the fiery airplane angled at the waffle-bottom skyscraper. Debris raining down. People tumbling like injured seagulls, soaring out of windows, their neckties like nooses. We listened to the garbled audio, leaning towards our TV, wanting to put our ears to the screen to hear the voice of our friend Ed, the battalion fire chief. We were hypnotized by TV news, scanning images of shocked parents, wives, husbands, and children. Some, near cordoned-off yellow-taped sidewalks around Ground Zero, hawked photos of their missing loved ones.

September 11th marked the decline of my husband and my retreat from him.

Later that day, Josh told me what had happened. That morning, he did not the take his usual route to his office—riding the train into the World Trade Center subway stop. Instead, he took the subway to downtown Brooklyn to pick up Blumberg law forms. He carried his Gibson guitar in a hard vinyl case. He wanted an instrument at the office to play the handful of songs he knew and that the kids and I teased him about, like Phil Ochs' "I Ain't a Marching Anymore" and Elvis's "Heartbreak Hotel."

I imagined what it would have been like for him taking the A train into the World Trade Center stop. Would he have come up into darkness? Plumes of smoke? Fire? Falling debris as I frantically tried his cell phone only to get his long-winded voicemail message? Would he have struggled for his life that morning like the other thousands of people sipping coffee at their desks before huddling into smoke-trapped conference rooms stuffing suit jackets under the doors?

Instead, after hearing "all circuits are busy," he answered my call on that perfect cloudless morning from his office, one block from the towers. Relief flooded me and after that I was afraid to hang up even though he insisted "I'll call you right back. Stop, I'll call you."

He told me that once he got into his office, the building management wouldn't let anyone leave, thinking it was too unsafe. His office was in an old building with crusted thickly painted window panes that shakily slid up and down. He described what he saw from the window: people jumping out of the window as billows of white smoke and office papers danced in a devilish whirl. From the windowsill, he scooped ash into a jar that he kept on his dresser, until we were forced to sell our home some years later from the financial wildfire whose flames were set that very day. He said, at times, the smoke grew too thick to see anything, then it would clear for a moment and he could stick his head out the window and glimpse the building engulfed. When he opened the window he heard a din of voices and sirens screaming. He kept hanging up and calling me back.

"That tower's gonna fall, I tell ya," he said, panic in his voice.

The prospect of the tower falling was an outlying thought. I was more concerned about having access to his voice, his breathing. I heard the righteous certainty in his voice, despite the fear, and sensed he was telling me this because he wanted to predict something accurately, he wanted to be right. He always wanted—needed—to be right. Little did I know he was terrified about which way the building would fall and if it would be in his direction.

When the South Tower fell, Josh had already moved to another floor to wait it out with Ted Zip, a computer specialist who had once given him a camera wristwatch as a gift. The tower didn't collapse as he expected, but imploded and as each floor folded into itself—all 108 stories—he heard mini explosions until the final avalanche of white smoke crawled down John Street like a tsunami. He closed the window and the blinds, raced under the desk, locked his knuckles around his head and froze like a little boy in a 1950s air raid exercise.

CHAPTER 2

I grew up in the Gravesend section of Brooklyn in a tidy two-family Italian-American home with my parents and two older sisters, Laura and Christine. My Aunt Martha, Uncle Tony, and three older girl cousins lived in the apartment upstairs. We shared holidays together, called a dish towel the *moppine*, had "gravy" and macaroni every Sunday, and watched our mothers bite their clenched fists as a warning before they were about to blow their tops. On occasions when the families were gathered, we ended the night around the kitchen table singing Neapolitan love songs, like Oh Marie, my father strumming guitar while Uncle Tony played the harmonica. As the youngest, I was the mascot, the pet, and loved to soak up everyone's attention. They called me the baby until I was twenty-one.

My oatmeal complexion, framed by Asian-black hair and a sprinkle of freckles across my nose, gave me a sickly pallor, one that begged to be rescued, though I was 100 percent healthy. To make matters worse my pale eyelids were often crusted over by eczema. It was sometimes so bad that they were shut closed when I woke in the morning. My best friend, Lydia, once drew a sidewalk-chalk picture of me kissing Steven Goldbaum, a neighbor boy who also suffered from eczema. A sparkly, pronounced goldenrod decorated our lids in Lydia's rendering on the pavement in front of her house.

Legend maintains that I took an hour to finish half a bologna sandwich on Wonder Bread while I read the bread bag and stared off into space. "One good wind will carry you away," my mother sighed. I stashed a Kleenex in my palm to catch the nasal drip, the result of frequent head colds that earned me "most frequently absent from school." And the lack of "meat on my bones," as my mother delicately called it, coupled with my shyness and fragility made me the recipient of constant coddling from my whole family. Were my personality just a bit different, this unconditional love might have produced the next Nobel Peace prize winner, but it did not feed my confidence. I took the other route. I craved the attention and support of an aging Hollywood starlet.

Once, when I was about eight, I twisted my ankle playing Jingle Jump, a hot toy at the time: a plastic skipping rope, with a bell-shaped ball that jingled on one end and a ring that attached to your ankle on the other end. You'd get the ball rotating with one ankle and as you got momentum, you'd jump with the other foot over the rope as it rotated around your ankle. No one counted my Jingle Jump exercise as a strength-builder. But I was good at it. I Jingle-Jumped up and down the sidewalk, skipping in front of our house, for hours.

The twisted ankle wasn't serious. It hurt just enough. So I dug out a roll of white Red Cross gauze from underneath the bathroom sink, wrapped it sloppily around my ankle, and limped around until someone noticed ("Oh, poor baby!"), grabbed me a pillow, and insisted I put my foot up.

The following year, at nine, I ached for a dog, but my parents wouldn't budge. "You can't even take care of yourself!" they said. So I hounded my sister's cute boyfriend, who believed every child should have a puppy, to lobby on my behalf. He won my parents over. We adopted Sam, a white-pawed pooch we had for fifteen years. I learned a lesson: rely on others to get what I need.

The overprotection from my family didn't lessen as I grew. "Don't go off the block," my mother directed me. As an obedient child, I took her warnings seriously. *There must be something dangerous beyond East 9th Street. Surely something I can't handle.*

So as a teen, I spent countless summer afternoons lounging on our plastic-covered couch beneath the velvet portraits of Jesus, studying *Cue*, the *Time Out* of the '60s, memorizing the names of French restaurants like *LeGrenouille*, so I could be ready for the call. I longed to be a refreshed Holly Go-Lightly and simply couldn't wait to sport a cigarette holder, peel off elbow-high white gloves, and bug-a-loo at a house party in a Greenwich Village walk-up. There I'd meet painters, writers, musicians, and other assorted bohemians.

I wanted to go to Woodstock but I knew my parents weren't letting me anywhere near Yasker's Farm. The news photos I saw of hippie girls with bandana headbands, painted flowers on their faces, and bare midriffs mesmerized me. I liked looking at the girls.

I'd read about art galleries in *Cue* even though neither of my hard-working parents had ever set foot inside a museum. How could they? My mother toiled nights at a Turkish Taffy candy factory in Coney Island picking and packing until her fingers ached. My dad worked long hours as a procurement officer in a dependable government job at the Brooklyn Navy yard. He napped until midnight then drove our Buick LeSabre to pick up my mother. I went with him a few times in the summer and the klieg lights from nearby Coney Island and Luna Park gave the industrial area a late-night party glow. When my mother climbed in, the scent of caramelized sugar that clung to her pores filled the car.

The Daily News, complete with the *Jumble* and *Dennis the Menace* comic strip, was our family's newspaper. By fourth grade I'd noticed my classmates' current events clippings came from *The New York Times*. The layout of the columns and smaller font suggested this was a more serious newspaper, and I thought I should learn about it.

I joined the Columbia Record Club so I could order original cast albums of Broadway shows I would one day see. Finally, I did take myself to my first show, the musical *Hair*, complete with full frontal nudity—the very thing my parents were shielding me from. My three friends and I purchased tickets at the box office giggling and lying to our folks that we were seeing *My Side of the Mountain*, a kid versus nature flick.

As I approached college, and felt the urge to get out on my own, my sister Christine dutifully reminded me, "You leave this house in a veil or a coffin." We were well aware of this Brooklyn, Italian marriage manifesto. We learned it as girls, first from our dad's Uncle Alphonso, off the boat from Southern Italy, who pinched our cheeks till they hurt, and asked, "So when you gonna getta married?" as his wife, our rotund, toothless Aunt Jennie, stood by in her cobbler apron stirring the pot of tomato sauce.

By the time I was a student at Brooklyn College, the pear-shaped engagement ring—the "rock," as we called it—was as sought after as the bachelor's degree. I succumbed and married young, even taking a leave of absence from college to save up for the wedding. It was held in a Bay Ridge hall with a light-up dance floor. But the marriage was brief and disappointing. I had grabbed it to escape my parent's 1960's version of helicopter parenting and flee the familiar Brooklyn streets—the modest one-family attached homes, Virgin Marys in clamshells, and the Manhattan-fearing, provincial attitudes.

The East River spanned less than two miles between the boroughs, but it might as well have been 2,000 because I never heard of anyone from my Gravesend neighborhood ever moving into "the city." No one swapped my zip code for a tonier Manhattan address. But I longed to venture and sample the grittiness of New York City, the unpredictability, the two a.m. last calls, the weirdoes. Nothing reckless, just a move to catapult me out of the cocoon into a Bright Lights, Big City adventure in a place shimmering with its own pulsing creativity. I was ready to pole vault into my real life. I just needed a guide.

✦

It was 1979. I was sitting at my desk at my job at the legal publisher. My boss's office was three feet away. She was the editor-in-chief, an earnest, single, middle-aged woman with a heaving laugh. She discussed case law, passionately, with her male colleagues who congregated outside her door. The cloying sweetness of English Leather cologne floated in the air.

This was my career path to publishing. I had jumper-cable hair, having had my strands permed into a collection of frizz, and wore a navy suit, pumps, and floppy paisley necktie, my best dress-for-success outfit. I couldn't help notice, in the group, a young not-yet-admitted lawyer, Josh, often part of this cohort of suits. He was the only one wearing jeans, the latest Jordache. He sported a close-cropped, carrot-colored beard and dome of blond hair, arranged on his head, like that of St. Anthony. He directed a joke to me every time he passed my desk.

"And *that* goes for you too," Josh quipped, like Groucho with an ash-flicking hand motion, turning to me full body, away from the suits. I had no idea what "that" meant as my fingers flew across the keyboard of my IBM Selectric, typing citations, and ignoring the swirl of conversation. I smiled politely wondering when he was going to leave me alone.

✦

I hadn't seen Josh around the office for a few days. I wondered if he was sick or left the company or moved to another floor. I was surprised at how much I missed his flirty comments.

"Mark Josh out on personal leave," Josh's boss, Frank, told me, since I was in charge of time sheets.

"He's studying for the bar," he explained.

I nodded.

"He's a crackerjack, you know."

I nodded again.

"Gonna make a great attorney."

The world of attorneys, the law, people dashing to court, talking about statutes and case law, and districts, circuits, judges, and the New York Law Journal didn't spin in my orbit. Anything I knew about law I learned from TV dramas like Barnaby Jones and Perry Mason, where in the final scene the murderer breaks down and confesses after the lawyer corners him. I came from a world of butchers, construction workers, and secretaries. But now I felt smug, rising over my parents' lifestyle, gaining a level of sophistication unknown to them.

Josh returned the following week, bar exam behind him. I saw him by the cubicle of our copy editor, Maya. She was a few years my senior and another smart, quick-witted know-it-all who had been promoted from my position. Josh wore a black leather vest and Tony Lamas. He twirled a gold Cross pen, telling Maya he was going to write her up for talking to him.

"Unauthorized use of time," he said. Maya giggled.

"How was the bar exam?" I asked, strolling over.

"Think I did all right. If not I'll take it again. It'll work out." It was the most serious I'd seen him and looking beyond the swagger I saw warm, trusting blue eyes.

"Pretty soon, you'll be hanging the shingle. Attorney-at-Law," I said waving my hand like a magic wand.

"Yup. On my way to becoming attorney-outlaw."

Maya laughed. It took me a second to get the joke. I smiled and shook my head.

"Hey, I'm allowed to be corny," he said.

He then pulled a stack of vinyl record albums out of a plastic, J&R Music bag he was carrying. I was impressed. I'd never bought more than one album at a time: "Armed Forces," from Elvis Costello and the Attractions, Lou Reed's "Rock n Roll Animal," the Ramones, "Road to Ruin," and one or two others. He held up the cover of "Armed Forces" with the charging elephants. Sure I had swooned over Peter Frampton and his 'fro but mostly I was listening to Top 40 disco. I had never heard of Elvis Costello or New Wave music so I didn't say anything, just listened…then Maya asked who all these rockers were.

Josh smiled, dimples pushing through the beard. He walked me back to my desk.

"I gotta go out to Long Island and visit my parents this weekend but maybe," he spoke quietly, "if you're free, wanna do dinner Friday night?"

He shifted nervously.

"Sure," I answered, my knee-jerk politeness not letting me consider whether or not I really wanted to.

Friday we rendezvoused at Entre Nous, a stylish black-interiored French restaurant on Third Avenue, where I sampled paté, cornichons, and Pouilly-Fuissés. It wasn't *LeGrenouille* but I was getting warm.

"These are just little pickles," I said, holding the cornichon by its end.

Josh talked easily about himself, his parents —dad a dentist in a house practice and his mom, an artist—and his Uncle Larry, active in city politics, who had made him want to become a lawyer.

"When I didn't get into Colby College, Uncle Larry said, 'FUCK THEM'. So I went to Hobart, in the Finger Lakes, and dropped acid every day."

"You did not!" I gasped, I had never met anyone who'd tried LSD.

"Well maybe not every day. Think I missed a day or two." He paused. "What about you?"

"Never missed a day either…of class!"

He grinned. "A good girl. Well, we'll just have to take care of that."

I blushed, not sure whether his comment was sexual, drug-related, or something I didn't know about. Despite having been married, innocence still clung to me. Especially as I swam in the bigger pond of Manhattan.

He was heading over to the Bells of Hell, a gritty bar on West 13th Street, later that night, to hang with his posse—musicians and a bunch of trust fund kids. I was impressed that our date was an appetizer to his evening. He didn't invite me. I felt a bit envious I'd be missing out on the fun.

He held the door for me as we left the restaurant into the muggy summer evening and strolled to the subway.

"Sure you're gonna be all right getting home?"

"It's only eight o'clock," I answered, feeling good from the wine.

Then he took my hand, walked me to the corner, and hailed a cab hand up, pointing in the direction he wanted the taxi to go. An expert cab-getter! He swung open the taxi door and peeled off a twenty from his wad of bills held together by a dollar-sign money clip. I shook my head.

"I really can afford my own cab," I said. But he insisted, and folded the bill into my palm.

As the cab made a left to go west on 33rd Street towards Penn Station, my route home to my sister's house on Long Island where I had been temporarily living since my divorce, he waved and mouthed, "Get home safe."

The next day I bought "Armed Forces" and played "Accidents Will Happen" and the rest of side A until I wore out the grooves. Elvis's snarling, staccato lyrics, cryptic storyline, and wailing keyboard represented an attitude, an explosive punk world that felt sinister, energetic, and permissive. "Yeah, take it!" it screamed.

Many nights during that summer, Josh and I walked downtown straight from the office near Turtle Bay to his apartment on East 23rd, one block from the School of Visual Arts, where I'd hang with him, his dental-school brother, and his freakish friends, like Tom, a handsome, squared-jawed actor and bartender, who'd point to his cheek for a kiss then quickly turn his head planting his lips instead. The "bach pad," as I called it, was decorated fraternity-style: mannequin wearing a hockey helmet, the Wantagh LIRR sign ripped off somehow from the platform, and the backgammon board always open and waiting for a betting partner on the beat-up Con Ed wooden cable-spool coffee table.

Josh didn't stop moving or reciting lines from Firesign Theatre, "Are you sitting in the waiting room or waiting in the sitting room?" He was the first to jump up to the stereo to flip the album over, roller-skated on the carpeting, danced like a pogo stick to the Ramones, "I Want to Be Sedated."

Once he shimmied hand over hand on the wooden railing surrounding the loft bed only to fall hard onto the wooden kitchen floor. He got up unhurt, and we watched the bruises spread on the top of his thigh like a Technicolor stain. He was very proud of those spectacular bruises and showed them to anyone who cared to look. I found all Josh's leaping around entertaining. I never knew what he was going to do next.

A few months later, Josh moved into an apartment across the hall, an adorable duplex with a loft-style bedroom over the kitchen. My plan had been to find an affordable Manhattan apartment. But after I staggered home from the oral surgeon one evening, Josh at my side, half-holding me up on the sidewalk and guiding me gently to the comfy pillows and blankets he'd arranged on his sofa, I never left his place. I'd had an allergic reaction to pain medication and as I recuperated the next few days coaxing the analgesics out of my system, Josh waited on me—chicken broth, fluffed up pillows, milkshakes, and not-taking-no-for-an-answer instructions to call on him for everything. He surprised me. For all his tumbling around, he was quite the nurturer.

Our living together didn't sit well with my parents. But I'd been married already and earned the passport to live as I pleased, even if they didn't agree. They came to visit a handful of times. They appreciated Josh's taking care of me.

Josh's parents, Lillian and Mel, on the other hand, although Long Islanders, were frequent Manhattan-goers who loved theatre, the Metropolitan Museum, NY Philharmonic, Sunday brunch dates, and dinners at the Old Homestead, the venerated steakhouse near West 14th Street. They took us out frequently and when the waiter asked if anyone wanted a cocktail, Josh's father waved him away. "No one wants a drink," he would bark. Ignoring that Josh and I were about to order one.

"Jews don't drink," Josh said to me in a muffled voice.

"Really?" my eyebrows raised.

He shook his head, furrowed brow. "It's what my parents like to think."

Josh, who'd grown up on Long Island, came from a tight-knit family. His mom and dad regarded the powers of their first-born son as limitless. They were so confident in his future that they drove seven hours to see him in Geneva NY at the end of college waving a law school application, urging him to fill it out and give the world his gifts. The first time I met Josh's mother, Lil, I joked, asking if she was "responsible" for this young man, a wise-cracking smart-aleck. "I am proud he's my son," she told me, dead-pan, without any humor.

The first time I visited his parents at their home was for Rosh Hashanah dinner, Jewish New Year. I'd never been to a Jewish holiday gathering and didn't know what to expect. When we arrived I saw round tables with beautiful print tablecloths, fresh flowers, and cut crystal goblets. His mother's artist-sculptor's work--Italian *carerra* stone heads, smashed-pottery assemblages, and Henry Moore-inspired wooden figures—blended seamlessly with the stylish décor of custom-designed draperies and Persian rugs. I hesitated walking into the vaulted entryway, trailing Josh. He yelled out a booming "Hello!" and Josh's mother sprang from the kitchen, handing a platter to Elena, the almond-eyed Salvadoran woman who had worked for the family for years. Josh's younger sister, Wendy, a special ed teacher, bounded downstairs from the second level of the split-level home.

Josh's mom tackled him in a bear hug and then reeled me into her arms. "I just love what you're wearing," she gushed taking a step back holding both my hands. "You look so beautiful!"

✦

I was in it, the swirl of big-city activity I'd longed for—New York's combustible punk, rock, and blues music scene coupled with a drug scene that was everywhere. My model employee-by-day and party-girl-by-night lifestyle was far from unique. The city was a gritty candy store, if you wanted it: after-hours clubs, sex dens for any inclination, and a smorgasbord of the illicit: coke, heroin, and ecstasy, all available and deemed recreationally harmless.

Josh was a hotline to venues like CBGB's, Mudd Club, and Max's Kansas City during the days of its last exhale. He wrangled us into the Mudd Club by slipping the back-door security guard 20 bucks to see the Talking Heads, me standing on a folding chair close to David Byrne as he danced in his inflatable-balloon-man style as the band pumped out "Life During War Time," the chart-topper that immortalized the very downtown club. We even saw the Plasmastics, a notoriously loud, chain-saw-wielding band.

We regularly dropped by CBGB's and caught Richard Hell, one of our favorite punksters, and his band, the Voidoids. Standing at the back of the club in the dark, sweaty atmosphere, Josh standing behind me, arms around my waist, music too loud for humans, watching the parade of skin heads and hollowed-out downtowners, I was enthralled with my life and in love with Josh who, the day after we made love for the first time, called to tell me how much he had enjoyed being with me. I felt cherished. This man was a keeper.

Josh's friends became my friends—rockers, aspiring songwriters, actresses, costume designers, playwrights, photographers, models, and real estate investors who made a killing buying and flipping apartments.

They invited us to countless parties and events, including Doc Po-
mus's birthday party, Billy Idol's dinner table, and, a few years later the
hotel room of Earl Slick, David Bowie's guitarist, during Bowie's Serious Moonlight concert tour in Philadelphia. To get to that concert,
we hopped Amtrak to Philadelphia at eight-thirty p.m., landed in our
fourth row seats in time to hear Bowie perform "Let's Dance," wound
our way to Slickie's (Earl Slick's) hotel room, and got back to New
York City at five-thirty a.m., enough time to shower and get to work
on time.

We were friends with Kelly LeBrock, the Vogue cover girl and ac-
tress from the movies *Weird Science* and *Lady in Red*. I mock-interviewed
her one night as we sat on the couch at our apartment, pretending I was
Merv Griffin, to help her get ready for her appearance on his talk show.

On Friday nights, after the workweek, and after Josh had begun
his own practice and I moved to another company, I would fire up
the Osterizer for blender drinks. Around nine or so, Josh would pull
down the combination-locked attaché case from the back of the closet,
fingering the pop-up fasteners. Click! Click! The pharmacy was open.
The briefcase was filled with an assortment of illicit choices—from
black beauties to cocaine to weed. Sometimes Josh would hold up the
assorted contents for examination, as in a game for our drug-knowl-
edgeable friends.

"What's this? Is it a pickle?" he asked displaying a small green gel
capsule. Then he held up another.

"What's this?" A Sabrett?," he asked, fingering the small hot-dog
shaped pill.

Confirmation came after Josh thumbed through the PDR (*Physi-
cian's Desk Reference*) always at hand on the coffee table. Where or how
he collected such an assortment of pharmacopeia I had no idea. I felt
immune to this Whitman's sampler, rarely looked inside the suitcase,
and if I did it was to marvel at the idea of anyone having such a collection. I never asked for the combination to the lock and only knew that
the lawyerly briefcase had been a gift from his uncle. I was fascinated
but never hooked by the supply; I was lucky to have a non-addictive
personality. Because our lifestyle was so attached to the New York City

music scene, I never thought about feeling afraid or spooked by the amount of drugs people around me were doing. It was simply what everyone did. Plus, I was always in good hands: Josh was our circle's ring leader, in charge, letting our crowd know it was time to head downtown to the club, get to the movie on time, get some air, or go home. My chicken-soup provider took care of us all. This was before the crack epidemic, when the harmful effects of drug use became frighteningly real. The early 1980s were still an age when we hailed the Holy Trinity of sex, drugs, and rock and roll—and didn't think anything could harm us. We enjoyed a "live for today" attitude, and felt invincible. Plus, it was God-awful fun.

While Josh embraced his drugs, I sought after something else that was all mine. Maybe I needed to claim something of my own since Josh was such a strong personality. Maybe it was the allure of something loose and experimental. Or most likely, it was a need to tap into a deeply rooted attraction to women I had always had but kept muzzled. I didn't want to embrace this third option, however, since the prospect of being gay scared me. At thirteen, having had a crush on Alice, a female counselor at CYO (Catholic Youth Organization) day camp, I looked up same-sex attractions in the library and learned they were normal for pubescent girls so I let go of the worry that I could be "one of those." But in the swirl of unexpurgated fun and a daring, pre-AIDS climate, the butterflies in the belly excitement I'd had around that girlhood crush were resurrected into a longing to sleep with a woman. I shared my feelings with Josh, who was delighted and encouraged me. "Just don't fall in love!" he said.

The quest for the right woman became something we shared, even though he knew my desire to sample this venture on my own—without him in the bed. We even told our best friends, who lived around the corner, and soon they were scouting women for me, too. At first, it seemed like a light-hearted romp, a purely sexual seeking but then, even before I'd touched a woman, a yearning set in for a deep female connection, something that puzzled me because I loved Josh so completely.

One night, a group of us were having dinner at Kitty Hawk, a sprawling restaurant with a replica of the Wright Brothers plane dangling from the ceiling when I met Ellie, a twenty-five-year-old waitress from Daytona Beach with auburn hair, a dimpled chin, and a square gymnast body, who'd been cruising the New York City lipstick lesbian scene. Ellie bantered with us as she took our orders—lots of drinks and barbecued ribs.

"What's your desire, dear Ellie, our trusty waitron?," someone asked.

"It isn't any of you gentlemen," she said, staring at me with an impish grin.

"Oooh," our group intoned.

And by the end of dinner, Ellie and I exchanged numbers.

I was twenty-seven when Ellie dragged me to Van Buren's, a dyke club in the theatre district, one Friday night. I had no idea where to meet women. All I knew was Paula's, a cavernous dive bar on Greenwich Avenue, with a pool table and women with mullets and dangling key chains. I didn't even know that there were secluded lesbian joints like this until Ellie preached, "there's a world out there, girl."

Ellie and I arrived at Van Buren's by cab, skipping down a few steps and rolling into the mirrored, glitzy narrow barroom with the dance floor in the back. When I stepped inside the dim room, I was surrounded by a stable of gorgeous women, not a mullet among them. My mouth must have been open because Ellie looked at me.

"You see?" she nodded.

I'd entered a secret sorority of women—designer-dressed, Farrah Fawcett-hair-attractive, miles of cleavage, heads thrown back laughing, and no one apologizing for anything. And soon women fell easily into my bed.

✦

Josh and I planned to marry and held hands across the table in a high-backed booth at Molly Malone's, an Irish pub, on Third Avenue. I feared that our being from different religions would be a problem with our parents and for the ceremony.

"And what about my, you know, attractions," I said, hesitating, afraid to name it.

"We'll work it out. Everything, my dear, can be worked out," said

Josh, a phrase that always had the power to soothe me. And, he'd been right. At the end of April 1982, Josh and I exchanged wedding vows at the United Nations chapel. The non-denominational ceremony inside the stained glass sanctuary began at 10 a.m. on a daylight savings Sunday, the time change intimidating our party-going friends who feared not showing up on time. As I arrived at the altar, escorted by both my parents, in a lovely, non-traditional touch far removed from my first Italian-American Catholic parish church ceremony, I turned and peered into the rows of guests to see Nicholas, one of our besties, wearing his shades, black t-shirt, and a hung-over- from-last-night-aren't-you-proud-I-made-it grin. I was thrilled to see him!

My husband and I and a few close friends tumbled into a stretch limo to our downtown wedding party at the country and western club, City Limits, on Seventh Avenue in Greenwich Village. I refused to call it a wedding reception! Our friends the Dixie Doughboys, a country swing band à la Bob Wills and San Antonio Rose, got our families and friends up and two-stepping. Our friend Robert Gordon, the rockabilly performer with a slick pompadour and a red hot, gone daddy-o style, stopped by to wish us well.

On our honeymoon, we toured the rolling French countryside munching on baguettes and sipping from a bottle of Armagnac in our red Ford Fiesta. After spying cow after cow in meadows, we created a game in which the first person who could identify a bovine in the distance and yell *vache*, would be the winner. Josh pointed to his face and belly, declaring himself the winner saying he was a *vache* with pimples.

We enjoyed a night at Eugenie Les Bain, the chic spa in the southwest, a wedding gift from our friend Andre who also treated us to dinner at the Michelin three-star restaurant of Michel Guérard, the star chef. Michel even came to our table and invited us into the kitchen where he continued to work and entertain us, brandishing a chef's knife.

The next morning as we lounged in matching plush bathrobes in our French country-style suite filled with the same spring light that inspired Monet's paintings, I scribbled a thank-you postcard to Andre. I was still euphoric from the outpouring of love at our wedding only days before and felt overwhelmed with everyone's love and generosity.

"Gosh, I'm so glad I had fun at my own wedding," I said enjoying the memory of watching our friends and parents' friends swing each other on the dance floor.

"Hmmm," Josh nodded.

"What about you?" I nudged.

"I don't really remember."

I looked at him.

"It was four days ago, darling. How could you not remember?"

He tilted his head and gave me the sniffing signal, pretending to hold a spoon up to his nose. "Wish I could've enjoyed our wedding; it looked like fun," he sighed.

I had no idea he'd emptied one too many vials of coke into his nose that day! His behavior seemed so normal.

"What a shame. You missed a fun party."

I felt momentarily detached from him: *he was too high to enjoy our wedding*. I brushed it off, though, convinced Josh could manage whatever he was using.

But something else did give me pause. The previous summer, Josh and I had rented a cottage at the top of a winding mountain road in Greenwood Lake, a small boating community on the New York/New Jersey border. The carpenter who had owned the house renovated it in the style of an alpine chalet. We went in on the rental with a couple— Sammy, a pot dealer with wire-rimmed eyeglasses and a Bob Dylan look who lived in our building, and Nadia, his girlfriend.

We spent Memorial Day weekend together—us two couples in our Fiorucci jeans—and I had been naïve enough to believe that when they said we were going to play baseball thought they meant the game with mitts, ball, and bat. I found out quickly the first night they meant free-basing or smoking cocaine, the sport that lit the comedian Richard Pryor on fire. When the bulbous pipe with the glass bulb was passed I declined, not liking the jittery way coke made me feel. As I shook my head no, I felt Josh, Sammy, and Nadia's brief disappointment in my not joining in. But they turned back quickly to their huddle of free-basing with the thought, I'm sure, that there would be more for them. My exclusion from the trio set up an uncomfortable dynamic for the rest of the weekend. I was the fifth wheel.

What started out as me being a spectator alternately fascinated by the excitement and shadow of danger, however, turned to disgust as I found the threesome's behavior focused solely and desperately on two things: that bowl of coke and the mini blow torch—a sneering side-kick that seemed very much part of the experience. I kept walking out onto the screened-in porch to get away from them and fume at Josh for putting me in this position. I couldn't see the end of that weekend fast enough. Over that summer, I'd see Josh late at night by our kitch-en stove lighting the pipe, bubbling the water and inhaling deeply. He gazed at the pipe longingly when it left his lips. I insisted he throw the pipe away and after minor protest he tossed it down the incinerator. I never saw any sign of it again.

CHAPTER 3

Down to ground zero
with a rust colored rose
trying hard to close
that door
what have I opened
what have I done
that I'm not the one
it's for.

      —Jack Hardy, singer-songwriter
          whose brother Jeff died on September 11th

We kept vigil on our friends who never made it home from work that day. There should be someone to call, a central phone number, a source of information, an agency, a shaman, an elder. But instead information about our friends Ed, Jim, Andrew, and others filtered home through people we knew.

Within a week, Josh, the boys, and I were bringing pastry to our friends' homes where the husbands and fathers were missing. We paid our respects, yet there were no bodies, no death certificates, just the brooding knowledge that each passing day lowered the lid on their coffins. The slow, arduous days filled with a mixture of expectance and a bankruptcy of hope crept over the streets of our town. The "death" houses grew in number and the trees along the avenues sang a sick wail punctuated by the merciless toll of the carillon at St. Agnes Cathedral signaling one more funeral.

When we approached Coach Jim's house, his wife Mary was sitting in the front of their Tudor home in a lawn chair shaking hands, and occasionally smiling with vacant eyes. One night, our sons and their friends gathered around our oak dining room table to make sandwiches for rescue workers: a sandwich, a drink, a fruit, a napkin. Soon we joined services at packed churches and synagogues. Some memorials and masses were held quickly after September 11 and others stretched into weeks, even months later, depending on how steadfastly the family clung to hope.

Josh couldn't go back to the office for two weeks, the streets around Broadway and Ground Zero, as the site was now called, restricted by blue police Do Not Cross barricades. Josh and my older son Matthew took the train one afternoon because they wanted to pick up the Gibson guitar but couldn't pass through the streets. At home, Josh wandered the house without purpose, saying he couldn't focus. He'd lost the energy that seemed connected to his DNA. At night, he sweated through t-shirts, cried, and shook. He stopped watching TV coverage about 9/11 and isolated himself in the bathroom, on and off for hours.

When he returned to the office, he complained of the stench of burning, the unremitting clang of rescue workers extracting metal, the dust, the air, the tourists, the t-shirts. He missed Shah's newspaper kiosk and the friendly server at the bagel store, now deserted. He told me about the woman's shoe store whose front-window display was covered in a layer of ash, as if a volcano had swept and receded. Workers' papers still swirled around lower Broadway, though no more than the heartache that passed from person to person.

In those days following September 11th, I scouted the Long Island Railroad platform for familiar faces, always afraid that if I hadn't seen someone he or she was probably dead. If I did see a friend, even an acquaintance, we instinctively hugged hard, glad we were both still living. One night, I embraced Frank Leo, standing in the well of the train doorway as it pulled into the station. The dad of a casual friend of Adam's, he was someone I would normally greet with a nod whenever I saw him walking his dog near our house. That day on the train, he bear hugged me. One morning, I left a bouquet of flowers at the glass and metal train station door for those who never got to return home on the five-twenty-seven.

CHAPTER 4

Six years before 9/11, in 1995, we were in a conference room buying our first house.

"Now here's a deal breaker," said Gary in his characteristic sardonic tone. "Did you leave the radiator covers? We're talking high stakes here."

Gary, our attorney and friend from the legal publisher days of 1979, rolled his eyes. We remained friends over the years; he and his wife Bethany having met at the legal publisher and married like us. He offered to handle our house closing as a favor and wise-cracked about our small demands.

The couple across from Josh and me at the long, dark conference room table, the sellers, nodded and laughed.

"And the chandelier? Is it in one piece?"

After Josh left the legal publisher, he and Gary started their own law practices sharing space in a suite on Park Row in lower Manhattan.

Josh and I signed page after page of legal documents with his stubby Mont Blanc fountain pen. I couldn't sign them fast enough. I didn't want anything to go wrong. I wanted this house. The 1927 side-hall Colonial on a quiet tree-lined street in Rockville Centre had most of the features on our wish list: working fireplace, full basement, attic, parquet floors, front porch, high ceilings, and according to the engineer, "good bones." Everyone shook hands and the fixer-upper was ours. We had landed in one of the best school districts in New York and had gotten a good deal.

I was thrilled to get out of the ground-floor loft we'd owned in Boerum Hill, Brooklyn, where a drug addict put his hand through the window and stole our answering machine. Countless umbrellas had been taken as they stood drying outside our front door covered by the ornately designed iron gate. I had had it with the unrelenting street sounds blaring into our ground-floor windows—like Rob Base and DJ E-Z Rock's ubiquitous "It Takes Two" rap song flowing from sedans with blackened windows, hum of idling tractor trailers, and the far-off pop of gun shots—always six in a row—coming from the nearby Gowanus housing projects on Friday nights. One summer, awakened in the middle-of-the-night, I watched through the window blinds as a pair of cops wrangled our elderly neighbor, in his underwear, from the stoop of the half-way house next door. The following spring, a young man was shot dead in the middle of the day on the corner diagonal to our home. The police chalk outline marked the area around the body until the rain washed it away.

My parents, who had moved to the Long Island suburbs, visited reluctantly and when they did I prayed their car radio didn't disappear in a puddle of glass. Josh and I placed a small sign on the dash of our BMW, "We take ours in a Benzi box," letting thieves know we removed our radio in a little box with a handle when we left the car.

Inside the apartment, the boys' bicycles blocked the gated front entrance and I dreamed of the day I could open a screen door and say: "Go Play Outside!" I couldn't do that in Brooklyn. I had to teach Adam and Matthew, then five and eight, never to touch syringes lying on the sidewalk.

We had moved to Boerum Hill in 1987 when it was a crusty, tough neighborhood, but once I became a mom the edgy New York City I had once longed for held little appeal. I looked at my life through mother lens and traded in the disco ball at Studio 54 for fluorescent lighting at monthly PTA meetings and mother's groups. The closest I got to gay women now was through Adam's toddler playgroup when Amy and Beth, a lesbian couple, joined with their little boy Justin. Meeting them provoked the past for me and though I longed to tell them about my lesbian past, fantasizing they would welcome me as a legacy member into their sisterhood, I never did.

I no longer enjoyed the smell of beer and stale cigarettes from old man bars and could hardly remember what spontaneity felt like—not with bedtime schedules and my children's need for constant vigilance.

Shifting my focus to parenthood didn't mean I had no longing for my old party-girl self. I did! But I replaced these old indulgences with the sweetness of skinny arms around my neck and the savory scent of boys' hair that smelled like damp earth.

Josh and I took parenting seriously. We attended lectures by child experts such as Dr. Brazelton and devoured books by Dr. Spock, Giselle Ames, and other advice-givers. Just as Josh was a roller skater and runner in Manhattan, he kept it up in Brooklyn; Josh continued to be mercurial, living up to his nickname from college: Flash. On Sunday mornings, he ran to Prospect Park with toddler Adam strapped in the blue canvas baby jogger. And when Josh finished the New York City Marathon two years later, the photo he took with his medallion included Adam in his arms. As the boys grew, Josh became known as the superhero doctor because he repaired the limbs of action figure toys. When Wolverine's retractable claw broke off he engineered a new one and attached it with the skill of a micro-surgeon. His reputation grew and boys from the neighborhood arrived at the front door to drop off their beloved Hulks, Ninja Turtles, and Power Rangers. Josh kept a bucket with spare heads, legs, and arms and made his repairs with gusto, showing me his handiwork. He spent hours repairing parts when he could buy a new action figure for five bucks.

"Hey, look at this!"

I stopped what I was doing and acknowledged Batman's new smooth-moving leg that helped him jump into his Batmobile. Spider-man's suction cup hands were like new so he could scale walls again. Matthew and Adam just scooped up their mended "guys," not caring much about the effort that went into their rehabilitation. They were just happy kids with their toys fixed.

And, Josh got things done. Once I casually commented that our Chinese Evergreen needed re-potting. He walked into the kitchen snatched up an old newspaper, the bag of potting soil from under the sink, a big serving spoon, and sat on the living room floor, and re-potted the plant. It was one of the things I loved about him—he'd act immediately. Why do it tomorrow when it can be done today? I'd prefer to think about things, analyze them, get others' opinions. "Do you think it's time to re-pot? Is it the right season? Will it be too much of a shock to the poor plant? Does it fit into my plan for the plant?"

He also liked to sew. When our Danish neighbors moved they gave us their Singer sewing machine. Late at night in Brooklyn, I lay in bed listening to the whirrr-whirrr-whirrr of the sewing machine as Josh guided his fingertips around fabric. The sound of the machine, which Josh placed atop the Deco glass coffee table, was comforting, like the sound of a rolling ocean outside a beach house. One birthday I gave him a gift certificate for ten sewing lessons at a small shop in Benson-hurst. At his first class, Josh told me, the instructor was so perplexed at having a male student that she couldn't improvise a beginner's sewing project for him other than a blouse. The instructor could never quite reconcile his presence and continued leading the group with "Now, ladies," then look at him. He learned enough to sew a toddler-sized pumpkin costume for Adam, which landed our boy in a Halloween photo in the local newspaper. He also sewed a small, rectangular, plaid pillow for the car, which the boys fought over constantly.

Now married to Josh for thirteen years, I longed for a backyard and clean streets while he preferred not to make a move to the suburbs, es-pecially Long Island where he grew up. He viewed it as the land of san-itized strip malls, big hair, shopaholics, traffic, and cultural deprivation.

"Long Guy Land is death! One way in, one way out," he exhorted.

But when we finally accepted an offer on our apartment, he re-lented, and we searched for the house with the proverbial picket fence.

After the closing, we headed straight to our new house. Josh jiggled the key to open the front door. He held his red, metal tool kit in hand whistling through his teeth Jingle Bells. He always whistled a holiday tune or "It's a Small World," when he was nervous.

It was July. We entered and were greeted with a sweltering, damp hello. Our voices echoed across the boxy living room into the wood-paneled "full" dining room. The house felt sturdy, despite the lived-in smell. And the rooms look huge with all the furniture gone.

"Nine, ten, eleven," Josh and I counted in unison as we pointed to broken windowpane after windowpane. When he got to fourteen, we shook our heads in disbelief. We strolled through the house, descended to the basement, and stared at the seventy-year-old furnace. The asbestos didn't look quite as threatening when we were scouting the house but now the unit looked sickly, like it was sprouting white boils. We approached it gingerly. It looked contagious, explosive like a time bomb poised to detonate if we don't meet its demands. We contracted with a demolition company to remove it before we moved in. Upstairs, with the bath mats gone, the bottom of the bathtub was rusted orange like a Creamsicle.

Outside, there was more crab grass than lawn, the side steps leading to the yard had a rickety wrought iron banister, and the brickwork was crumbling. We'd always wanted a house with lots of light and were blessed with forty-four windows but now they would have to be repaired or replaced.

Josh and I traversed our new home in silence. As the parents of rowdy boys, quiet was a luxury but not at this moment. "I didn't think we'd have buyer's remorse so quickly," I quipped. Josh picked up his tool kit, hummed "It's a Small World After All," and headed to the front porch.

"It's all gonna be okay," he reminded me.

✦

We moved on the hottest day of the year. Standing in the middle of the kitchen beneath the white ceiling fan with the pull chain, I gathered my hair in a sloppy French twist to keep it off my sweaty neck. At five-foot-two, I was shorter than the pull chain but not so for others, like the moving men, who walked into it.

"Watch the chain," I kept saying, like playing hostess at a disaster site.

Everywhere I turned I saw something that needed updating— the tea kettle wallpaper was dingy and the doorknob to the side door reminded me of the industrial hardware on an old army footlocker in my grandmother's house. I opened the side door to let in air and an anemic breeze filtered through. I looked outside and saw Josh helping the moving men carry boxes in. He looked like a movie director, running, sliding, and standing with one hand on his hip pointing in the direction he wanted the movers to go. I stuck my head down the stairs and Matthew, Adam, and one of their new friends from the block, Tyler, had strung their super hero figures to the banister with string lying around from the movers. My kids thought you could do anything with string and scotch tape. I fell in love with the basement, even though there were only two greasy windows letting in light and a fat concrete pole in the middle of the room. It was the inside version of go-play-outside and the boys were giddy as they ran up and down the steps.

By midnight, I collapsed into bed, which my older sisters, Christine and Laura, had thoughtfully made up earlier in the day. They'd stuck white paper accordion blinds in place at the top of the window and I saw a piece of a yoke-colored moon between the blind and the window. Josh and I had a hard time getting the boys to sleep but now they dozed across the hallway in their bunk beds, Matthew on the top clutching Mitzi, his floppy-eared stuffed dog he carried in a box in the move, and Adam, below, a restless sleeper, whose sheets were kicked off and twisted like he'd done battle before succumbing to sleep.

Josh rummaged in the hallway sorting and stacking boxes. He came into the bedroom wearing a rolled-up red bandana around his neck to catch the sweat cascading off the top of his bald head. He was follicle-ly impaired he reminded everyone and loved to quote Wayne Dyer: "God only made a few perfect heads. The rest he covered with hair." Josh re-tied the blond strands that hung at the back of his neck into his signature ponytail and dusted smears of dirt off his white t-shirt. "How about not unloading your dirt onto the carpet?" I said.

He shot me a dagger look. "Why I oughta…" he said in his Three Stooges imitation, shaking his fist.

"Why don't you stop unpacking now?" I said sweetly, amending for my harshness.

"Yeah. Just gotta take care of a few more things," he said as he always did when he had no intention of stopping.

"I know, I know. You're a shark. If you stop, you'll die."

He came to my side of the bed and knelt down.

"What are these? Tissues?" He grimaced, lifting the end of my pillow. "Are you crying?" He pushed the hair off my forehead. His eyes expressed a combination of puzzlement and compassion. Plump tears fell down my cheeks.

"You know it always works out," he said.

"I know. But the house is such a wreck. I didn't know what I was getting us into."

"I already love it here," he said. "The yard, the basement, this nice street. There's so much for me to fix."

I chuckled.

"I love it here too. It's so quiet." We stopped talking and listened to the crickets chirping outside our window.

Suddenly, the sound of shattered glass shook the quiet. We looked at each other, mouths agape, then bolted downstairs to see the ceiling fan had fallen from the ceiling and pierced our beautiful glass coffee table. We approached the shards as if they were demons then looked up at the hole.

"Welcome to the neighborhood," said Josh.

CHAPTER 5

Bagpipes whined their plaintive plea as police barricades corralled hundreds—neighbors, family, friends, uniformed firefighters and police, dignitaries who emerged from long sedans—on the windy, sun-blinding afternoon of Ed's funeral. Our friend had been a battalion chief in midtown, held a master's degree in fire safety, and was one of the smiling, reassuring fire fighters wearing pounds of equipment as he stepped up stairs in the Tower while people were scrambling to escape. He was one of 343 firefighters lost, many of whom perished because of communications equipment that didn't work and the loss of the operations command center housed in 7 World Trade.

Ed had been summoned to the site from midtown after the planes hit. At six-foot-two, Ed cut a strong figure, trustworthy in his stature. He sported dark hair, a full mustache, and kind, dancing eyes. Ed's strength was so reliable that his wife Pat told me a few days after September 11th, "he's a strong guy," as if to suggest that if anyone can survive, it would be "Eddie." A devoted father and dedicated soccer coach, Ed, like Jim, the baseball coach, cared deeply about his three boys and wife, his community, and my son. Before every soccer season, Ed held parent meetings to talk about his approach—which was always to help his boys' team develop their skills and have fun. He was a coach who would instruct off the field but let the boys play to their strengths when they were on. Ed had an infectious laugh. He never shouted. Instead he offered a hearty pat on the back when a boy ambled off the field or a suggestion, at an opportune moment, to try something different next time. When he died, Ed, forty-six, trailed a legacy of kindness and authenticity that lived on in those who had the fortune to know him.

Our town of Rockville Centre, NY, had the dubious distinction of having the second highest number of children, thirty, lose parents on September 11th. Very little attention had been paid to those children whose parents, like Josh, may have survived but were never quite whole again.

By the end of September, Josh dropped five pounds, maybe just from sweating alone. He grayed at the temples (with what little hair he had) and couldn't focus enough to read—even the juicy Carl Haissen novels he loved and piled atop his night table. He traded his passion for running for milling around. He sniffled and shuffled.

Despite the pall of 9/11 we went ahead with Josh's fiftieth birthday party. Held upstairs at George Martin, a local restaurant, the gathering gave everyone a chance to be together during a difficult time and celebrate the lives we were so grateful to have.

Standing by his birthday cake, Josh looked like a shadow—gaunt and lifeless, a striking difference from the person I wrote about only weeks before in the invitation:

COME CELEBRATE JOSH'S 50TH BIRTHDAY

He's driving, he's running, he's never going slow
He's fixing, he's sewing, he's joking, we all know

He's strumming, he's chompin' a salad every night
He's folding, he's smoothing the clothes, they look so bright!

He's scheming, he's culling the props that he might wear
He's speeding, he's dashing, All right, I'll meet you there

If we can slow him down enough, we'll celebrate his day
Cause Josh is turning 50 and that's something kinda gay

Since he's agreed to take a break we're hoping you might, too
Join in the festivities for Josh's birthday rendezvous

The crowd of fifty friends and family—from Gary and Bethany, our lawyer friend Josh had shared space with, to my dad, Josh's dad Mel, his sister Wendy, brother, and friends and cousins—were our support. They huddled around us like ballasts to a drifting boat even if no one suspected how unmoored we were becoming.

"I want everyone to know how much I love my son," Mel announced when it was time for cake. The room quieted and we looked ahead at Josh and his dad, arms around each other's shoulders. Mel and Josh resembled each other, both balding, except that Josh's hair above his ears was patchy now, like that of a trauma victim.

"He's one of the most honorable people I know," he added.

Josh smirked, looking ready to spring a self-deprecating joke.

"Happy birthday, son."

When they hugged, Mel's arm hooked the top of Josh's shoulder, more to hold him up than share an embrace.

As the months passed, I grew impatient with Josh's shuffling and sweating.

My home no longer felt like the bastion of protection I had depended on; in fact, our house mirrored the uncertainty and soul-searching New York City found itself in in the wake of 9/11. My husband had been taken away, replaced with someone who looked similar but had the life drained out of him, as if he too had lain on an embalmer's table. Josh had always felt things deeply. He was someone who cried easily, like the time I saw him sitting in front of the TV crying while watching a *Today Show* segment that profiled two high school graduates: one, a white boy with a lavish commencement party, and the other, an African-American boy who lived in the projects and celebrated with a pizza. Now Josh's tears were chronic, seemingly over nothing, like the cliché'd joke of the housewife who can't get ahold of herself because she burnt the casserole.

"Look, I appreciate this," he said impatiently, not sounding appreciative, one night in our bedroom waving a brochure I'd picked up from the Rockville Centre World Trade Center Child and Family Counseling Program, a store-front set up after 9/11 and sponsored by the local hospital. I stopped in there and spoke to a young man who told me that counseling services were only available for people directly affected—wives, husband, children, parents. But he gave me a brochure, which I'd left on Josh's night table, which listed web sites and organizations that could help.

"I'm fine, really. Stop making this more than it is."

"There's help, you know. Maybe Dr. Grossman," I suggested.

"Yeah, all right," he said waving his arm dismissively. "Stop bugging me. I'm gonna make an appointment."

He saw Dr. Grossman, our family doctor, insisting on going by himself, and told me she said he was experiencing post-traumatic stress. She prescribed Wellbutrin, which he took for a while, but I wondered if he followed the prescription, since he had always self-medicated, paid little regard to the effects of substances, and claimed to have super-human tolerance.

I could not report any improvement in him—he continued living but with an ill-defined listlessness punctuated by bouts of anger. And my impatience grew with his growing isolation and my rebuffed attempts to pierce his shell.

"Okay, it happened," I finally said to my husband. "We're all getting on with our lives. Even the victims' families." As Josh sank deeper and deeper, I started spending more time at work.

CHAPTER 6

I first spied Claire in spring 2001 at the pink swirl marble bathroom sink in the ladies' room of our office, long copper-colored hair flowing past her slender shoulders. Strikingly pretty in a Nicole Kidman-esque way, she washed her hands vigorously, leaning straight into the mirror, to examine a blemish on her chin.

I tried to catch her eye because she was new and wanted to welcome her, remembering what it was like to be the newbie, that awkward "no one to have lunch with" feeling. I stole a glance at her, then my own reflection—my dark brown chin-length bob unstylish next to Claire's couture fresh-faced appearance. I finger-picked my strands and smoothed my cardigan. She stole a goodbye glance at herself in the mirror, tossed a balled-up paper towel into the trash and, without so much as a look at me, exited.

I scurried down the carpeted hallway, giving the receptionist an eyebrow nod, and through the password-protected locked door. I slid into my office, a large corner cubicle, with a cream-colored oval desk floating in the middle of the room, on the eleventh floor of a Manhattan high rise overlooking Fifth Avenue.

Two years after we moved into the house, I returned to full-time work at the non-profit, lucky enough to land in the same publishing department I'd worked in before my children were born. Within four years, I had become editor of the national magazine, a hefty responsibility given its readership of one million.

My routine at home churned smoothly, however, with Josh driving Adam to the middle school and Matthew to the high school in the morning before boarding the railroad into Manhattan. He hated the hour-long commute compared to the fifteen minutes it used to take to get to lower Manhattan from Brooklyn. The Izod sweater and Armani suit-wearing fathers heading to their Wall Street trading desks irked Josh as well—something about their upward mobility, hefty bonuses, and competitiveness got under his skin. I figured this poked at some sense of inadequacy. At home he picked up a number of other home duties, too, like cooking and paying the bills, which I was happy to scrape off my plate. He'd been paying so many of our bills out of his lawyer account that it seemed easier to just hand over the whole business. Craig, our twenty-three-year-old babysitter, showed up in the afternoons. Though Craig wasn't great at riding the boys to get homework done, he could cook up tacos even if he left the stove covered in grease stains.

Josh, with his loving blue eyes and skinny runner's legs, continued as solo law practitioner, coming on his twentieth year, one year longer than our marriage. At the office on John Street, across from the World Trade Center, he shared space with Donald, an accountant. Josh's clients were an eclectic mix of small business owners, executors of estates, and some criminal clients, a holdover from an earlier time when he took on litigation and defense. Now, his clients were owners of shoe stores and print shops; some were wealthy, established business people while the criminal clients lived at Manhattan Correctional Center.

We enjoyed our lives in our side-hall Colonial on the maple-lined street in our charming suburban town, watching Adam shine at soccer, Little League baseball, and basketball and Matthew showing a flair for guitar. At home, Matthew blasted the music of the Beastie Boys, Rage Against the Machine, and Taking Back Sunday, and since Josh and I were such music fans we loved it too. Married to a lawyer, I felt I had surpassed my mom and dad—eschewing their working-class humility and high-stepping in the spoils of an upper middle class life: boys attending one of the best school systems in the country, expensive sleep-away camp, private beach club, requisite mini-van, and stylish couples parties.

To top it off, as editor of the magazine, I enjoyed a modicum of status—invitations to conferences where Martha Stewart spoke and gave away goody bags with high-end steel potato peelers. I was often sought out by co-workers in other departments who wanted to promote their events or have me include photos of families who'd done something "extraordinary." Many times as I was waiting for copy from someone in the building, I'd run into that person in the elevator, and he or she would fumble apologetically about being late with their content. I felt like the school principal everyone was afraid of and I wanted to say, really, stop it, it's okay. I reassured with a nod, saying that a few days late wouldn't matter, even though it did matter because I would be scrambling at deadline to make up the time.

Our publishing unit churned out a national magazine, books, brochures, and reports with a staff of fifteen: editors, editorial assistants, an art director, and graphic designers. Everyone was tucked away in a maze of fabric cubicles.

Blossom, our editor-in-chief, headed our team. A slim, tall fifty-ish Texas woman who loved barbecue, she had recently replaced Maggie, our director of thirty years, who had died of ovarian cancer. With Blossom at the helm, things had shifted.

Unmarried, Maggie treated her staff like family. Like a loving parent, she brought us exquisitely wrapped little gifts—like a crystal angel ornament from Scandinavia. She loved Russian poetry and didn't own a television. Once when Josh and I traveled to Spain, she lent me her travel diary, a beautiful, red palm-size journal filled with her tiny, tight handwriting. It detailed her travels through Madrid and Catalan. I carried it on my trip and studied it daily. Maggie had died in 1998, the same year as Josh's mother, whom I'd grown to love dearly, and a year before my own mother passed away. Even though I shared a deep, intricate, "in it together" bond with my sisters Laura and Christine, who still doted on me even in middle age, the loss of my mother, Lillian, and my boss, Maggie, within a year left a visceral, chasmic loneliness.

Right before Claire came, our department plowed through a stable of freelance graphic designers, none of them meeting Blossom's liking. So I was surprised when Blossom called me into her office to ask how I felt about having the new designer, Claire, take a stab at laying out the magazine.

"We can have a full-time staff designer for what it costs us to have the design company lay out four issues a year," she said. We sat at her small, round meeting table nestled in the corner of her office. Small purple and red origami cranes sat with us at the table.

"It's fine," I responded, but really I felt reluctant to change just when we'd gotten the cycle of deadlines handled. Plus I was fond of the designer at the small firm we'd hired. He was patient, soft-spoken, and accommodating, even when we changed things at the last minute, which was all the time. He provided a measure of safety, someone to rely on.

"Good. Glad you're ready to be bold," she said.

I rushed around the office. Lena, my sidekick and production manager, handled circulation, copy corrections, photo permissions and a stream of other things. I set the themes of the issues, conceived article ideas, hired writers, edited, wrote captions, and arranged photo shoots. Every issue, Lena and I culled through dozens of submissions for photos and stories.

With light-brown hair mixed with gray, Lena exuded calm and strength like a teacher who'd seen scores of students pass through her classroom and wasn't fazed by childish pranks. A fiercely private person, Lena had no interest in office chatter and sometimes responded in ways I could imagine her stoic German father, a North Dakota farmer, would reply: with the facts and no embellishment. Growing up on the plains left Lena with a sturdiness that was both foreign and reassuring to me.

"We're like two halves of a good brain," Lena said about how well she and I worked together.

"Yeah, together we actually get it all done," I added, even though I was nervous most of the time. I once heard that magazine editors were always anxious. Probably because there were so many moving parts and tight deadlines. I felt suited, however, for my job and good about how I'd handled it. As someone who'd grown up relying on other people, I surprised myself at being able to take charge of such a big project. I knew I could do it only if I had others to help me.

Lena and I sat side by side at a rectangular conference table in the art room combing through the letters and photos. A six-foot high green cabinet, against one wall, held skinny drawers that slid out smoothly. It was a holdover piece of furniture from the days when graphic designers had to store oversized poster board illustrations and photographs.

"That letter's a keeper," I said, handing the sheet to Lena. We judged the entries independently then compared our choices. Most entries weren't particularly interesting so when a good one came along we got excited.

Lena and I turned as heels clicked on the floor. It was Claire—her body half in and half out of the room. I'd been noticing her as she strode through the floor. She was hard to miss in her cowboy boots, walking with purpose, like she always had someplace to go.

"Looking for supplies." she said. "Post-its, stuff like that."

"Hallway closet." I pointed. I was about to jump up but Lena did instead and walked Claire to the cabinet. I heard chattering, then polite office laughter. "If you need anything else," Lena said, "We sit down there." I pictured her pointing to our end of the floor.

"What's up with her?" I asked when Lena rolled her chair back to my side.

She shrugged.

"Nice enough," she answered.

We sorted through the buoyant piles of looseleaf papers. Lena neatened the "No" pile; that pile would receive rejection letters.

As I approached my desk, the phone jangled, one ring—interoffice.

"Would you mind talking to Claire about the booklet going to the Smithsonian?" Blossom asked.

"What about?"

"Tell her it doesn't have to be perfect. To finish up." I wondered why she was asking me to do this but was glad that I had an excuse to speak to Claire.

Claire worked in the tiny, temporary freelancer's spot—fabric cube, computer monitor that dwarfed the desk, not much space to maneuver a swivel chair.

I poked my head into her workspace tentatively, manuscript in hand.

"Hi," I said, voice rising as if it were a question.

Her right shoulder faced the door. She turned, smiling warmly, not what I'd expected.

"How are you doing?" I asked, syrupy, with the accent on "doing" like a nurse visiting a hospital patient.

I introduced myself and extended my hand. She shook it firmly and I was glad she didn't have a wet noodle handshake.

"I love this project," she said pulling the word "love" out like soft, unwieldy taffy. I heard a surprising twang of Southerness. "So excited. This book is gonna be shipped to the Smithsonian for that exhibit on women athletes."

I wasn't impressed. I'd seen dozens of booklets get published and forgotten, but over the years I'd learned not to shake a newcomer's enthusiasm. Let her enjoy the sense of importance she imagined this project had.

"When do you think you'll be done with it?" I asked.

"Today. Just kerning a few lines then saving the files." She spoke with certainty. I'd never heard the word kerning before but later learned it meant tightening up spaces between words on a line. A rich palate of yellows and blues caught my eye on her screen.

"I love those colors," I ventured.

"I'm good at color." I glanced at her russet hair and blue gray eyes.

"Yes, I can see that."

Later that day, Claire poked her head into my office.

"Supposed to talk to you about the magazine," she said.

Before I could say, "come in," she stood before me, then sat easily in the armchair across from my desk.

"We're ready to design the fall issue," I began.

I swung my chair around and grabbed a handful of back issues from the shelf behind my desk. I fanned them between us, then thumbed through the pages telling her about the regular columns and how they gave our magazine its distinctiveness. She looked at me intently, unlike in the ladies room. Now she seemed enthralled by my words.

She broke my gaze and stared at my family photos on the file cabinet behind me. There was one of me and Josh sitting on the black-and-white striped couch in our basement holding our guinea pigs in our laps. I wore a sleeveless burgundy button-down shirt holding Rodney, the golden one, and Josh held onto Reese, the black and white pig, between his knees with one hand underneath. Our heads leaned into each other and we mugged for the camera, me with a shiny-faced, eager smile and Josh with a mock frown. The other photo was of me, Josh, Matthew, and Adam on the shore of Cantiague Lake on Long Island waiting out a rainstorm during a canoe trip.

"Your family?" she asked as she got closer to the photos.

"Yup," I said as I looked at the photos with her.

"How old?" she asked, pointing to my boys. She seemed entranced by the photos as I told her their names and ages.

"Wow. A teenager. My son is fourteen months old," she said, eyes wide. She pushed her hair behind her ears and I noticed how delicate they were.

"Who watches him during the day?"

"My husband. We don't leave Jamil with babysitters."

Oh boy, one of those moms who's a slave. I thought of the joke, "Next time I'm comin' back as the only child of forty-year-old parents." I didn't say it, of course. And she wasn't forty; she looked closer to thirty.

"What's his name?" I asked, needing clarification.

"J-a-m-i-l. It means handsome in Arabic."

"Be right back," she exclaimed before darting out of my office.

She returned with a photo of her son sitting on the floor and staring right into the camera. The toddler's skin glowed a beautiful coffee color and his eyes appeared dark and knowing, like a sage, intensity in those orbs. His features mirrored hers, high sculptured cheekbones, delicate nose, strong chin.

"He is handsome! Looks just like you."

"You think? My husband is Pakistani."

"What a beautiful combination."

She scrutinized the picture.

"Relationships are everything. Don't ya think?" she asked.

✦

Over the next few weeks, I sighted Claire darting in and around the cubicles, tresses shimmering, space around her charged electrically.

She moved into an office across the aisle from me. Her formerly antiseptic space was now lively: outside her door hung a print of a poster-size rigatoni pasta; inside on top of her file cabinet sat a carousel of brightly colored markers, design books flooded with typography and bold spreads splayed open on her desk, along with glossy photos of Jamil. A wall poster broadcast the Barbara Kruger quote: "I shop, therefore I am." Outside her office push-pinned to the wall was a row of illustrations she had penned—a gallery of bistro chairs labeled with personality types. A whimsical, flowing ornately designed chair was called "grandiose." Another drawn with sharp fibrillating lines was labeled, "neurotic." I thought them clever. She strolled into my office freely now, especially in the mornings, eating organic pears, her favorite, bought from the Park Slope food co-op.

One night as I packed up to leave, I heard movement in the hallway. I crossed the aisle and spotted Claire sitting cross-legged on the floor of her space staring into the guts of her Mac, the side panel removed and lying on a pristine white cloth she laid down. I was surprised. Not because I'd never seen anyone tinker with a computer before—Josh, the fixer, always seemed to be pulling our computer apart and talking about motherboards and schematics, something I knew little about—but it was startling to see in my office where everyone called tech support and followed procedures. Nobody sat on the floor, on their haunches, with computer guts strewn about. The only people allowed to tinker were in IT.

"Wow! What are you doing?" I asked. It was just after six o'clock and the late-night stillness that comes after the vents shut down had set in.

"My God. There's no tech support here. What does anyone do when they need help? Wait for IT?"

I nodded.

"That's ridiculous."

"Well, just watch out for Blossom," I warned. "She doesn't always appreciate people taking matters into their own hands."

"Then whose hands should I put matters in?" she asked with a laugh. "She told me she liked self-starters."

"Amazing, you can fix things like this!" I said. "Such a tech-savvy girl!"

"Nah, just takin' care of business," she replied, her accent peeking through.

We chatted easily while she reassembled her computer. I liked that she flaunted the rules, unlike my scaredy-cat self. Once, when I was 10, my sister Christine held me hostage for months telling me she was going to tell to our mother that I said "shit" in front of the dollar store. I was so afraid of being found out that I polished her shoes and made her lunch for a week. Even months later Christine resurrected the threat whenever she wanted to strong-arm me. And I complied.

"Help me up," Claire commanded as she extended both arms. Her limbs were long and lean like the rest of her. I grabbed her fingertips.

She climbed up on her cushioned swivel chair then stepped onto her desk with her clunky boots. She pointed to the honeycomb-patterned fluorescent lighting panel on the ceiling.

"How can I get rid of those?" she asked pointing to the bulbs. "It's way too glary in here." Without waiting for an answer, she jumped down, ran into the hallway and shut off all the overhead lights on her part of the floor. The few remaining people in the office grumbled.

"Oh, don't get your knickers in a twist, darlin's," she hollered. She grabbed a screwdriver and paper towels from her drawer and climbed back onto her desk and removed the lighting panels. She handed them to me. She used a paper towel to unscrew the fluorescent bulbs above her work station.

"That's better," she declared. She darted into the hallway and turned the lights back on.

I watched all this, nervous that someone would come by and catch us. I didn't want anyone to think I was her accomplice.

Removing any property—even light bulbs—was clearly against the rules.

"So, about Blossom," I said, left hand on my hip.

"Oh, I should be careful, right?" she asked as she replaced the panel. "Like get permission before removing anything?"

I nodded.

"Oh, sure. It's just that the lights are, you know, no good for me."

She was out of breath, exhaling heavily, her head cocked pleadingly. I eyed her incredulously; it wasn't the desktop-climbing I couldn't believe—though her spring to action fascinated me—it was her exquisiteness I couldn't turn from.

✦

Claire laid out the magazine quickly, working over the weekend to present a deepened color palate and refreshed design. She was in my office first thing Monday morning, waving pantone color swatches like a kid brandishing a good report card. Her ribbed black turtleneck sweater hugged her torso. She smiled broadly.

"I really wanted to design a new masthead but I couldn't do everything at once," she said while dragging the guest chair next to me. She sat.

I scanned the printouts quickly and felt a surge of excitement: the design looked clean, young.

"Wow. It looks great," I said.

"Remember, my machine isn't calibrated so the colors aren't totally accurate."

I turned to the Contents page. The Meta font she'd chosen for headlines looked sharp and contemporary. But I knew immediately Blossom wouldn't like it. The change was too abrupt. She hadn't authorized this much.

"It's like someone opened a window into a musty room," I let slip—and I meant it.

Later that day, I walked to Blossom's office with the printouts.

"How'd she do?" she asked pointing me to the round table.

"I really like it," I said.

Blossom studied the pages, her silver-rimmed reading glasses dropping to the end of her nose.

"I didn't want her to redesign. I didn't give her the okay to do this. Where does she get the idea she could do whatever she wants?"

I inhaled. "I think she just wants to do a good job."

She circled a few colors on the page.

"Tell her to tone those down."

I nodded and shimmied out of her office, glad to be leaving. I practically skipped down the hall and into Claire's workspace. She had headphones on and her back was to the door. I touched her shoulder lightly. She spun around startled then slipped the black headphones off to rest around her neck like a collar.

"She wants me to what…change the colors?" she asked.

I nodded.

"You can't just pull a color out of the air; it's part of the palette."

"I don't know what to tell you."

"You know, I met a lot of divas when I worked in fashion but they had something to be divas about. This one doesn't know what she's talking about."

"When did you work in fashion?" I *knew* she had a past.

"Oh, Malik and I had a design business. 'The business,'" she repeated, air-quoting the words.

"A men's line," she said. "We made it to Barney's windows."

My eyes widened.

"It nearly killed me," she intoned, folding her arms tightly. "Worked all the fucking time. Before we had Jamil. We had an apartment on Central Park West and our line appeared in French *Vogue*. Bendel's too. It was incredible."

I had seen the book *Failing Forward* by John Maxwell sitting on her desk. Now I understood her guardedness when she first arrived. She was working as a freelance graphic designer at a non-profit after thinking she was set for life with a successful business.

"What happened?"

"Got screwed. Money, always money. Someone owed us a hunk of money, didn't pay, and we had to close the business. Right after that I got pregnant. One of us had to work," she said, turning her hand palm side up like she was weighing an imaginary parcel.

"Well, glad you're here," I said. "You're very good. I appreciate your talent."

"Thanks." She blushed.

Later she came by my office and showed me the corrections.

"You know, thanks, for your help," she said, "You I can talk to. You understand."

I shrugged, embarrassed.

Five minutes later, she was back.

"I have to ask you," she said pointing to the framed picture of my family. "You know about kids. What am I supposed to do when my son bites me? He left teeth marks in my shoulder," she said turning her chin to the injured side.

"Put him down and walk away."

"That's it?"

"Kids hate to be ignored. He'll get the message. Tell him you cannot play with him because he bit you."

She grinned. "How do I keep him from throwing things in the garbage? He screams if I move the garbage pail. Last night, he threw away a set of house keys."

"Put the garbage pail on the kitchen counter—high."

"How can I get 10 minutes to talk on the phone when he's there? He's impossible."

"Let him stand on a chair at the sink and fill it with soapy water. Throw some bath toys in the water. Better yet kitchen utensils. Stand near him when you call. I used to save that for when I really, really needed to make an important call."

She shook my hand as if we'd just signed a proclamation. And for the first time around her, I was tingly. She looked at me with the same intensity she gave herself in the ladies room mirror.

"Working mothers under fire," I said.

✦

Throughout the summer, Claire and I worked side by side. We crafted a short-hand like an old married couple—I would take her Aquafina water bottle and fill it without asking if I saw it empty. She slipped me a macaroon from a snack area down the hall.

The day didn't start without Claire charging in to say good morning. If she got in before me, I'd find a little yellow post-it note stuck to my computer screen. It would read, "Hey," the signal that she was in and waiting for my hello.

As we worked, she left yellow post-it notes on page proofs, too: "If you cut 10 lines here, I'll be your slave" or "I prefer to be called crabby, not surly," referring to a joke I had made one day about her insolence. We crammed in the work of an entire staff, just Claire, Lena, and me.

One morning as I arrived, Blossom stood at the entrance to my office. I got an instant headache. Blossom was rarely in early. Wearing a below-the-knee, dark, loose skirt and flats. She was reading a quote posted outside my doorway that Claire had push-pinned. It read, "A woman radiates what she really is. Not what she imagines she is, and attracts what she radiates." I loved that Claire had given me that. I slowed my pace as I walked to my workspace.

"Good morning, Janet," she said when I reached my office.

I nodded hello and walked into my office. My eye went to my computer screen for the post-it note to see if Claire was in. She wasn't. I offered my boss a seat as I slid my bag off my shoulder and slipped out of my khaki raincoat. My bag hit the floor with a thump. I tossed my coat onto the shelf that lined the area behind my desk. We stood face to face.

"How's it going with Claire?" she asked, taking her time pronouncing the letter "L."

"She's a good idea person. Excellent designer." As soon as I said it I knew that wasn't what she was fishing for.

"She certainly is creative. You know those artist types, bless their hearts." Blossom used the "bless her heart" expression often, polishing it with her Texas twang. Claire told me that Southern women tacked that expression onto the end of sentences to come out looking good.

"I hate that man-stealing bitch, bless her heart," Claire had said, citing an example.

"Does she think I don't know anything about publishing?" asked Blossom. "Only been in the business thirty years."

I said nothing.

"You're not her supervisor, but I know I can talk to you. I asked Claire to fill in for Trevor while he was on vacation to move the work along. I ended up getting a call from the sponsor. She changed the style of the entire book. No one asked her to do that."

"Did you talk to her?"

"Oh, I talked to her all right. Listen, keep an eye on her, okay?"

"Ok," I said, my cheeks growing red.

"I like Claire," said Blossom. "She's got a lot of enthusiasm. But I won't let her run my department and neither should you."

Later, when Claire got in, I asked about the incident. She rolled her eyes.

"Jesus H. Christ. I couldn't believe they were gonna let that book go out like that. Design was horrible. I saved their asses. They should be thanking me."

"Just do what they ask, ok? I know it offends your sensibilities but who cares? It's not your business. You work for them."

"All right, all right. But it's hard for me to abide when I don't re-spect. You know me."

She flashed a wide smile and caught me staring at her.

"What?" she asked.

The morning sunlight danced through my office and landed on her glistening baby-pink skin and gold Sedona landscape hair.

"What?" she repeated.

"Nothing."

"Come on," she insisted.

She had no way of knowing I had started singing "Sunny," the 70s R&B song, in my mind when I thought of her. When I was a teenager learning guitar, I strummed the chords to "Sunny." I remembered the chord changes. "Sunny, yesterday my life was filled with rain....Sunny, you smiled at me and really eased the pain. You're my spark of nature's fire. You're my sweet, complete desire…"

"You're so sunny." The words spilled out.

"Ha! Sunny to hide the storm clouds maybe."

She backed up and shot me a devilish grin. She turned to go and I studied her body, boyish, no curves but a delicious androgyny that appealed to me, like a Helmut Knut photograph I'd once seen: spikey-haired boy/women in black ties, crisp white shirts, and boxy jackets with the cuffs rolled up. The models gazed into the horizon with intoxicating aloofness. I had seen those photos back in the 80s when I had explored the New York City lesbian scene with Ellie, the waitress.

✦

At the end of the summer, Josh and I drove to Paradox Lake in the Adirondacks and turned onto the manicured road with the tidy white sign, "Private children's camp." The thick August air hung still amidst luxurious pines standing defiantly like verdant fur soldiers. The woodsy aroma lured me as I stepped out of our minivan and onto the soccer field that served as parking lot. I loved the camp. I loved the manners our boys displayed when they came back home. I loved the activities—they played hockey on smooth asphalt, shot hoops, swam, sailed, and had tribal wars. I imagined that allegiance to a team might give our children a leg up in the business world. But sleepaway camp was a must dictated by Josh's dad. I was told that it was a Jewish rite of passage where boys forged lifelong friendships. Josh's dad, in his seventies, counted his camp days among his best memories and still kept in touch with his bunkmates. Josh attended Camp Towanda and later B'nai Brith with his cousin Martin.

"Hey. There you are," I said spying Adam in the sea of campers walking toward us. I lunged with outstretched arms. This was Adam's second year and Matthew's third. I imagined this was a hard day because their bags were packed and the time had come to say good-bye to their friends and this paradise. Adam squeezed me tight. He looked taller, especially wearing the white camp dress shirt with the Southwoods logo.

I kissed the top of his brown buzz-cut hair that smelled sweet. I knew the counselors must have insisted on showers that morning.

Around us were reunions of parents and kids igniting the atmosphere as birds tweeted, kids shrieked, and parents exclaimed how tall or how beautiful or how amazing their children were. An observer of this scene would think these parents and children had nothing but love and admiration for each other. Josh hugged Matthew in a tight, brief embrace, and then I squeezed my fourteen-year-old.

"We love this kid," declared the clean-cut counselors, two college boys, who walked over and pointed to Adam.

"And this guy…," they said, fake-shoving Matthew, "he's an awesome DJ. Should've heard his radio show. This place'll never be the same." Everyone giggled. All the hyperbole felt genuine though, not like overblown chatter. My kids were incredible.

The boys led us to their bunks with cool names like Noonmark and showed us where they'd slept, patting the mattress for the last time this season. We headed to the lake and watched the boys cannonball off the inflatable climbing wall. Then we all took a speedboat ride, choreographed by the lakefront counselors, while the kids took turns bouncing in a giant black tire tube tethered to the back of the boat. I was excited that my kids had the opportunity to be here; something my working class parents could never have afforded for me.

That September, 2001, the boys were in their new schools. Matthew arrived as a freshman at the high school and Adam as a sixth grader. Josh had built his law practice at his downtown office, doing what he did best—lawyering, counseling, reassuring clients not to worry about the small business violation or contract discrepancies, and the slow process of ushering the probated will. It was all going to be okay.

CHAPTER 7

"An ice cold beer. Whaddaya think?" I asked Claire. She sat in the guest chair in my office handing me color proofs. It was right before Christmas 2001. The air held a chill, settling in for a long stay and New Yorkers walked quickly as they pulled up their collars. I felt an inexplicable connection to strangers since the terrorist attack. Our city had been violated, but instead of viewing everyone as dangerous I felt the opposite: I clung to a person's gaze longer than usual searching for wisdom or an answer. People seemed gentler with each other in those few months, taking an extra minute to hold the deli door open or waiting for folks to exit the subway car before barreling in. Whenever I noticed some kindness, my heart felt satisfied for a moment.

I asked Claire about the beer in what I hoped was an off-handed way. I had actually rehearsed how to ask because I'd been thinking about her—her sturdy walk, her refreshing, cheerful determination, the way she glided through her computer glitches, her beauty. I knew my attraction to Claire was more than friendship, something I acknowledged to myself even though I would rather have relegated my same-sex attractions to the past. Gary, our attorney-friend who knew me back in the day, once asked Josh and me, after we'd become parents and homeowners, whether I still was interested in women "like that."

"That's playing with fire!" I answered quickly. "I have no desire to poke that hornet's nest."

"It's a perfectly natural part of you," Josh, sitting with us, piped in. "Stop being so afraid of it."

As some men would be, Josh was titillated by the idea of his wife with another woman and didn't see the harm, but I knew the depth of anguish it could cause me. At least a year before meeting Claire I had confided in my neighbor and best friend about the female lovers I'd had B.C. (before children). It was the first time I'd told anyone in my sub-urban circle, a much more conservative bunch than my city friends. My best friend Amanda and I had gotten cozy over a few glasses of wine and once I revealed, it was as if the lid of a box had been lifted, stirring feelings of desire I hadn't even know I'd repressed. I instantly felt dif-ferent. Previously, when I'd thought of myself with another woman, my feelings vacillated between shame and confidence. But after my brief conversation with Amanda I felt free, sexy, and renewed.

Now Claire stoked that desire. And despite my head launching warning flares, my heart's momentum to engage Claire picked up speed. Was it Claire and her androgyny that ignited this resurgence in me? Was it my determination to soak up every gorgeous morsel of life in a post-9/11 world? I had not told Josh about my wanting to wander. It was no longer the 80s and there was too much at stake with a family, a house, and a whole revolving world. And since the towers, I felt it would hurt Josh; if I could hide my attractions I was sparing him.

"Love to," Claire responded

We dropped the printer's proofs for the spring issue at the Fed Ex office and strolled into Mulligan's, a dimly lit Irish pub on Madison Avenue. We sat on high stools at a small, round table near the jukebox. A wall sign read: First World Series American League Boston Red Sox versus Pittsburgh Pirates, October 1, 1903. Miniature American flags on sticks were planted everywhere. I slid off the stool and brought us Bass ales from the bar. I placed our drinks on the table, then sidled over to the jukebox. There's something inexplicably sexy about standing at a juke box selecting tunes in a dark bar, like kneeling at an altar.

Back at the table, I faced Claire, her gray-blue eyes dancing.

We rode from topic to topic effortlessly, like a city cab weaving around traffic. Movies we loved, office gossip, our childhoods, beliefs, and philosophies.

"I feel like such a grown-up being out after work," she said. She rested her chin in her hand and looked around dreamily. Her slender hands cupped the golden ale as her lips grazed the top of the glass.

"Don't get out much, huh?" I said. I was excited to be out too. My body felt loose, like I could drape myself over everything.

"Let's both pick out something on the jukebox," I said, pointing with my chin.

I turned the knob and album covers appeared and disappeared.

"How about Rod Stewart, 38-0-7? 'Do You Think I'm Sexy'?" she said.

"I remember when that song came out, child."

We finished choosing songs and hopped back onto our stools. When one of our songs played I gave her a feigned surprised expression, mouth open like a capital "O."

"Tell me a secret," she said playfully. "You tell me one and I'll tell you one." I hesitated, not sure if I should take the bait.

"Ok, you first." I cleared my throat nervously as Rod Stewart sang, "Come on, baby, let me know."

"Ok," she said. She hesitated, looked down into her drink and laughed, "Ok," she repeated. "Malik was only, like, the second person I've ever slept with."

"And you're telling me this—why?"

"Secret, darling. That's my nasty little secret I don't share with anyone."

"What's wrong with that? You're married to him," I said.

"I've only slept with two people! That's pathetic." This launched us into a conversation about how everyone sleeps around these days and we speculated about people in the office.

"Now, you," she said, her voice rising at the end of the sentence teasingly.

"What's your little secret?"

I took a deep breath and exhaled forcibly, smiling.

"I like women's bars," I said, my heart beating despite the beer analgesic.

"You mean like a lezzy bar?" She laughed out loud. "I'll be goddamned. That's great. I used to hang out with all these gay people at college. They loved me." She paused. "Why lezzy bars?"

"It's like a big sorority. No men. Best place in the world to dance," I said, even though I hadn't been to one in years. "We should go sometime?"

"Next time I'm paroled from the domestic prison, I'm going with ya," she said, her Virginia accent spilling out.

"When?" I asked. "Next Friday? Is that good?" I knew in this moment I was steering us down a dangerous path but went gleefully.

"Yeah," she said breaking into a fat grin. "Hell, yeah. I could use a little adventure," she said. "I can't believe you do that. God. No one would ever suspect you. Mother of the year wants to go to a dyke bar. Does Josh know?"

"About my past? Yup."

She smiled through an intense gaze. "Listen, come to dinner at my house. I want you and Josh to meet Malik."

"Sure," I said with unease. "Gotta pee." Then I tumbled off my stool and headed for the ladies room.

✦

The following Friday evening, Claire and I emerged from the West 4th Street subway station into the cold, clear December air. We made our way to John's Pizza on Bleecker Street. Despite the chilly temperature, Bleecker teemed with people carrying holiday packages; we walked in the street at times to avoid groups of teens clogging the sidewalk. After a short wait in front of John's we made our way to a wooden booth in the back. Our conversation didn't have the same fluidity as the week before and I thought maybe we should just have dinner and go home. But we made our way to Henrietta's, the lesbian bar. The cold made us walk faster and our heels clipped quickly along the cobblestones on Morton Street until we finally spilled into the storefront with the darkened windows and the beefy woman bouncer outside.

Inside, the place was dark and packed and there was an electricity that suddenly connected me and Claire: a plunging neckline, someone applying lipstick, a striped shirt open to reveal a black brassiere, a tiny rose tattoo, tight black pants that hugged a sculpted ass. We looked at each other and smiled. She appeared relaxed, though her cheeks flushed as we took off our coats and stepped to the back where wooden benches lined the wall. We got drinks, then cleared a place among the piles of coats and plopped down. Conversation was impossible as the music pulsed, Mary J. Blige, singing, "leave your situation at the door so grab somebody and get your ass on the dance floor."

I started dancing with a couple of Latinas. I felt good about being there but wondered how responsible I was to look after Claire. I beckoned her up to dance. She shook her head and as I danced I felt like I was defining my territory, perhaps, and feeling more comfortable. Even though I hadn't been to a gay bar in a long time, I felt experienced, like I knew the ropes. I turned my back to Claire as I danced, not wanting to look at her as I lifted my arms overhead and gyrated, pretending I was belly-dancing, trying to be sexy. I slid into an "I don't give a shit" dance zone that Josh always recognized and said "Oh boy" like I was headed for trouble.

When the music slowed, I scooted down next to Claire with no idea what she was thinking. I was afraid that maybe I'd brought her to something she wasn't comfortable with.

"How ya doing?" I said into her ear. I smelled a tinge of lavender as I got close.

"My God," she replied wide-eyed. I could hardly hear her with the music so high and the bass thumping in my chest. Then she pointed and I looked behind me. Two young women: one perched on the edge of the bench, her back arched against the wooden pew. The other woman straddling her, facing her, wearing a baseball cap over her buzz cut, which I noticed earlier. She had an "NY" razored near the nape of her neck. They were taunting each other, bodies undulating. I looked to Claire and rolled my eyes skyward. I was enjoying watching and reminded myself I was a lurker. Something I could watch but not taste. If I had sex with a woman—if I abandoned myself to the possibility and the experience—I feared I would lose the life I'd chosen, of being a wife and mother—I didn't want to extinguish something I held so dear.

Yet here I was with Claire, recklessly dipping my toes into the pool of desire. And the water felt so damn good. I couldn't figure out if I was resurrecting my lesbian leanings now because I found Claire so irresistible, or I was having a mid-life crisis, or I was feeling empty because of the loss of three significant women—my mother, Josh's mother, and

Maggie, my old boss. Or maybe it was because Josh was distant and not himself? In the past, a wrinkle in our relationship could be smoothed over by making love; it was quicker than a dozen conversations and always brought us safely back to home base. But that seemed impossible now. Or—was it the possibility I'd feared the most? Was I a lesbian in denial, someone who cloaked herself in heterosexual privilege and refused to accept herself as gay? One former lesbian lover had admonished me with these parting words: "It's not going to go away," when I had refused to leave Josh. Now, I looked over at Claire, so pretty, and imagined kissing her. But no, that would scare her and push me beyond lurker. So I got up and walked away.

I fished my cell phone out of my bag: one-fifteen a.m. Two missed calls. A pang of fright stabbed me because I knew it was Josh checking in. I'd have to explain where I'd been all night. And already I started mentally calculating where Claire and I were at what time so I could offer a flawless explanation, like a teenager coming home past curfew.

Claire and I walked north on Hudson Street towards the A train. I was all business now, going uptown and she going downtown, so we paused in the grimy white-tiled area between the subway stairways. We looked at each other in an awkward moment, smiled, and hugged. I embraced the cold fabric of her bulky black coat and touched her icy cheek with mine. "See you Monday," I mumbled as we parted.

I got to Penn Station and realized I'd read the train schedule incorrectly. After midnight, the Friday night schedule became Saturday morning, and I'd missed the train. The next one wasn't until three-ten a.m. I hadn't left my car at the station so I had to call Josh to pick me up.

"Where the hell are you?" he asked when I phoned.

"I've missed the train. Can you pick me up at four o'clock?"

"Of course. Claire's husband called me looking for her."

I paused. "Oh boy," I said.

"He said, 'Our crazy wives, out having fun,'" Josh mocked.

"So he wasn't mad?"

"No. He isn't the one who's mad, sweetheart. What are you up to with her?"

"Nothing."

I heard a heavy sigh. "See you at four, front of the train."

I milled around Penn Station, observing the teenagers stumbling drunk. Girls with loud personalities running in stilettos to the train platforms. How ugly it looked to be drunk.

When I got home, I noticed a Christmas list Josh had written and fastened to our refrigerator door.

Merry Christmist
Finish Christmas List
Under mistletoe Kisst
Cut out always being Pisst
No more parents being Disst
Limit all teary Mist
Eliminate Opportunity Missed
Hear it all and get the Gist
Learn the card game Whist
Never hear "malignant Cyst."
The baby born is Jesus Christ.
Now I'm done, I'll rest my Wrist.

✦

On Monday morning, I wandered into Claire's cubicle. I wondered what kind of reception I'd get. Would she be skittish? Friendly? Cold? We had shared quite a night with me as tour guide into a secluded world. As the youngest of three growing up, I reveled in showing someone something new.

"Hey, how's it going?" I asked casually. Her face, which usually opened when she saw me, was flat, her skin dull. I got afraid that her husband was pissed off about her coming home so late.

"Haven't slept for three nights," she whispered. "I'm exhausted." She pronounced "I'm" like a Southern-accented "ahm."

"Oh?"

"I finally understand something…everything," she said. I glanced behind me to make sure no one was standing nearby.

"Everything?"

"Yes. It's all falling into place."

"Uh huh."

She looked down. "I'm gay." She grimaced. "It's been the missing piece my whole life." She rolled her chair closer, head bent, as her hair swayed. I leaned over.

"Wow," I said looking for something to say.

She nodded tightly.

"There was this woman, Carla, in college. Everyone told me to stay away from her. Now I know she was after me. I shoulda listened to myself back then. Wouldn't have wasted all these years."

"Well, everyone goes through a questioning period with these kinds of things," I offered.

"Yeah, but at thirty-five? How could I not know this? I've been absent from my own life." She paused. "I can't stay married to him. Don't know what I'm gonna do."

I backed up to the doorway recoiling at what felt like a hot poker. She wanted out of her marriage? Because I took her to a lesbian bar?

"It was a lot to take in, the other night," I said.

I thought of the moment I chose to invite her to Henrietta's, knowing I was making a decision to steer her down the path of potential lovers. Now guilt swallowed me. She's done? Ready to throw her family away? How do I put out this fire? Yet even in her glassy-eyed expression her face's delicate features were exquisite. She appeared thin and vulnerable as a wounded starling. And now I knew her age, too. I felt ancient at forty-seven.

"How do you do this?" she asked. I looked at her quizzically. She had a scary honesty.

"Do what?"

"Be two people? What's the secret to that? How do you cut yourself into two?"

"Ah, come on. All women are two drinks away from being lesbians."

A flash of anger.

"I can't do that," she said. "This cutting myself in half."

✦

By afternoon, I was relieved to see Claire's stamina return. She was laughing with Timothy, Blossom's admin, at the other end of the hallway. When she and Timothy parted I ducked into my work space before she could see me watching. On her way back, she stepped in, her face close to my ear.

"So, you had lovers before you were married?" she began, peppering me with questions about my past.

She sat in my guest chair and in whispers I told her about the half-dozen women I'd slept with before I was married and how being at a gay bar felt so refreshing, like soldering a lost connection with my past.

"Something about being there fed me," I said. "I don't know what it was exactly but I felt open, free." I shrugged.

"Yes, you were all sparkly."

"Gotta get back to work," I said after forty-five minutes, conscious of how much time we'd spent talking. Claire's boss, Helen, sat in an office next to me and I could hear her on the telephone talking to a vendor. I got the feeling Helen was watching us.

"Well, don't forget the dinner at my house after the holidays. Malik wants to meet you." She touched my arm.

"Ok. As long as he doesn't ask me any questions about my past," I laughed. Her gaze pierced me.

"I told him all about you. How you take care of me here. He was glad we went out."

"I hope not *all* about me. Well he won't be thanking me if you're gay," I said in a stage whisper.

"It's okay. I trust you." Her voice was not hushed.

Perhaps, I'd said too much. I didn't really know her very well, only some months as co-worker. And she latched on quickly. I'd mixed personal and business, not a good idea. Yet her allure was magnetic and I'd climbed onto a high wire to show her my courage, to usher her into my world.

One day, I came back from lunch and found a CD, wrapped hastily in a brown envelope, on my desk. I knew it was from Claire, her chunky script unmistakable. It read "Madonna's Erotica," and I felt like my fingers were singed from its touch. She poked her head in my office and saw me staring at the disc and beckoned me with her eyebrows to listen to it in her office. She slapped bulky headphones over my ears, like a mother putting a hat on a little girl, then played the first track, the Peggy Lee song, "You Give Me Fever." I must have blushed. "You should see the look on your face!" she shrieked.

"Well, my God," I said.

"Listen, girl, you haven't heard anythin' yet," she said sliding into a soft drawl which I heard when I tipped the right headphone up.

She searched for another track on the CD.

"I'd like to direct your attention," commanded Madonna. My heart pulsed. Claire stood back and watched me listen to the third track, "Where Life Begins." I grinned nervously. *How does she know she wants this?* She seemed so sure.

CHAPTER 8

Josh had always been an agile skater and skier. As a boy he'd been taught to downhill ski by a Swiss instructor by keeping his woolen hat gripped between his knees. When we'd ski together—me on familiar beginner and intermediate trails and he on the double diamonds—I'd see him coming down the mountain in his jet black jacket and ski pants and marvel at his form. He traversed the mountain powerfully, his body bent like the letter "Z" absorbing the moguls with grace. But Josh's body—always so reliable and sturdy—was changing.

That winter, he coached Matthew's indoor roller hockey team and joined his own outdoor men's roller hockey league, with teams made up of guys in their twenties and early thirties. "You didn't know me when I was a scoring machine," he said when he signed up. At forty-nine, he was the oldest player on the team but was undaunted. It was one of the few places I saw his old, pre-9/11 spirit. Captain of his high school tennis team and 11-time marathon runner, including the Boston, Josh still had a touch of "Flash" in him.

When they let him off the bench, he sailed over the smooth black asphalt and skated backwards smoothly. He guarded his territory with the fierceness of a Marine, a look of intensity that came through the helmet's face guard, even though he could be knocked over just from the force of the young players whizzing by. Sometimes he would spin like a ballerina atop a music box because the other players were fast and powerful and they didn't suffer aging athletes.

The players often included him in after-game stops at the local bar and one or two called him for legal advice. The one time he scored a goal, he ended up on the asphalt and later in the hospital emergency room, and weeks later in the operating room for a laminectomy—back

surgery to treat ruptured discs. But he was a quick healer, and the afternoon after the surgery he roamed the hospital looking for a spot to
make phone calls. Since I'd been up that morning at five-thirty a.m. to
take him, I fell asleep in the hospital bed, hoping they wouldn't mistake
me for a patient.

Even as a coach to Matthew's roller hockey team, I'd see Josh gesticulating, pointing, and pacing in the box on the other side of the rink
and I felt some relief—he showed signs of his old self. But he could
change so quickly.

On the day of the first car accident, I picked Josh and Adam up
near the entrance to the parkway. I was relieved to see Adam in his
soccer team's red sweatshirt, unharmed and waiting on the sidewalk. He
clutched his soccer ball and Gatorade. I hugged Adam hard and glared
at his father, who I was sure had been driving too fast and distractedly.
While driving, Josh had been known to fiddle with the radio, clip his
fingernails, or, if he was in a "trying not to bite his nails" phase, paint
his stubby fingertips with "Thum," the anti-bite polish with a bitter
taste. "I have seven or eight good nails I could show in public," he had
said. On the drive home, after waiting for the car to be towed, I willed
myself to wait until I got home so I could talk to Josh privately about
the accident. I drove home.

"What the hell happened?" The words spilled out a few blocks
from home; impatience trumping my intention to delay the conversation, like a bully shoving to the front of the line.

"Why do you always take everyone's side but mine?" Josh asked,
skirting the issue. "I made a left-hand turn with the light," he yelled. "I
don't know what your problem is."

Suddenly we were arguing about why I don't support him, the
topic of the car accident shoved aside. I looked in the rearview. Adam
looked indifferent, peering out the window.

"Dad, you were asleep."

The words thudded.

"Oh my God," I said.

"Absolutely not true!" Josh's nostrils flared. He took off his navy
blue Yankees cap and wiped his bald head, one of his nervous gestures.

But the indignant expression on Josh's face made me hope he was telling the truth.

"Adam…?" I said calmly, my voice rising as if asking a question.

"Yes, mama?" His intonation matched mine.

"Did Daddy really fall asleep?"

"Well I couldn't see under your sunglasses but I think your eyes were closed."

"Are they closed now?" Josh asked as he turned to the back seat while setting his Ray-bans in place on his nose. His sunglasses were like clothing, always on.

"Maybe it looked like Dad was sleeping…maybe," I implored with a refreshed tone for my 11-year-old.

"I guess," Adam replied, singing the word into two syllables. "What about my game? When are we going?"

"Uh. Don't think you're gonna make it to this one, buddy," I replied.

Adam kicked the back of the seat.

By the time we got home I considered that Josh and Adam were fine physically but a bad taste lingered in my mouth. Josh was unsteady and unpredictable.

The Saturday before Christmas, our friends Paul and Francoise, part of the circle of couple-friends from town, had us over to their "Country Hoe Down" night at the Hempstead Country Club, where they were members. That evening we drove to the club in a white van, the kind churches use to transport congregants. We'd rented it for the night along with three other couples so no one had to be a designated driver.

In keeping with the country and western theme, I wore an oatmeal-colored straw cowboy hat along with a red gingham dress that flounced. Josh, having been a fan of country swing music, had a lot of the costume components already at his fingertips—Levis, gray ostrich cowboy boots, a chunky black belt with the turquoise and silver buckle, black leather vest, and those ubiquitous sunglasses. As the van wound its way through our suburban streets and stopped at each of our friends' houses, we sang "Love Train," by the O-Jays, clapping, and replacing the word "train" with "van." "People all over the world, join in, join the love van, the love van!"

Inside, the country club was lively; a country swing band and a square dance caller were on stage. Paul and Francoise greeted us, having decided not to take the "love van," but their own car; they wanted to get there early and get a good table. I stood at the buffet line with Amanda and noticed Josh sitting next to Paul at the other end of the room at the round catering-hall table with the white tablecloth. Both their plates already piled high with food. Paul was talking and gesticulating to Josh. Paul was looking ahead or at his food and didn't seem to notice that Josh's head was hanging close to his plate. Amanda nudged me, noticing Josh just as I had. His head was falling closer and closer to his mashed potatoes but Paul kept talking. Then suddenly, Josh's eyes opened and he lifted his fork and knife chin-high, paused, then his eyelids fell while his hands clutched his utensils like a mannequin poised for a still-life photo. At first, Amanda and I chuckled. But then my pulse raced because I remembered the car accident and Adam saying his father had fallen asleep at the wheel. Seeing his fatigue so blatantly amidst the festivities and noise of the ballroom frightened me.

I darted over to Josh and shook his shoulder.

"Josh!" I shrieked.

"What's wrong?" he asked, eyes springing open.

"Let's get our coats. We're leaving."

"Why?" he asked, bolting awake, half-standing now. "I'm fine."

"No, you're not." I steered us over to the coat check and Paul came with us, asking Josh if he was feeling all right.

"I'll take you home," said Paul, an audiologist, switching into emergency mode. I hated taking Paul away from the party but agreed because I wanted to leave quickly. I felt embarrassed and worried.

"Really, I'm fine," Josh said, shrugging my hand abruptly off his shoulder. "We don't need to leave."

"There's something wrong with you."

His insistence that everything was fine was something I might've deferred to if his sleepiness hadn't created such a public display.

We drove home, Josh and I sitting in the back seat of Paul's Volvo sedan, as he drove like a chauffeur. No one said a word.

When we got home, Josh fell asleep in bed immediately. I, on the other hand, lay awake all night next to him, imagining the worst—brain tumor, aneurysm, cancer. I'd never known anyone to have narcolepsy. The next day I told him he had to see a neurologist and that I would make the appointment.

"There. Is. Nothing. Wrong. With. Me," he insisted, angrily.

The night of the doctor visit Josh told me the neurologist was not concerned but sending him for tests, a CAT scan. Weeks later, he reported, "Everything is normal." He punctuated this announcement with a told-you-so smugness.

CHAPTER 9

Claire and I stepped into the Wine Merchant in Park Slope, Brooklyn. It was early Friday evening, February 2002, on our way to her apartment for dinner with Malik, Josh, and her son, Jamil. Petite linden trees dotted the avenue, the bottoms of their trunks encircled with scalloped metal grating. Tips of the trees waved amidst gusty wind in front of a black-blue sky.

"We're friends," I had said to Josh earlier that week, when he asked why Claire and Malik wanted us to come to dinner.

"From what you're telling me, now she's gay," he asserted. "What are you, her guru? Or are you looking to get into her pants? Just be honest, okay?"

"Really, you're making too much of this," I said.

"I'll come to dinner cause I want to be with you. Clear? "

I nodded, uncomfortable.

After buying the wine, Claire and I saw Malik pushing Jamil in a stroller. I recognized him as he came towards us. I had met him once when he came to the office with their son. His unexpected appearance startled me even though his approach was warm and unguarded. He hugged me as I was about to extend my hand. He was a handsome man around forty with a thick charcoal mane graying at the temples. At about five foot six, he was shorter than I'd remembered. When Claire pecked him on the lips she stood a quarter head taller. Her flaming redness and his charcoal complexion merged like combustible earth and fire and I understood how they would be attracted to each other. They were different, yet complementary. Jamil, their toddler son, arched his back to get out of the flimsy stroller. The wind whipped at my pants. I was cold and anxious to go.

"On my way to the Met Food," said Malik. I noticed the way he said "the Met Food" and not just "Met Food." I wondered what time we'd be dining if nothing had been prepared. It was already six and Josh would be coming at seven-thirty, after meeting a client in Manhattan Correctional Center, a local jail. Claire reminded her husband of the grocery list, while kneeling next to her son. Say hello to Janet, she said in that mother voice while Jamil clearly wanted nothing but to get out of the stroller.

We parted with Malik. Seeing her family sobered me. I had looked forward to some time alone with Claire. We'd talked about getting a drink somewhere before dinner. But now I'd switched into wife-mother mode and worried about the dinner that hadn't been prepared.

"Why don't we just head over to your place and get things started," I suggested.

"Yeah. I'd like to get things started."

"No, really," I said, serious now.

"Relax," she said soothingly. "Let's go to Blah Blah, this cute little café on 11th."

"I don't know." I hesitated. "We really don't have time. Malik will be back at your place and won't he need help?"

"I'm not worrying about him right now. Let's cross," she said, walking ahead of me.

We settled into a cushioned banquette near the curtained window. I slid in and she started to take the seat across, then sat next to me. The waitress took our drink orders, a white wine for me and a Bass for Claire.

"Can you lower the lights, please?" Claire asked her.

"We need them on so people can eat dinner," said the waitress.

Claire nodded and the waitress walked away.

"There's no one in the place but us. Jeez."

She rested her cheek against her palm and I rested my hand on her back.

My white cotton boat-neck sweater left the top of my shoulders half-bare. There was no one in the café except the two of us, the waitress, and the bartender lugging cartons to and from the bar. The waitress was doing busy work. I moved towards the window, away from Claire, on the banquette.

"Sit closer to me," Claire pleaded.

I moved towards her. "See how obedient I am?" I said.

I folded my arms to warm myself from the drafty window and Claire rubbed my shoulders then took my hand. The touch made me sizzle and my breath responded with an exhale. We didn't say much, just gazed like teenagers, grinning, searching each other's faces until the heat rose like the temperature on a muggy July afternoon. Our desire rolled over the banquette like fog, like a child's homemade tent over our heads and it didn't matter that there were people around.

Claire's lips made their way to my neck. She nibbled, then moved to my lips and soon we were kissing, plunging, hungry kisses. I felt light headed. We truly didn't care who was near because our lust was greedy, demanding; we pitched over everything for that moment.

"Anything else?" the waitress asked, handing us the check.

"No. I think that's enough for now," Claire said, turning to me.

The three of us laughed. The waitress looked relieved we were leaving.

Claire's apartment was a second-floor walk-up in a slim, tidy building. The stroller folded upright near the door told me which apartment was hers. I was trembling slightly and flushed; I needed to be a good actor. Plus I smelled of sex; I felt it leeching from my pores, even if we'd only been making out. At the top of the stairs, I straightened my clothes and she stopped, cornered me by the wall and—despite my anemic protest—kissed me deeply before thrusting the key in the door.

I didn't smell any cooking when we entered and Malik was sitting at the table reading. The chicken wasn't even in the pan. He got up and greeted us eagerly. I wondered if she would say something to him about the lack of progress in the food prep but she just took off her coat and set about in the kitchen, adjacent to the living room. The space, which would have felt claustrophobic were it not for the loft-like ceilings and brick walls, was decorated sparsely with dashes of color in the lampshades and prints. I remembered her saying how good she was with color when she was redesigning the magazine. How important the palette was. How she wanted to get it just right and spending the week-end developing the color scheme. Her apartment was like her magazine design—clean, nothing extraneous.

We uncorked the wine and Josh arrived as I was sipping. He looked harried after his visit with a client in prison. My face was scarlet. Having the oven on high in the small apartment didn't help my body temperature. Josh gave me a once-over, then pecked my cheek before I introduced him to our hosts.

Jamil was climbing on the couch, making it impossible to sit there, so Josh and I joined Malik at the table. Josh was friendly and funny making a joke about "Crooklyn" and parking our minivan on the street. We were all tight in the kitchen so I was grateful when the food was finally served. Claire gestured at me to come to the living room—only feet away. There she and I sat crossed-legged on the couch facing each other with our plates on our laps. At one point, she got up and took a photo album off the shelf. Josh moved to a spot at their computer across from where Claire and I were sitting while Malik was left to put Jamil to bed. I didn't hear any crying, just Malik's British-tinged voice and its melodious assurances.

Josh was searching furiously for information about his client on the computer. Every so often he would spew a "thank you, God," and "yes, I knew it." I was glad he was engaged in his own quest. It gave me space. Lately he was obsessed with this guy he'd been researching, talking about this client in federal prison, someone who identified himself as the illegitimate son of a former high-ranking official in the Philippines.

With the hangover from 9/11 still making us queasy, and Josh's behavior so erratic, I'd cautioned him about getting too intimate with a prisoner he'd claimed the US government was trying to keep incarcerated. I'd also steered him away because this was just the type of client for whom Josh would end up working hundreds of hours for and not get paid.

"Don't worry; I'm getting a retainer," Josh had told me, meaning that the client was signing an agreement for legal services. The agreement signaled to me that he would get a fee. It was important because Josh had a list of clients he no longer charged for legal services; clients who had crossed over into Josh's "friend" category. People he wanted to "help out."

"You're not a charity," I'd reminded him. But something in his temperament made him want to give his skills and knowledge away. Perhaps he didn't value himself enough, I'd thought.

Yet, I was intrigued that Josh was following the trail of this guy; not only because it felt like a spy novel, but also because this investigation had given Josh renewed energy. Except for the narcoleptic episodes, which had waned, Josh seemed more himself. His tightly wound, focused self, replaced the aimless, depressive person I couldn't understand.

"This was our fashion business," Claire said, emphasizing "was" while laying the photo album flat. She showed me magazine clippings from French *Vogue* and I understood right then how successful their business had been and how painful its failure must have been. Her husband hadn't worked since the business folded two years before, just when their son was born. They had decided that Claire, with her graphic design skills, was the better choice for employment. So Malik stayed home with their boy. Now I understood even further why she had been reading *Failing Forward* when I first met her. I gazed at her sitting with her legs crossed and imagined making love to her, getting tangled in her Sedona-hued hair, getting folded into her purpose and wondering whether I could ever get out.

That night, Josh and I lay in our bed, stiff as ironing boards.

"What's going on with her?" His tone was tentative but his intrusion made me angry.

"Just tell me the truth," he pleaded. "I don't care what you are."

"You're crazy; we work together."

But my body defied me: I was hot with the fever Peggy Lee sang about. And my husband of twenty years knew my temperature was high for someone else. During the night, I tiptoed downstairs to the porch room and turned on the computer to a hotmail account I'd created just for messages with Claire: tourguide1@hotmail.com. There was an email waiting in my inbox. It began: *Your shoulders, your neck....*

CHAPTER 10

Claire left small magenta-colored notes on my desk. The paper was stiff and by her folding them in half, she created a matchbox-size canvas.

My Smooth J, read the cover.

Inside: *Are you aching?*

Each note was printed in small letters, no caps, black, fine-point pen.

Cover: *Did I tell you?*

Inside: *Your hands are soft like rose petals.*

She decorated the notes with tiny drawings and scrawled her signature script, flowing and painterly. On this note, she's sketched delicate tulips with faces, the stems long, tube-like, and intertwined, like us.

Cover: *Valentine's Day stickers: Kiss-Kiss; Just 4 Us*

Inside: *I'm having a "your shoulders, your neck," week. That's why I'm on the cliff. Good crazy. But damn. I need some relief. Thinking about it in bed this morning.*

Cover: *SJ (Smooth J)*

Inside: *I want to glide my tongue across your sweet, crooked bottom teeth.*

Note from Claire:

I don't know how all of THIS will turn out (hmmm…turn "out," see I can be a cornball too). But there are some things I AM certain about. We found each other because we needed to. I've been searching a long time, but I wasn't sure of what. Now I know 2 things: I needed THIS and I needed to find myself, release myself, allow myself to be ME (backwards E). I believe you were looking for the same things as ME (backwards E).

I was afraid to write her back because I didn't want any evidence. No evidence of my hand in a desire that was overflowing, like a river in

danger of wiping out everything. So I corralled my lust, took the prickly insistence that rattled my heart and pulsed my blood, and stepped on
it. I told myself: I can control this. It cannot flood me. I won't allow it.
I will make myself not want her.

Note from me to Claire, February 21, 2002:
*My dear: I am becoming undone. I am not a person who gives into my
impulses easily. But I, too, must open the steam valve. I don't know where to go
or what to do with this. I keep trying to shut it but Jesus, it's too fucking hot to
touch. I need your help. I can't work. I need to be able to go home, be comfortable,
honest. I don't know how to be. I love your notes. I can't look away but this is
dangerous. We have families.*

Despite the danger, I agreed to long walks at lunch time, to the
back steps of the Morgan Library where they display banners for exhibits of illuminated manuscripts from the thirteenth century, reminders of
ancient love, art, and duty. I told her we needed to find something in
between and she looked at me quizzically, irritation in her eyes.

"And, exactly, what is that?"

I mumbled something about not getting so swept up in emotion.
As we sat on the cold slab steps and held hands, she slipped a little ma-
genta note and walnut shells into my coat pocket. I found them when
I returned to the office.

Magenta note:

Outside: Illustration of a walnut

Inside: *The toughest nut to crack.*

We sat at small round tables at Starbucks on Madison Avenue holding hands through cups of latte and green tea, which she pronounced
"grain tay." At the table, I felt like all things were possible. I was drawn
in by the blue-gray of her eyes, her lovely breath, her ability to coax me
into playfulness. She had, at Christmas, gone to a diner with Lena and
me. Next to our table hung glass ornaments of a crèche scene—baby
Jesus, Mary, and Joseph. She unhooked glass Mary, supplicating on bent
knees, and dared me to wear the chunky Jesus parents as a pair of ear-
rings, which I did by slipping the hooks into my ears. I ate lunch with

the crèche dangling.

Then next time we were at Starbucks, I got serious and told her to get some "perspective." She called it the Big P.

"There has to be some middle ground."

"What the hell is that?" she asked. "What the hell is middle ground?"

Note from Claire:

Outside: Illustration of a coat hanger

Inside: *Did you know I always hang my coat facing yours in the closet?*

I hadn't noticed. But after she told me I noticed all the time. The closet became our shorthand. If her coat was not there I missed her. I wanted our coats face to face.

When Josh called me at work in the afternoons now, he asked what I did for lunch.

"I ate lunch," I would respond.

✦

Letter from Josh, March 1:

I thought you should know that because of your steadfast refusal to keep me informed as to the C&J events of the last few weeks, claiming an invasion of private space, I will try to honor your request and rely on the trust and honesty you profess. You know how important it is for me to be able to trust you and how much I want to believe what you tell me.

At this point, Blind Faith is very hard to justify, however. I want to believe that your refusal is stubbornness, childishness, or philosophy rather than the fact that the information is just so horrible you can't say it. I'm not giving up yet though because I love you too much. Help me out? Josh

At home, Josh was continually angry with me, and I found myself dodging him because he questioned my honesty. He claimed it wasn't my relationship with her that was infuriating; it was my lack of telling the truth. Late Sunday evening arguments took place behind our closed bedroom door, where I sat on my side of the bed, leaning against the inlaid mother of pearl oak headboard as Josh paced in front of the windows where the moon peeked in.

"The secret self is the feelings, not the facts, my dear," he snarled. "The facts are the truth of what is, not what we feel or wish it to be. If I were in your shoes," he laughed, "I wouldn't want to tell me either. And I know you're getting angry now because you can't win, right? No matter what you say, I don't believe you, right? Nothing has happened, right? I know you fooled around and it's probably gone too far once or twice. And I know you feel you deserve it because you have that lesbian component. That gives you permission, right?"

"It doesn't give me permission," I said, exhaling. "Please let's pick this up tomorrow. I'm tired."

"Nobody likes to come clean," he shouted. "Everybody denies responsibility and wants to blame outside factors, or rationalize, minimize, maybe, or at least ignore unpleasant truths. We're indignant. Aren't we? Aren't you?"

I stared at the dream catcher hung in the corner of the room, fixated on how the feathers got tanner as the eye followed their form and how intricately the netting was sewn. I didn't even know what the questions were. What was he asking me?

"Lies become truth, you know," he continued. "Silence can become the truth. The significant can become the insignificant. Truth can become a secret shared only by those who know the facts." He was giving a summation before a jury and I the defendant.

I nodded in agreement. My body recoiled towards the headboard. I just wanted this to stop.

"Sure. And tomorrow you're back with her. And she can hammer you too. I know how aggressive she is. How she needs you to be like her. But you like being hammered by her. But not me. Sure we can talk about it tomorrow."

As unpleasant and horrible these encounters made me feel, I absorbed them not only because I felt guilty and that I deserved it but because I had unwittingly agreed to be a receptacle for the frustration and despair molting off him since 9/11. His anger at my indiscretions pointed to some return to normalcy. At least he was animated, not the depressed, listless person who had lost all interest in living. He was beginning to stop his swaying and to bolt upright like the inflatable toy punching-bag clown at a standing position. I had gotten his attention.

Magenta note:

Cover: *Drawing of a heart pierced by an arrow, tears (blood?) dripping.*

Inside: *We talk so intimately about so many things, but we've never even hugged a full hug, no coats, not sideways, you know?*

Note to Claire:

I'm having a love/hate relationship with your notes. The duality of things. How can you write that, then go about your business? Face your husband? I guess it's a release for you but for me, it's all so real. Your writing is cold water in my face. You're forcing me to face the reality and intensity of all this: how I feel about you, how you've changed my life, how I look at women, how I feel about my body. These notes are hot potatoes—like in the game—get rid of them. It all feels serious. And I hate that feeling. I want to be released from it even though I love your letters.

Magenta note:

Outside: *HJ* (Hot J)

Inside: *I can't help it. You make me wanna be so bad.*

Letter from Claire:

So the only way I can get any kissing with you is to take you to a straight bar, sit in the window, pin you up against the wall, and move in. You squirmer. What yummy kisses. I have nothing to compare them to. Maybe teenage kisses. Like when I was fourteen or fifteen and played spin the bottle. Kissing you was simply luscious. And dangerous. An intensity I could not have imagined. I could have kissed every inch of your body right there in the window. And never looked up to see who was watching. I'm not leaving this earth without making love to you. I mean it.

I told her about a book of lesbian erotica I owned with a story by the brilliant Kim Chernin. *An American in Paris* describes two women who do a dance of sexual circling. I'd read this book secretly at home and stored it in a locked backpack at the back of my closet. In Chernin's story, the Parisienne seduces the American who, in describing how dangerous it felt, compared the act of becoming sexual to standing at the edge of the woods watching teenage boys play with knives. The author offered long, delicious passages about how it felt to be with her Parisienne lover as they double-wrapped their woolen scarves around their necks and walked arm in arm through their Arrondisement on the cold, cobblestone streets towards the apartment and exquisite con-summation.

Days later, I happened on another incredible book by the same author, *My Life as a Boy*, at a library sale. I snatched this gem and savored every word about a woman entering middle age who wishes to live her life like a boy entitled to venture and explore, unlike girls who are left behind to care for others:

> *If a woman in her thirties turns into a boy that may mean she's having trouble getting out of the place she is in. She requires the instinctive, wholly natural ruthlessness of a boy. He will leave home; everyone expects it of him. He won't move in next door to his mother or around the block and raise children, not likely. He won't give it a second thought: he's off into the world, he's a boy, he's going.*

I passed it on to Claire. I wished us to be boys and ride a wild adventure. I wanted her to go with me. I recognized the thrill of being a boy, a man, even for a few hours at a women's bar where I might join feminine mysteriousness and possess the essence of what women own. Yet I also knew that the woman who lives around the corner from mother was me.

Soon, Claire started dressing like a boy. She wore steely black Doc Martens paired with camouflage pants and apricot cut-off t-shirts. Her boss, Helen, took notice and reminded her that jeans and camouflage trousers were not appropriate office attire. The dress code notice got push-pinned to the department bulletin board.

"I don't care," she said. "Let them send me to the principal."

One day she wore a light-blue sailor-boy top and told me she was going to get a tattoo.

"Don't make it an anchor," I joked.

The blue of the sailor top coupled with her cascading golden hair resembled art. She rollerbladed in the hallway and pinned up pictures of Cindy Sherman, the performance artist who photographed herself as characters like deranged housewives.

"You couldn't look like a boy if you grew a penis," I told her. Yet her growing androgyny—her transformation—had lassoed me. I admired her unequivocal leap into the lesbian arena, a place I'd once longed for, yet struggled with, a place I hadn't accepted, despite the years of stops and starts. My hot and cold relationship with the lesbian world gnawed at me like a small animal, telling me I was a fraud, a lukewarm liver of life, safe and disgusting. I argued with it as if it were a long-lost sibling who showed up when she needed something. I felt like I belonged nowhere, an empty inhabitant of the walnut shell, the meat scraped out and discarded. I felt disgustingly tepid in my actions but not in the depth of love for my husband and boys or affection for Claire's illustriousness, outpourings, relentlessness, boldness, and unwillingness to settle. I was stuck in a classic mid-life triangle: I didn't want to give up anything.

✦

At the end of April, Josh, Matthew, three of Matthew's friends and I climbed into our Plymouth Voyager. Matthew was turning fifteen and wanted to celebrate his birthday at Skate and Surf, a punk rock festival in Asbury Park. Josh had been accompanying him to concerts in New York City—at the Bowery Ballroom, Roseland, and other venues where they caught bands like MXPX and the Movie Life. Skate and Surf featured the boys' favorites: Good Charlotte, Saves the Day, the Descendants, Dashboard Confessional, and Alkaline Trio. On the trip driving south, Matthew, his wavy black hair hanging to the top of his shoulders, sat in the back with his friends. He'd brought along a toy we called the grabber, a dinosaur head at the top of a stick, whose mouth opened and closed by a lever. Matthew kept grabbing my elbow with the grabber and I kept falling for it every time, thinking there was a bug on my arm. Josh, who wore a "Less than Jake" Lego Man t-shirt, kept clicking photos of me from his wrist-camera.

I really didn't want to go to the weekend-long festival but Josh had been so suspicious and angry about my entanglement with Claire that I had no choice but to say yes. We parked Adam with a friend for the two nights.

It was rainy and bone-cold when we arrived at the beach in Ashbury Park, a once-glorious resort town on the boardwalk. Ocean waves sprayed the shoreline boulders as we checked into a fleabag—formerly palatial—hotel across the street from the cavernous concert hall. The boys were anxious to get to the concerts, scheduled throughout the day and nights. While the kids went off to the shows, Josh and I faced hours alone together, something we'd been avoiding. At one point, we walked to the concert hall where, as we got closer, the bass vibrated in my chest. Pierced lips, boys in hoodies, and thick spikey belts congregated outside as skateboarders practiced their moves on home-made ramps, even in the rain. Petite bleach-blond girls with streams of colorful tattoos on their arms and chests waited outside to get their hands stamped along with us. Josh, a veteran concert-goer, brought ear plugs and gave me two marshmallow-y Hearos which I plugged into my ears. I appreciated it.

Once inside, we climbed the wide stairway to the yellow-taped bar area, drank beers, and watched from a balcony the crowd surfers and kids in the mosh pits. Below, scruffy-faced boys spun their arms like windmills, ran as if in a whirlpool, and dared anyone to enter their space. This must be what it's like to be a boy, I thought: *defend your territory.* But the more I watched, the more I saw that moshing was more posturing than anything else. I looked at Josh. He caught me staring at him.

"Like the old days," he reminded me.

"Yup. Let's stand on a chair and watch the Talking Heads. I'll change into my huk-a-poo blouse and you can wear your parachute pants."

He squeezed my hand and for a moment I felt safe again.

Later, we walked over to the main stage where Dashboard Confessional was about to perform. They sang a song I'd been hearing the boys play at home, called "Hands Down." *Just kill me so I can die happy*, went the lyrics and I couldn't help but think of Claire, Café Blah Blah, and our kisses. I fought back tears I didn't dare show.

Josh and I had dinner alone that night at a nearby Spanish-style restaurant. The furnishings were old-world decor: heavy dark-wood chests with metal draw pulls, scalloped sconces, and high-backed velvet chairs. We ordered sangria and as the night unfolded Josh kept drinking after I'd stopped with my second glass. Soon he was into shots of Cuervo Gold and looking very red in the face.

"So I'm sorry if you don't like it that I'm the meddling watchdog up your butt and into your innermost sanctum," he began.

"What are you talking about? I told you what you wanted to know. Didn't I?"

"Yes, my dear," he sticks on the "r." "I know she's given you letters, which you refuse to show me… And regardless of your belief that she is motivated by her pure and unadulterated love for you, the truth is she needs you to be gay and leave me for her, nothing less."

I exhaled hard, ready for the emotional pilfering that had become such a part of our time together. He wanted answers about my feelings towards Claire. I was afraid to spill them, scared of him, fearful of the truth, which I really didn't know for sure any more. I was compelled by her, yet I found her intensity as frightening as it was intoxicating. I was not in love. I tried to convince myself, like the song from 10 CC, the band from the 1970s.

"The only reality here is that if she doesn't stop very soon, it will likely erode our marriage, my dear." Again, emphasis on the "r." "Despite what she tells you, you are not gay. You may be attracted to women, and I could even live with the occasional encounter, but if you continue with this obsession, this fantasy, I will stop loving you."

The words plunged into my chest.

I braced myself for the onslaught and I stopped saying anything about his coming home from work past ten p.m. most nights and his lack of explanation for why he kept visiting his client—this so-called "Filipino illegitimate son"—in prison nearly every day and not tending to his law practice. He shrugged when I showed him a bottle of pills I recently found in his sock drawer, refusing to tell me what they were and if he'd been taking some. When I pressed him, he said, "You don't tell the truth. Why should I?"

After the Skate and Surf weekend, which our son told us was the best weekend of his life, I found a greeting card Josh slipped into my work bag. I found it before I'd returned to work and read it sitting on my bed. The cover, which showed the backs of two bears hugging on a hill looking at a heart-shaped star formation, read: "I'd rather do nothing with you. Than something with anyone else." In his loopy, impossible-to-read handwriting it said:

I Love You. It's not the "I love you," but the I LOVE YOU, the one where I pledge my life to you for better or for worse. During hard times and harder times when it really counts. I give you this commitment now and forever. If you want it and are ready to accept the responsibility of this commitment, together nothing and no one can stand in our way. My love, just say the magic words, "I love you" and I'm yours. Just say the magic words, 'I choose you Winkie,' like in Best in Show, and my heart soars."
— Josh

On Sunday night, the day before my return to the office, I felt so clear in my resolve to stop "seeing" Claire that I reassured my husband. I wanted nothing more than to stay married, I told him. I meant it when I said it.

CHAPTER 11

Note from Claire:

I've never told you what I like about you and how THIS started for me. The gay bar: I like how you were: bold, at ease, so comfortable. That got me going. I liked that you were comfortable talking to women there and you approached them. That's what I want, too. I'd like for you to approach me sometimes. (I know conflict, conflict, so goddamn annoying, isn't it?)

"What is this?" I asked, standing in Claire's cubicle, puzzling over a piece of art. I held a glass jar encircled with black electrical tape in a strangling maniacal way with a little opening to view a dash of potpourri.

"Butch in a bottle."

"Is this being butch?" I laughed.

"It's the state I'm in. Having to shut down these feelings because of my situation."

Claire's artistic output grew: drawings, collages, and photos, assembled in bulging hardbound sketchbooks. They spilled from her file drawers, which she kept locked, except to show me. She couldn't keep it at home and dared not show anyone else. She was very careful with the keys, always nervous someone would see and judge the personal nature of her work.

She handed me a light bulb covered in duct tape, then a harmonica-size box with a tiny play hammer covered in electrical tape and heavy twine. The box contained a note with a drawing of a nail attached to the hammer that read: *Nail me*. And two small, plastic toy clocks—children's blue and yellow, mounted next to each other on thick white posterboard lined up neatly. She labeled the blue clock set to eight-thirty a.m. *THIS WAY* and the yellow set to five-forty p.m. *THAT WAY*.

"This is the time when we can be ourselves," she said pointing to the eight-thirty clock, "and when we cannot be ourselves," she continued, pointing to the five-forty clock. The words *THIS* and *THAT* signified the time we were together and time we had to go home to our families. Then she graduated to photography books of runaway trains (her, she said) and Petroishka dolls (me) one nestled inside the other inside the other.

Her art thrilled me. I admired her facility and unstoppable need to create. She called me her muse and I conjured up Henry Miller and Anais Nin and Georgia O'Keeffe and Alfred Steiglitz. Art consumed us and I felt drunk with its power to transform us.

Now, she was reporting daily on the events at home. Her husband knew, she told me one day.

"Exactly what?" I asked, nervous he would hold me responsible.

"He knows I'm interested in girls…since that night at the bar. I had to tell him. He sees how crazy I've been, how I've been dressing. He's making me answer questions on a questionnaire he made up. He told me I had to. I can't rile him up."

She pronounced "rile" like "doll" with an "r."

"He can get mean," she continued. "I've seen it; I'm afraid if he finds out I'm out, he'll try to keep Jamil away." She hung her head.

"What are you gonna do?" I was frozen, wondering if he was going to contact me or come to the office like a crazed, jealous, hatchet-wielding ex. The conversation made me want to run to the comfort of Josh and home.

"Gonna answer the questionnaire. Buy time until I can figure it out."

Her husband's growing knowledge did not concern her enough. She started leaving me tablet-sized "flip books," as she called them because the pages flipped over the top rather than left to right. When I came back from lunch, a new one appeared in the discreet brown inter-office envelope, with the figure-eight string tie. Someone will see it, I thought, but then I couldn't imagine how. Her artwork was as combustible as a tinderbox because it held my explosive passion. Feelings I had stuffed down. Feelings that terrified me. Feelings I wanted to detonate. Yet I unwrapped my prize from the stiff brown envelope, so proper and far away from love and giddiness. I slid the flip book out and savored her and our delicious world. When the book descended into my fingers, it was as if our souls kissed.

Cover: *LONGING...FLIRTING...ACHING.*

She penned the word "flirting" in a delicate lower-case script with the ascender of the "f" leaning into the "l." The "g" curled like a hopeful lover waving good-bye. The "c" was capped and backwards because that is her initial and she was not too steady on her feet right then. Oh, and the *LONGING* and the *ACHING* are upside down and backwards and to be read from left to right. Things are topsy-turvy in the *LONG-ING...FLIRTING...ACHING* book.

Inside were her observations about me/us:

You being ambivalent

You saying you don't allow yourself

Me saying you put me into a tailspin

You smelling watermelon perfume in the bathroom and saying, If I smell that on a woman on the train it sends me into a tailspin

You wearing that tight lavender camisole and pulling your shirt closed all day

Me being tortured out of my mind and drinking and not sleeping because you are two people and me wanting desperately for you to be one, be you, and crying because I think you just disconnect from your feelings, so you don't have to be in pain because of THIS.

Me saying we have to get into bed and you saying you can't because it will put you in another place and me thinking maybe that's the place you're supposed to be and that's why we met and fell in love.

We are a bomb [illustration of ticking bomb] in a briefcase tick...tick...tick.

You wanting desperately to find the right color wire to cut to stop the ticking, me wanting to let it explode.

✦

One morning she pled with me to come with her, leave the building for one minute. I agreed uneasily and we walked along the city streets at a brisk clip.

"Stop," she said. "I'm in love with you."

Later that day, the flip book had a new entry from our stroll:

Me touching your cheek on the street, you pulling back saying, "don't," me telling you looking into your eyes, "I'm in love with you." You looking irritated, uncomfortable and saying you don't allow yourself. Me feeling, "this is right."

A few days later, she showed me the questionnaire her husband had asked her to answer and sign.

It asked questions like, "How long have you known about your confusion?" and "Do you think it's good for a married woman and mother to be acting like this?" I didn't say it, but I thought maybe he was right. I shouldn't be acting like this. I'm a mother and a wife with responsibilities. But Claire, oh God, how could anyone say no to her? My body felt hot to touch all the time. I was in love, though I desperately denied it.

I'm trying to work, I would tell her, to get a magazine out: assign articles, set up photo shoots, stick to a production schedule, plan meetings. Whenever she came into my office to view a slide on the light box, her lips grazed my ear, "I want you." One day, she pressed a business card in my palm. I looked at the card, Metro Hotel, then back at her. I grinned, embarrassed. My body was pulsing with need, especially when I smelled the sweet lavender scent she wore, the one I first smelled at Henrietta's. I put the card in my pencil drawer. She turned and left. I wondered if it would ever be possible.

Josh called my office three times a day now. He gave me letters, poems, lectures, and warnings about the threat to our family should I choose to love her.

He left me a poem:

YOUR BOAT
ROW ROW ROW YOUR BOAT
GENTLY DOWN THE STREAM
MERRILY MERRILY MERRILY MERRILY
LIFE IS BUT A DREAM

ROW ROW ROW YOUR BOAT
I THINK I SENSE A THEME
YOU SET A COURSE FOR GOD KNOWS WHERE
WHAT MOTIVATES THIS SCHEME?

ROW ROW ROW YOUR BOAT
HAS SURELY SPRUNG A LEAK
YOU LOOK AROUND AS YOU GO DOWN
WHAT IS IT YOU SEEK?

ROW ROW ROW YOUR BOAT
IS THIS SAFE HARBOR PORT OF CALL?
THE LAND OF MILK AND HONEY
WHERE YOU CAN HAVE IT ALL?

ROW ROW ROW YOUR BOAT
ADRIFT UPON THIS SEA
WEARILY WEARILY WEARILY WEARILY
WON'T SOMEONE RESCUE ME?

Flip book entry from Claire:

I don't know the rules of somewhere in between. I just wake up at night with you on my lips. We are in between two lives. Not completely in one or the other. Blowing back and forth like wind kissing spring leaves.

After a few weeks, I said yes to Claire's persistence that we "go somewhere; get out of these cubicles, please." So, on a Friday afternoon, we took off, bound for Central Park. It was a glorious spring day and we walked north, passing hyacinths and daffodils in cement street plant-ers. The pungent sneaky scent of the purple flowers trailed us as we sauntered shoulder to shoulder, me wearing my khaki raincoat over my black and white jersey blouse with the three-quarter sleeves, the one that made me feel Parisian. We were free, out of the eyes of scrutiny. She went to grab my hand.

"Don't be skittish," she remarked when I pulled away. "It's New York. We're allowed."

We held hands inside my coat pocket. Her hand felt like an artist's, rough in the middle.

We approached the 57th Street entrance to the park, past FAO Schwarz, where hansom cabs lined the curb and horses swung their tails rhythmically and looked straight ahead between their blinders. As we walked on cobblestones, I suddenly felt very old.

"Remember the movie, *Age of Innocence*?" I asked. She had gathered her hair up in a clip on top of her head and I squinted to see her freck-les drawn out by the sun.

"Yes."

"The scene where the two lovers—who are not lovers," I said, "held hands in the back of a horse-drawn carriage? That physical con-tact was all they would ever have. And it lasted them a lifetime." She looked at me.

"That's how this feels," she said. "Two little rose petal soft kisses and some sun-warmed hand-holding has to last us a lifetime."

We planted our bodies at the top of a hill, underneath a tree, to avoid the sun because redheads burn so easily, she reminded me. I laid my raincoat on the damp grass for us to sit.

"Grass stains," I said. She laughed.

"Who cares? You're so neat. I'm gonna call you Ja-neat."

"I like that. It reminds me of Janootz, my mother's nickname for me. I hadn't told anyone that in, probably, ever."

The sun poked through the trees dappling our space.

"Do you ever want to kiss me again?" she asked. I let her hair down out of her barrette.

"You know how sometimes when we're talking I start smiling?," I asked. She nodded. "That's why. I'm thinking about kissing you. And when I think about kissing you I think, 'I won't hold back.'"

And then we were on it, kissing like teenagers. I took her face in my hand.

"My dear," I moaned and kissed and kissed her as if I were afraid she was going to run away.

On Monday morning, I found a cardboard orange-colored note in my pencil drawer:

Outside: Blank

Inside: *What is this? This is…you, me, getting to be free, alone, together, sharing ourselves, no censoring, no apologies, no rules to follow, physical heat like a blow torch, skinny-dipping in a warm emotional pond, knowing ourselves for the first time all over again, alone, together, racing to us, going to the unknown in the physical world, but known only to us.*

She was a speeding train—a Japanese train, she said, like the ones that don't run on tracks. "They're magnetic. No friction because there's no touching of metal." She gave me a photo of a runaway train and labeled it "rascal." "The rascal is unstoppable," she wrote. "I don't know him/her very well. I didn't even know I had it in me. You brought that out too, you know."

When I packed up my things to leave the office on Fridays, I was hoping for relief. I wanted to be in my home safely with my husband. The exhaustion of these emotions—and trying to pretend they meant nothing—felt heavy as a house.

Then, one afternoon, we left the office at lunchtime to shop at the Gap.

Claire leaned against the entrance to the fitting room while I rifled through the clearance rack. Looking at her out of the corner of my eye, she looked tall and slender, I thought, what my father would call legs that go from here to there. The luster of her hair rivaled the coat of an Irish Setter and I swear she had the whitest teeth I'd ever seen on an adult. She smiled and plucked her copper colored-hair in a bunch on top of her head then let it fall to her shoulders. I backed up, pretending to look for a bargain while stalling.

Claire suggested we share a dressing room so we can get done quicker. I knew I was walking into the lion's den but I liked being led. I told myself, "this is what friends do when they go shopping; they share a dressing room."

The woman stationed at the dressing room ushered us.

"We'll share this one," Claire said, pointing. We tried on black low-rise jeans and I wondered about the state of my underwear. Which ones did I wear today? Then came the moment when I could no longer avoid her gaze which she'd been trying to catch through the whole dressing room charade. She was a half a head taller and I looked up at her. She put her thumbs through my belt loops and pulled me toward her. She was leaning against the wall. We were both in our socks.

I smelled her clean soap-scent up close, the one I inhaled every day as she brought me page proofs or a photograph to look at through the loop. Her delicious aroma was now on me. This was the first time we'd had even a modicum of privacy and I let go and kissed her, devoured her. Her lips felt like pillows and I thought this is what a man feels. I was sure everyone in the store knew what was going on behind the slatted door. Her breath was sweet and as refreshing as a drink of water at the park fountain. I ran my tongue along her lips before I circled her mouth moist, ready, begging. She had her hands on my waist and I leaned into her as I pressed my knee between her legs. I thought of people waiting to use the dressing room and pulled away but she wouldn't have it, being pushed away. We finally took a break, looked at each other incredulously, then giggled.

"We gotta go," I said, always the voice of reason.

She later wrote me that kissing me was like adolescent kissing, sweet boy kissing, flowery trying-on kisses like when you're thirteen and it all seems so dangerous and unbelievable. Someone would actually want to kiss you! Yet I pushed her away because I knew Josh would ask what happened today and I am a very bad liar. When we got back to the office, I was shaking. I felt delirious with love and fear, my synapses firing.

The next morning, I wrote her that this had to stop.

Note from Claire:

You wrote about your fears and I understand all of them. And I respect them. But you know what scares me? Holding back. I have this urgency to live my life fully. Up until three months ago I thought I had been. But now so many things have changed. Me. So with this change comes a different life to live. I know we are living in those other lives but there's another one to nurture as well. They can never merge. That's the big problem. So what to do? Live two lives? Can you do that?

From Claire: Photograph of a walnut, open shell, flesh exposed, chunks of smashed shell strewn. Handwritten script in a circle around the photo: "And you wanting to climb back into the safety of your shell, that makes it so much worse. Because once the shell's been broken, and we've split it wide open, you can't get back in...."

Later that week, Claire, Carson, Lena, and I sat at a table in Mulligan's, the East Side pub where Claire and I had our first beer together in November. We left the office for lunch and had been out for hours, a move I rarely made. But it was Friday, we were having a good time, and the beers were flowing so I thought, "what the hell?" I seemed to be in trouble with Josh all the time anyway, so why not? The luxurious light of the May afternoon trickled in and illuminated the scuffed hardwood floors, rickety chairs, and electrical workers sitting at the bar.

We were sitting at the back where the lighting was dim. Claire was drawing on a white, paper placemat with a flair pen. It looked like she was drawing designs but I could make out the words in her flowery lettering: "You are my smooth J." No one noticed because the design camouflaged the words. I gave her "the Look," since neither Lena nor Carson knew about us.

Lena told a story about when she was a kid growing up in North Dakota and her brother Marvin grabbed a snake near the dam. On the way home, Marvin tried to wrangle Lena by lassoing the snake around her neck. Once they reached their yard, he killed the snake and hung it on the fence. Lena laughed.

"I love stories about snakes," Carson, our openly gay fifty-year-old co-worker, said clasping his hands playfully.

He kept buying pitchers of Bass ale and pouring it into tall glasses, his colorful Mickey Mouse tattoo sliding out of his shirt sleeve when he poured. Carson's eyeglasses were a stylish tortoise-shell amber that covered half of his wide handsome face. He loved gossip and shared it dramatically with sweeping hand gestures.

"What's with you two?" he asked when he caught Claire and me in a gaze. We looked at him and laughed.

Lena said, "What?" Her face showed a serious don't-leave-me-out look.

Everyone giggled and Lena's eyes widened.

"You two?" she asked cautiously.

It was obvious now and I was oddly proud of it, having let go for the moment of my fear of judgment. It was all okay right then, that hated fear eclipsed by a serenity I'd forgotten I could even feel.

Claire, sitting to my right, reached over and rested her arm on my right thigh. Heat like a spark. I couldn't believe her boldness. I ignored my impulse to swat her hand away. It felt too hot to halt. Soon I put my hand under the table and interlocked her fingers until she placed my fingers on her thigh. I pulled back.

"I'm going out for a cig," she said. Carson and Lena followed and I saw them through the storefront glass under the awning and I wondered whether I should head back to the office. I had to pee bad but I waited for them., There was something about me not wanting to leave the table alone, as if someone would take it.

"I'm going to pee," I announced when they returned. Sitting in the bathroom stall, I heard the outside door open. The light went off. It was dark as a cave.

"I know it's you," I said as I peed. We laughed.

As I came out, she grabbed hold of me at the door. We sighed with the relief of holding each other.

"You know…" I began, "no." I shook my head even though she couldn't see it. I moved past her and she let me go. I headed back to the table, to Carson and Lena. To a rush of disappointment.

I got up a to pee a second time a bit later and found both of us in the ladies room again. The floor was black and white subway tile. She touched my shoulder. We were both sweaty, sticky scotch-tape skin. I caught a glimpse of her wavy firecracker hair in the mirror.

"Where's that proper kiss?" I asked, referring to the one she was always asking for.

She kissed hard. She meant business. She turned off the light and pulled me towards her.

"Not here," I murmured. "Not here."

"If not here, where?"

I stopped resisting. I smelled cigarettes on her and liked it. It reminded me of a hard-driving Marlboro man. The air felt tropical, hot-shower humid. Within moments, our bodies were entangled, desperate to relieve all those months of longing.

"Tell me what you like," she pleaded.

We emerged from the ladies room, our faces flushed. Carson and Lena had left. We put on our sunglasses and faced the interrogating sun, my knees shaky but chest thick with affection, feeling the presence of my lover beside me as people rushed toward us along Madison Avenue. She had her elbow crooked on my shoulder and I put my arm around her waist.

"Did I act like a virgin?" she asked.

"No," I chuckled. "You are there. You've been there a long time." And just the act of putting these words onto the busy street, people racing towards us, watching my words evaporate, made me feel safe like this was right and good and beautiful.

✦

On Monday, I found a letter Claire had written to me over the weekend:

When I got home Friday night I couldn't stop laughing because I was so in shock, so unbelievable what we did. I can't stop thinking about it. And so concerned about you. Are you freaking out? Please don't tell me Monday this was a mistake. Dread.

When I saw her we were like giddy schoolgirls. She bought a notebook for us to write in, to record our feelings everyday.

The cover read: *For you with love.* The words were embraced by a hand-drawn heart. She wrote:

You putting my hair behind my ears with your warm soft fingers. This was drawn around a simple illustration of an ear.

You wearing those cute little Christmas socks, the colorful, striped ones, off season (you're so arty).

You paper clipping the little red notes I give you.

You telling me to listen to Angie Stone, track 4, "More Than a Wom-an" and me listening in the morning while I make my cup of green tea. "Girl, you're the blood in my veins, you're the air I breathe on a hot summer day, you're like a shirt with no sleeves."

You being the voice of reason.
Me being impulsive.
Us not being able to stop.

✦

One Friday after work, Claire and I took in the Gerhard Richter exhibit at the Museum of Modern Art. I was nervous. Not only was I lying to my husband about my whereabouts but Claire knew a lot about art and was very opinionated— I was afraid I wouldn't be able to hold my own. Museum art could be intimidating if attending with an artist and I wanted to be smart. She was my lover now. We moved to a new plateau and so much was at stake.

As we strolled through the galleries, filled with too many peo-ple—students with sketch pads and sleek Italian men with Bruno Magli shoes—she was overcome. She needed to sit when she saw Richter's landscape and ice paintings—so ephemeral yet palpable. Something felt ominous. She said the paintings were her, the storm clouds were inside raging and crashing. Her expression of sadness and beauty was perfect to me.

Later she wrote in a flip book:

You putting your arm around me at MOMA while I'm looking at Richter's painting of the sea with a slit for the horizon and saying, 'Storm clouds are coming baby.' Me feeling the dread.

CHAPTER 12

Josh moved his office from the shadow of the World Trade Center to a suite on Seventh Avenue and 28th Street, just north of the Fashion Institute of Technology, where nose-ringed students clustered. It was a well-lit space with assorted accountants and lawyers, including Norman, a ninety-year-old practicing attorney who occupied the corner office. Norman sent his wife flowers once a week with a note, one of which I saw tacked to the bulletin board in the hallway: *I love you as much as the day I met you.* His wife had put it there; she worked for him on occasion. I became teary as I read it, thinking of Josh's cards and notes, which had always been full of his devotion. That was the one thing that remained unchanged in the mess: Josh declaring his affection and loyalty. I thought of our years in Manhattan when he had arranged for bouquets of irises to be delivered every Friday from our friend Sasha's flower shop. Reading Norman's note brought a poignant sadness and a stab of guilt about Claire.

Josh occupied a compact office with a large square window overlooking the top of Madison Square Garden, the roof of the arena a circle with a knot at the center like a big top. We were both hoping this move would help Josh's mood swings. He had tried Welbutrin, prescribed by our family doctor for post-traumatic stress disorder, but he had stopped taking it. He'd always been cavalier about medications (the former college drug tester!)—trying them, stopping when he felt better, and claiming to know more than most lay people about prescription medication. He was still a student of the PDR—the printed authority on pharmaceuticals. Even though we no longer played the guessing game with illicit drugs—holding up the pill to match the photograph in the PDR as we had in our younger days—Josh still kept the reference book on the lower shelf of his night table.

One day, I found another jar of pills in Josh's closet. I couldn't identify the various tablets and capsules in the small Ponds' cold cream jar. They were different from the pills I'd found in the prescription bottle in his sock draw. With a feeble attempt to assert control over my husband's flirtation with drugs, I stashed the bottle in my own closet, next to my cocktail purses. I had taken them away like a mother withholding a toy from a first-grader. I didn't even hide the jar and would never have dreamed of throwing it away—too much respect for the sanctity of one's possessions. I just placed the jar on the shelf, inviting him, practically, to take it back. Perhaps I wanted him to claim the jar to demonstrate everything was fine and even hoping that whatever he was taking would help him cope with the irritability and isolation he'd shown since 9/11.

I mentioned to him in passing that I'd found the pills. Soon afterwards the bottle went missing. I never asked about it. I didn't want to believe his dabbling was a problem so I brushed away the resurfacing memory of Josh from the early 80s, hunched over the coke pipe, freebasing by the gas flame of our stove, looking like an addict.

✦

A year after 9/11, since Josh left the Ground Zero area, his crying and inability to focus had subsided though he still startled easily when he heard loud noises. If we were in the subway, I saw his body tighten and his face contort from the sound of the galloping train. Even though the narcoleptic episodes had passed and he was burrowing back into the fabric of our family—his eyes showed a vacancy. And he had another car accident in our Volvo station wagon when he stopped short and hit the trailer hitch on an SUV in front of him. The collision bent our license plate, cracked the windshield, and deployed the air bags. Fortunately, Adam and a friend who had been sitting in the back seat were not hurt, and neither was Josh.

Most days, Josh wore a black cap emblazoned with the word, *Truth*, which he ordered from an anti-smoking campaign. He was consumed with the truth, always talking about veracity, how the US government set people up, and manipulated citizens to gain money and power. How 9/11 may have been set in motion by the government. He cited his client who claimed to be the illegitimate son of a former Filipino official as an example of such maneuverings. The client had claimed to be invited by the Bush administration, then incarcerated in federal prison. Josh was after the truth about his client and the hidden fortune he claimed to know the whereabouts of. He was after the truth about Claire and me, demanding to know the details of our time together. He appeared like a camera lens opening and closing. Aperture exposed to let in hyper-focus on the things he was consumed with knowing.

Josh continued to step up his interest in the client who claimed to be the illegitimate son and a bevy of businessmen who were arranging international finance deals—something that had to do with medium-term notes, gold certificates, and bank guarantees. As many times as Josh tried to explain it, I never understood.

The Filipino client was in federal prison awaiting a hearing and sentencing over a felony charge—presenting a phony gold certificate (called a "fictitious instrument") to a federal agent. Josh researched his past. On our bed, after coming home after ten p.m., Josh laid out photos of gold bars stacked in vaults he said were in the Philippines. I had no idea if the photos were real and wondered: Was this client really the illegitimate son of such a well-known former official? Where was the birth certificate? Was he a scam artist?

"The more time I spend with this guy, the more I'm believing him," asserted Josh as he rifled through a dozen manila folders and the client's bank statements. "A number of legitimate businesses; an expensive apartment in New York; videos of him opening medical and dental clinics; a Lamborghini," he said listing the reasons to believe in the client's financial veracity. "If this guy's real and I support him now, that could mean some serious money for me," Josh said soberly.

I saw Josh's compulsiveness shift into overdrive, awaiting the big payoff down the line, as promised. Mostly, I was skeptical but a sliver of hope was present within me too. I wanted it to be true as well, especially since the client started sending me beautiful greeting cards, bought from the prison commissary, with lovely handwritten notes wishing God would bless me and my family.

✦

The day I saw the flowery note from Josh's ninety-year-old office suite mate, I'd come for lunch. The office had a tidy kitchen area with a cheerful speckled countertop and Black and Decker coffee maker. The air felt light and refreshing after the dreary office on John Street. Josh told me he was bartering lawyer services in exchange for rent and that Cory, the accountant who brought him in, owed him cash. When I asked about the hours he had worked in exchange for the rent, the amount of which he seemed to revise every time I asked him, he told me, "I got it in my head," and not to worry. But I did worry. Though he'd always been cagey about discussing money, now he got downright hostile when asked. I did not know his income and was feeling so guilty about Claire I didn't feel I could ask. He gave me checks to pay bills; that's all I needed to be concerned about, I told myself.

I sat with Josh in the conference room, at the long teak table. His new office was not yet unpacked. Our lunch started out very sweetly with the getting of paper-plates and doling out of the chicken tikka masala from my favorite Tandoori restaurant. But soon I was sequestered—this time in the conference room—as Josh spewed about me and Claire.

"Why are you telling me you are only friends?" he yelled.

He placed his hands flat on the table and leaned forward as if he were about to spring. We'd had this conversation many times so I could predict exactly where it would go—me in tears and him exasperated. But this time it was in the fluorescent den where lawyers squeeze depositions from people, the same way I was now being questioned about this secret part of my life. I responded as usual, with a modicum of assurance and composure about this feeling that I couldn't will away or exorcise as he would like me to. He paced the length of the table, gesticulating, presenting the evidence, summoning. I was no match for him.

Soon, we started seeing a couple's therapist, Shari, who treated patients in her split-level suburban home, a few towns from where we lived. We had a standing seven-forty-five p.m. appointment to which we often arrived late because Josh almost always missed the train home. Our lateness had become a habit, for which we continually blamed each other. But there was something odd about his absences. For example he would leave the house for hours at a time on the weekends—without much explanation about where he'd been. I chalked it up to his impulsivity, a trait we had joked about. At his birthday party the previous year, our friends had made a booklet with a poem about Josh with a punch line that read, "Where the hell is Josh?" We all jokingly sang "where the hell is Josh?" in unison.

"You seem like such a physical guy," said Shari, our grandmotherly social worker, pushing her glasses in place. She had a Long Island accent, pronouncing guy like "goy," and I thought of her as a mature hippie, with long dark hair and chunky jewelry. We'd been seeing her for six weeks.

"I wonder how you feel about the lack of intimacy in your relationship," she asked Josh.

"Not pleased," said Josh in a small, constrained voice. We sat next to each other on the finely upholstered couch. He took my hand and I wanted to protect him. I looked down at his crazy sneakers, Converse high-tops with yellow and red flames on the sides. *If it weren't for my burgeoning relationship with Claire, we could actually try to make a go of sex and connect in the way I knew was so important.*

"You need to get Claire out of your bedroom," Shari said. I couldn't believe the name of my new lover was open for discussion. My eyes welled up and my face flushed with anger at their willingness to serve me up. Yet, I was guilty and sad and hated that I had to let these two parts of my life intertwine like Claire's graceful drawings of two starry-eyed tulips embracing.

I told Shari and Josh I would stop.

+

I told Claire it was over and avoided her now in the office when-ever possible. I spoke to her only when it was work-related. I didn't let myself get caught alone in the same room with her and if I saw her coming I slipped into my office. I was firm when she wanted to discuss "us." I told her I couldn't help her. I told myself I wasn't being cruel, just clear.

We exchanged demure hellos in the hallway. One Wednesday morning, the only two seats left at our weekly staff breakfast were next to each other so Claire and I sat. Our boss Blossom pointed to the tray of danish and asked, "Can you please take the lid off, Janet?" And Claire piped in, "yes, please take the lid off." Claire then plucked a little frosted pastry off the tray and said she was taking it back to her desk to photograph.

She left me artwork now that consisted of a piece of twirled thin wire attached to a medical photo of a vibrant crimson heart with scis-sors poised to snip. *Feel it?* the caption asked.

She must have known she was embedded in me like a tattoo. When her foot grazed mine in a meeting, or I smelled the trail of her scent, or heard a patch of her accent I ached with a sadness that was bone-deep. Even thought I acted as if I were detached, my heart was bleeding.

Journal entry:
The very thing I have to do—end it, cut it off, finish it, is the very thing causing this pain. And I don't know how to be—ignore, engage a little, I don't know what's ok. No talking about the "relationship?" This all seems so impossi-ble. One part of me wants to just up and leave my job but the other part doesn't because I still want to be near her. How did something so pure and innocent nosedive into such pain and suspicion?

Note from Claire:
Only three weeks ago you were writing with an orange grease pencil on a little yellow sticky note: Track 4 on my Angie Stone CD. I used to play it in the mornings when I made my tea and it warmed me. And now you've turned

AWAY and it makes me wonder if you were ever facing me. Your husband is
telling you to stop [stop sign], your therapist is telling you to stop. Your head
is telling you to stop. I am outnumbered. My heart is outnumbered. You are the
head. I am the heart. I feel cut open from Neck to Navel.

This was usually the point I reeled her back in, just when I couldn't
bear the pain, right when I wanted to extinguish the agony of not
having her, not having my female lover self. But this time I released the
drag and let the line rip, watching her flounder in circles.

The art I received now was mostly about death—choked flowers,
baby birds falling out of the nest, illustrations of talk bubbles with me
saying "I can't help you" and her bubble filled with desperate-looking
question marks, their stems heavy with ominous shadows.

> *Live while you're alive,*
> *You'll be spending enough time*
> *In the cold, cold ground.*

One day, Claire passed out in her cubicle, flat on the floor. Someone saw her and the paramedics came quickly. They wheeled in a gur-
ney, gave her an IV, and took an EKG.

"Please get me my camera," she whispered as she lay on the
white-sheeted, monstrous, medical team bed that dwarfed our office
furniture.

"Really?" I said. I was standing nearby.

"It's an art project. Please?"

I fetched the camera and she took photos of the paramedics, the
EKG print-out, the IV pole.

"Documentation," she murmured.

She was into self-portraits so, of course, she'd take a health crisis
and turn it into art.

Our boss pulled me aside and asked if I would take her home in a
car service, since I was her closest friend.

"Of course," I answered, immediately nervous about being so close
to her.

We drove to Park Slope in the back seat of the car service, with her head on my shoulder.

"Thank you for taking care of me," she whispered

The next day, she reenacted her fainting spell so she could document it by lying on the floor of her cubicle and pointing the camera through her legs, her point of view when she had passed out. The photo caught her silver belt buckle and black pointy cowboy boots, her feet turned out, her body flat as a table. She made note cards out of the photos and gave me one that read,

Thank you for taking care of me when I passed out and for the egg sandwich. Love, C.

✦

Over the next two years, Claire and I swung toward and away from each other like a garden gate. Our coats were hung haphazardly in the closet, no longer facing each other. I saw her life unfold as we talked to each other cordially, sometimes intimately. Her husband, Malik, had taken their son to Virginia to visit Claire's mother, but had not returned to New York, though he kept telling her he would. Most days she was frantic about not being with her son and enduring the ten-hour Greyhound bus rides every other weekend where she carried bags of her son's clothing, shoving his things into the overhead bins.

Jamil was now in nursery school and she couldn't drop him off or pick him up; she wasn't there for the spring tea party or the mother's day breakfast or class painting project where the children all added their handprints to a quilt. I watched the ends fray as she struggled with the prospect of divorce and getting Jamil back. She had a new girlfriend in whose apartment she spent most nights as they worked on their art and later at a graphic design business. They read Jacques Derrida, Heidegger, Paul Celan, and Helene Cixous who wrote about women and writing and identity in a circular style, deconstructing language to make writing come from the body. Cixous, Claire told me, wrote about "blindness."

"We are all blind even if we think we see," she reminded me.

Her lateness in arriving to work resulted in a written warning from Helen about her absences.

"You gotta keep your job," I told her, "even if the circumstances are not ideal."

I had once again become the voice of reason. Somehow we had come full circle and managed to stay friends.

Him

CHAPTER 13

Life at home took on its familiar rhythm. Two 9/11s had come and gone and it was time for our congregation beach cleanup through the Unitarian Universalist church we belonged to, the boys' basketball registration, PTA meetings, Matthew's P-SAT test, and tryouts for the middle school 50s music revue which I insisted Adam appear in. He later told me was the most hateful thing he'd done in his life. Josh put poems in my lunch bag.

> *On a Fresh Start*
> *So glad to have another day*
> *To try to do this right*
> *So we could work together*
> *And we don't have to fight*
> *Good luck today*
> *With what you choose*
> *I know you'll be just fine*
> *Look deep into your heart, my love*
> *It's there, you'll find the sign*
> *Whatever's meant to be will be*
> *I'm with you all the way*
> *I know we'll be just fine, my love*
> *This choice is right, you'll say*
> *I love you!*
> *Josh*

In December 2003, Josh flew to Manila in the Philippines for ten days, on behalf of his client. It was a long, expensive trip and I didn't fully understand why he had to go. There was something glamorous, however, to this kind of business travel where Josh was unraveling a puzzle, accessing "bank codes," and locating his client's birth certificate so Josh could present evidence in federal court that he really was the former high-ranking official's illegitimate son, and save him from sentencing. When he spoke about this client, Josh grew excited.

"If I can find the right people in Manila, we'll be rich!"

I tended the hearth fires while Josh was away. Adam, now fourteen, shoveled the walk when it snowed, and Matthew, a junior in high school, studied for his mid-terms. I only had to throw them out of the house once for rough-housing and occasionally yell at them to quit playing video games. The best part was that I felt clean again, released from the shroud of longing and anguish. And I could sleep without fear of my duplicity being exposed by my counterparts: Josh castigating me for lying, Claire chiding me for my fear of coming out and not embracing my sexuality, "who I really was," as she called it. I'd been an electronic ping-pong ball, caught in the corner of the screen, hitting the wall, hitting the wall, hitting the wall, unable to free myself. I had been waiting for someone to save me.

A few weeks after Josh had returned from the Philippines, on a Monday in February, my father died suddenly.

I had seen my father the Friday before for lunch at his house, just a few towns over from mine. With the renewed calm in my life, I'd made time to see him on my days off. Since my mother had passed three years earlier, my dad stuck close to home, going to the cemetery, "walking the mall" in the early morning, or visiting one of us, his daughters. At eighty-seven, my dad, Joe, a five-foot-five, olive-skinned, first generation Italian-American, loved to tease, offer Mr. Goodbar candy bars and pistachio nuts to visitors, and had perfected what we called the "hand jive," the hand-tapping movement my father "performed" to accent the beat of a song. My father said the hand jive was like golf: looks easy, but takes years to master. He had been astoundingly vital, driving well, cooking, and cleaning the house on his own.

He had fallen down the stairs at home carrying a laundry basket. At the hospital, they released him with a sling for a dislocated shoulder but from Sunday to Monday morning, he had died in his sleep, from a heart attack, we later discovered.

We will be like constellations without our moon, I wrote in my journal. *Will we twinkle and show our luminosity? Or will we die out like red stars, turn into stardust from sadness? We have lost our loving reflector.*

When I looked at him in the satin coffin at the funeral home, before I deposited my tears and a Valentine's Day card, the one I had in the envelope ready to mail, I thanked him for making death look easy, like the hand jive.

Lena and Claire made the trip to Long Island for the wake. Claire wore her cowboy boots and a red Armani leather jacket and approached me wearing the sunniest, most comforting smile. She and Josh hugged and chatted in hushed tones and I was relieved that Josh was so welcoming to her.

✦

Josh generously laid out the $11,000 payment for my dad's funeral service by putting it on a credit card. He then stepped in as the estate's attorney since trusts and estates were his specialty. It was great to have someone we could trust. He would handle probate and distribution of assets.

My sisters and I had no idea that our working-class parents had squirreled their dollars away so readily, but really I should not have been surprised since I'd watched my mother keep an eagle eye on the family finances since I was a girl. She had paid our family bills at the kitchen table ritualistically: the stack of money orders, her good pen, and the list of monthly expenses written in her perfect penmanship. My father told me once that he couldn't hold onto a dollar and that if it weren't for my mother, they wouldn't have anything. But by the time they passed away they had a house that was paid for, IRAs, CDs, and life insurance. My parents had always wanted to protect me; so I knew the money they left was meant to take care of me and they would approve of my spending it on home renovation, since house and family meant everything to them.

My oldest sister, Laura, served as executrix of the estate. As the months passed, Laura began to press Josh with questions about the estate. Things didn't seem to be moving forward in the resolution and as patient and accepting as Laura could be, she probed.

"Estates take longer than everyone thinks," Josh responded.

Just as anyone might be nervous when a spouse was involved in managing family money, I was doubly uncomfortable with Josh's responses since he was cagey about money and irritated with Laura's insistence. While I understood Josh's point about estates taking time to resolve, I also wondered what was taking so long. He had muttered something about waiting for the accounting. But the estate was not the only thing he was being obtuse about. Some months earlier, I had insisted that he pull together all his business numbers—income and expenses—so we could visit Marge, a local bookkeeper. She did tax preparation and accounting. When we got to Marge's office on the first floor of her tidy suburban home, Josh handed her a Macy's shopping bag filled with hand-written ledger books and receipts. "I made so much money last year, I couldn't even add it up," he quipped. We left the bag on the chair in Marge's office. I was hoping she could bring some sense to this.

When we returned a few weeks later, she had recorded the figures into Quikbooks but there were holes: months of recorded income were missing. Marge turned her computer monitor towards us and we all looked waiting for Josh to supply the missing information. He said he frankly didn't know and wanted to get Quikbooks himself and do it. Later that week, he went to Staples and spent $200 on Quikbooks software, which he played with for a day and never opened again. His late hours at the office—sometimes until two or three a.m., the obscure business trips to the Philippines and another one to Geneva, Switzerland, and his reluctance to discuss income or expenses made me wonder if his skittishness wasn't another wave of distress from 9/11. I had read that severe symptoms can emerge months or years after traumatic events.

With my inheritance, which finally came through much to my and my sisters' relief, Josh and I moved ahead in the renovation of our house. I was grateful for the inheritance, the result of my mother's habit of saving over the years, even amounts like 5 and 10 bills into a coffee can. My parents had worked hard and were frugal. I had had dreams of renovating the kitchen since we moved in eight years earlier. Though the room's teakettle wallpaper and the pull-string light fixture had been part of our fixer upper's charm, I did want to expand the space. We hired an architect who lived a few blocks away.

We forged ahead like homesteaders. By the time the funds from the estate arrived, the architect and contractor had limned the area of our backyard where the addition would go. We decided to add rooms on the second floor of the house as well as the first. While Josh and I did a quick estimate of the cost, we never created a real budget. Like so many monetary decisions we winged it, confident in the hope that there would, magically, be enough.

"Bull nose or rounded?" Frank, the kitchen designer asked referring to the edging of the granite for the kitchen counter, soon to be thirteen feet long.

"I like the one that has no lip," I answered, preferring the less ornate style.

"I like your lips," said Josh, eliciting a smirk from Frank.

I shrugged and smiled.

The shop's windows let in streams of light, so when we moved to the cabinetry area we could see the grains of wood, particularly the light maple. When we were done surveying, Frank showed us the sketch of the kitchen design. I liked the pillow-style cabinets, edges rounded and smooth. They blended in with the sleekness of the appliances, and gave our soon-to-be-renovated kitchen a modern, warm feel.

At the housewares store, Josh called me his "cucina Italiana," when we passed the aisle of pasta bowls. He organized the pretty cloth napkins, straightening the piles for shoppers. "I'm straightening them, so I can decide whether to buy any," he said. We took a visit to New Orleans that fall where we walked down Magazine Street and spent a whole afternoon choosing hardware at a funky store with an endless stock of antique knobs and drawer pulls. We both thought it was one of the best days of our vacation.

Back home, we chose our kitchen counter color easily—a lively Brazilian black and brown granite to offset the natural maple cabinets.

And we were both drawn to the same stainless stovetop built into the counter. We'd never undertaken such a large, expensive, complex project together and the frustrations—of which there were many, including a contractor who didn't show up, an architect who moved in the midst of the job without telling us, a garage that had to be moved and rebuilt because of town regulations, sub-contractors who didn't get paid even though we paid the contractor, and no usable kitchen to speak of for months—pulled us closer. My husband and I embraced each other's strengths—he was the doer who stepped in when the general contractor was M.I.A. and I was the patient researcher who found the best store for our purchasers. Even the boys were in sync—no complaints while they slept on the couch for weeks while their bedrooms were rebuilt.

Josh designed and constructed a loft bed for Adam with space underneath for a friend to sleep over and even helped the carpenter knock some nails into the Ipe, a hard Brazilian wood, we'd chosen for the deck. In the end, we fell in love with our new home. The house became everything we had hoped for, right down to the office with the eyebrow window Josh and I shared that overlooked our neighbor's majestic maple tree.

Along with our house renovation, Josh and I started seeing Erica, a new couples therapist. A tall, elegant woman with soft blond hair, Erica embraced a self-possessiveness that made her trustworthy. She spoke in clipped sentences, definitive yes and no's, as if she'd heard about the deposition instructions Josh had once told me: "Say, 'yes,' 'no,' and 'I don't know,'" if you're ever deposed or on the witness stand.

Along with the colorful Kandinsky's *Composition VIII* print hanging on the white wall, Erica's windowless office contained a metal desk, high-backed black leather therapist chair, two swivel chairs, and a telephone perched on a small, square table. An area rug balanced the room's therapy-required neutrality with warmth.

"You have a right to speak about anything in your world," she told us at our first session.

"What do you mean?" I asked.

"You each have a right to express your perspective. Your world," she shrugged like it was the most natural thing.

"What are things like in your world, Josh?"

I was relieved he was going first.

"She's always had this side of her," he said, describing my sexuality. "And I can live with that. I just need to know that she wants to stay married for real."

"What's your world, Josh?" Erica repeated. "That's her world."

Josh paused, thinking.

"I don't matter."

"What do you mean?"

"I feel insignificant in her world," he answered.

"Do you hear that?" Erica asked me. Their eyes were on me.

"Yes, he wants to matter," I answered sticking to the deposition rules: 'yes,' 'no,' and 'I don't know.'"

"So, Josh, what's at the core of who you are?" I was glad it was still his turn.

"A need to be important?" he asked.

"You tell me," she replied.

"As long as I can remember," his voice rising on the word remember, "I've had a need to be seen as someone important. To my mother, I walked on water."

"First-born Jewish son," I said, throwing in my analysis, wishing to stand on the same ground as Erica.

"But I always felt it wasn't real, wasn't true. No one is perfect and I could never achieve what she believed I was." A scrim of sweat formed on his forehead.

"So you want to be important," Erica repeated. Her right hand karate chopped her left palm to make the point.

"Yes, you could say I want to be important."

"Like Uncle Larry?" I asked.

"My uncle, who died, I don't know fifteen years ago, was a big mucky-muck in New York City politics, friends with Abe Beam, and those guys. Made a lotta money. Yeah, he was a lawyer and I wanted to be like him."

I thought of a home movie from the 1960s taken by someone in

Josh's family. All the cousins were talking about what they wanted to be when they grew up and Josh, about fourteen, mugged for the camera saying he was going to become a district attorney. He had a full head of blond curly hair then and dimples deep as parentheses.

"And you?" Erica turned to my side of the room, left of Josh.

"What do I have inside?" I asked, clarifying. She gave me the go-ahead nod.

"I have no idea," I laughed. "Don't know what I'm after. I've never been able to discern who I am." I stopped, hoping she was done with me, at least for the moment. I thought about my growing up the youngest and relying on my family to tell me who I was.

"You don't have any idea how powerful you are, honey," said Josh, chuckling. "And for someone who doesn't know, you've done a good job of wrapping the world around your finger."

Erica shot Josh a look that quieted him.

"You have something inside," she said, clutching her fists into her sternum, "we'll figure it out."

Josh latched the black metal gate as we left and we walked hand in hand back to my office. Our visit to Erica protected us in a bubble as we walked, but when we got to my office, I felt uncertainty crawl back inside me. I was afraid Claire would see Josh and me, while we stood on the plaza. Even though she had spoken to Josh at my dad's wake and even met with him once, as a lawyer, about the divorce and custody issue she was facing, I was afraid the sight of us would irritate her. My relationship with Claire was over, and we were cordial, but hurt and disappointment hung in the air.

I didn't see Claire on the plaza but walked into her office when I got upstairs.

"How are the proofs?" I asked quickly, before recognizing she'd been crying, eyes puffy.

"I don't know what I'm doin'," she said. "Malik's just not coming back. I'm afraid he'll take Jamil and go."

"Where's he gonna go? He's already in Virginia."

"I don't know. He's getting desperate. I don't know what he's capable of."

She looked frightened and I didn't want to get sucked back in.
"Listen, we gotta get those proofs out. I'm sorry. I know this is a bad time but Blossom's leaving and she needs to see them."

"Don't worry. I'm gonna stay here late and finish. I'll leave them for her."

Later, after I'd been talking to a group of co-workers about the travails of the house renovation, Claire approached me at my desk. She must've overheard.

"What the hell are you doing?"

"What do you mean?"

"Why are you renovating your house? You don't even know what's gonna happen to you and that marriage. You're putting money in a house you may not even be living in. You're gay, remember?"

"I know," I agreed uncomfortably. "I'm just trying to live in the question, you know."

"Yeah, yeah, I know. I just don't get it," she said shaking her head. "You really could do whatever you want. You could sleep with me and he'd take you back. He's not going anywhere."

I blanched, not sure which words to react to first: "he'd take you back" or "you could sleep with me." She was being brutally honest, as was her way, but I bristled on hearing "he'll take you back" because I did not want to hurt him. I didn't want to say one thing and do another anymore. I didn't want him to "take me back."

"You don't understand," I said. "He and I have a deep bond. We love each other."

She grimaced and looked away. I later realized how much she needed me to break up with my husband, to embrace the same bold act she was confronting, to help ameliorate her pain.

By summer 2004, our home renovation was nearly complete. We had spent over $100,000 of my inheritance to have the house we'd always dreamed of. Josh and I rewarded ourselves with a weekend stay in Manhattan—an offer from the Hilton Hotel timeshare company. He was always quick to say yes to representatives who called about time-share deals where you could stay at a resort for cheap if you took a tour and listened to a sales pitch. I usually hung up on these reps but I heard him say, "Angela Anderson? Is that your name?" to the voice on the other end of the line. "Were you always called on first in class?"

The Hilton suites—thirty-six flights up overlooking Central Park, in the Hilton NY Hotel were plush and elegant. We were treated like VIPs at a happy hour where we sipped wine in flutes, viewed the luxurious suites, and listened to the pretty salesperson, who had a new baby, explain we could stay anywhere in the world if we purchased a time share. And with Josh's international trips and the prospect of cashing in soon with his elaborate business transactions, a $22,000 time share purchase seemed like a meager investment and endorsement of our future together. And even though I knew we should sleep on it, signing on the dotted line felt like signing a refreshed marriage certificate.

We told our therapist, Erica, about reinvesting in our marriage with the timeshare purchase and weekend in Manhattan. Her steady manner continued to draw us out.

"So, you were at dinner at Zanzibar and Josh wanted to feed you with a spoon, correct?" asked Erica.

"Yes, we sat at one of those small tables and he wanted me to taste the eggplant so he held a spoon up to my chin and I really didn't want any but felt obligated to taste it because I didn't want to disappoint him. So I ate it and he was right. It was delicious."

Josh, sitting to my right, looked down as I was questioned. Erica pinpointed her questions precisely and the lack of wiggle room made me squirm. I didn't like telling the truth.

In an earlier session, she asked me if everything was okay. And I answered yes. She asked me again and I said yes. She brought up the reason we were there, so we could repair a faltering marriage.

"Everything's not fine," she said, "And you are a liar."

The words stung. I let them sink in. Pretending that everything was fine and wearing the veneer of pretense like a painted smile on a porcelain clown was my own brand of fakery. We'd always said, "Fine, everything's just fine," in my family even when it wasn't. After that session, I saw the possibility, that truth, even unpleasant, was still the truth no matter how I wished to dress it up.

"And did you eat from the spoon?" asked Erica.

"Yes, I did."

"Why did you eat something you didn't want?"

"He seemed so intent on my trying it. I didn't want to hurt his feelings." I had thought my desire not to disappoint him came from a giving place within me.

"But are you telling the truth when you accept something you don't want?"

I felt the shame creep into my throat. What had seemed like a self-less gesture, opening my mouth to the spoon, as she said this, instantly felt dishonest and infantilizing, like a baby taking unneeded nourishment from an insistent parent.

"But he insisted," I blurted. "You know, you can be very persuasive," I said turning to face Josh. He looked at me sympathetically and gave me a "you're on your own" grimace. The heat rose in my face. I wanted him to bail me out, let me blame him. He said nothing.

"Look," said Erica. "If you don't want to eat something all you have to do is say no thank you. You have the right to do that."

I glared.

"Why didn't you say no thank you if you didn't want to eat any?" she continued.

"I didn't want to disappoint him. He seemed so eager to have me try something he was enjoying. Plus, he's usually right. He knows what I need more than I do."

Erica paused, looked at me. "You know," she said, "it's not your job to manage someone else's disappointment. When you do that you're not being truthful."

In that moment, I felt defensive of my truth: I wanted to hang on to my dishonesty. But I listened, staying open-minded, an entirely cerebral exercise because my body was tight, fighting to hold onto the comfort of dishonesty. But by the time we left the session, I considered that maybe I could be honest—even if it was only with myself and even if it didn't feel good.

A few months later, Josh had stopped going to his office, which happened to be near Erica's, so it was no longer convenient for him to join me at the lunchtime appointments. I didn't understand what had happened with his office arrangement, but apparently he and Cory—his accountant friend—had argued about the rent and the money Josh owed. When I pressed Josh about the details he responded as he often had when the subject of money arose—he left the room, his voice trailing as he went.

"You never take my side, you know."

I said nothing.

"And," he added, "you're making a big deal out of nothing. These kinds of arrangements are worked out all the time. It's not that black and white."

I backed away. He'd always been such an unusual man—full of surprises and the ability to size things up quickly and confidently. For years, I had jumped on the wagon of confidence he imparted, feeling my loyalty was at stake if I didn't believe him. But this time, I wasn't so sure I could trust.

I had wondered if his working at home hadn't been prompted by something he had told me a few months earlier: two men had come to his office and threatened him if he didn't pay back $200,000 that his client—who claimed to be the son of a former high-ranking official in the Philippines—owed.

"Why do you have to pay?" I asked on hearing this unbelievable tale.

I didn't have the courage to ask for details. Josh wanted to borrow $40,000 from our home equity line; some of it to pay his client's defense costs and the rest to keep the goons at bay. The story frightened me and I agreed he could tap the equity line.

Soon he worked exclusively at home, yet doing very little law work. I'd come home and hear him on the phone with a new business associate, Oscar, a name I'd never heard, talking about methods for securing funds from investors, a trip to Berlin he was planning, and money that had to be fronted. Many afternoons all he did was blaze a trail to the liquor cabinet, filling up his big, red party cup.

I continued seeing Erica on my own, willing to work with her to understand who I was and what motivated me.

"You mean there could be other reasons," I asked Erica, "other than my not wanting to hurt Josh or ruin my marriage, to explain why I'm reluctant to look closely at my sexuality?"

"Guilt, you know, can be a distraction sometimes, a smokescreen. Think that could be the case?" Erica uncrossed her legs and leaned forward.

"I don't really understand," I said, shaking my head.

"Look, sometimes guilt can deflect a deeper look into yourself. It could be easier to say I feel too guilty and blame someone else, rather than own the truth."

I paused, looked away from Erica, to the dancing shapes in the Kandinsky print.

"If I acknowledge that, then I may have to take responsibility and not blame him?"

"Exactly."

"I have something to confess."

She stayed quiet.

"I met two gay friends at Henrietta's one night. You know, the gay bar."

"How long since you'd been there?" she asked.

"Hadn't been there in a very long while. No agenda, just meeting up with old friends."

"And?"

"You know how I used to 'fall off the wagon' with Claire, then beat myself up about my actions?"

"Uh-huh."

"Wish it would all go away and promise to be a good girl?"

"Yes, I do."

"I'm ready to look at my motivations instead of beating myself up."

I told her about meeting a woman at Henrietta's, Veronica, and confessed that we kissed. "She invited me home but I said 'no.'"

"What are you thinking about it?"

"Well, usually I'd go to that place of guilt, even bringing this up is hard, Erica. But I remember what you said about guilt being a hiding place so there must be something else going on here. Quite simply: am

I gay? And if so, what do I do about it?"

"What if you are? What does that mean?"

"I can't be married."

"Says who?"

"Claire would say that. She asks me all the time how I could be married and be gay."

"Let's do two things, okay?"

"Sure."

"Let's set the marriage aside for one. Being married and being gay don't have anything, really, to do with each other. And let's set Claire's beliefs aside too. Let's talk about your truth."

"Okay," I said.

"Did you enjoy meeting Veronica and kissing her?"

"Yes."

"Did you want it?"

"Yes."

"Why did you not pursue her?"

"I didn't want to hurt Josh. If I ended up in her bed, I would've betrayed him."

"But you wanted it, right?"

"Yes, but I could make myself not want it. That's what I've been doing. Pushing it away."

"And pretending everything's fine." She raised an eyebrow.

I cringed. "You know, I was afraid to tell you about this incident. I'm ashamed of it now. I would much rather have reported that I didn't go the bar at all. That I was being 'good.'" I signaled air quote marks.

"Listen, you cannot make yourself not desire something you desire. It's impossible. You can say I want that but I won't take it. When you tell yourself you don't want it, it's not your truth."

"You mean the desire to stop something can't be because someone else wants you to?"

"Yes."

"So blaming someone for not doing what you want is avoiding your truth, correct?"

"Yes, Josh is not really the obstacle here. You've set it up to make him the obstacle so you deny yourself what you want or resent him for keeping you from it. Why not just take it or not with honesty because it's your choice? Do you like being at a gay bar?" she asked.

I nodded.

"Maybe you are feeding your essence, the true you. I'm sure there are other circumstances where the true you comes out too."

"Yes, there are. You know, I just realized what I've been doing is trying to make my denial be the truth. Make the truth be that I don't want it."

Erica stopped, leaned forward, and said, "Yes, you're creating the truth as you wish it were."

"How could this work?" I had asked Erica, referring to a fractured marriage.

"With honesty. Sexuality may not be a choice but you don't have to act on every impulse."

I was relieved. I could embrace my sexuality but also choose when and if to act.

At the end of that year, 2004, I moved to another position in the company. When the offer came along, I knew it was time for me to move on. I was ready for a new work challenge. And my days with Claire no longer held the sweet falling-in-love feeling we had embraced in our secret life.

As a going-away present, one of my coworkers gave me a stamp-size four-leaf clover from her family's collection gathered from worldwide trips. I was very touched and when I took the shamrock out of the cellophane to show Claire, the delicate stem detached from the leaves. Claire asked if she could scan it to make an image of it. She loved gossamery and found objects and I recalled all the pressed flowers, feathers, stones, and trinkets she had given me. I said, "sure."

A few days later, she came to my cubicle on a new floor and hung a poster she'd created with the image of the four-leaf clover beautifully rendered with its detached stem and the words "Broken Luck" scrawled at the top. I loved the sensibility of the poster with its dreamy ethereal flavor. But what did she mean? I couldn't tell if she was wishing me what she felt I deserved, or for a change in luck for the worse, or a lost chance. But maybe they were simply the words that came into her head when she noticed the broken stem. For me, "broken luck" meant a shift, a shuffling of the deck and a turn for the better. But deep down I sensed luck had nothing to do with it.

By Christmas, Josh was back home from a month in Berlin, arriving Christmas Eve morning. The boys and I had bought a Christmas tree and celebrated the first night of Hannukah while he was gone. While in Berlin, Josh made late-night phone calls to me as he walked frantically along the Spree in this city he now adored. His pilsner steins were always full and he remained in a house with investors to work on a deal, and wait for them to deliver cash so he could come home and declare his success. It still sounded implausible to me yet Josh's attachment to "a good outcome," as he called it, was fierce. He seemed caught in the grip of need and hope there would be that large reward for his loyalty and hard work on behalf of his Filipino client. He was in deep now; I sensed he was teetering on the brink of either a soul-crushing depression or an explosive outburst if I even hinted he should come to his senses.

The day he got back, empty-handed, he strung lights across our bedroom windows on the second floor, fashioning our family name. I found it funny that he would display our name rather than a symbol of the holidays like a Christmas tree, menorah, snowman, or sled. Josh, Matthew, Adam, and I smiled as we viewed it together from the street but I couldn't help but think Josh was asserting his identity by putting his name in lights on our street for everyone to see.

That May, Claire moved to Virginia to be with her son, now a kindergartener. She had been torn for so many months about being in New York and returned to the small town in the Shenandoah Valley where she had grown up. She didn't relish the idea of returning to the Bible Belt, where she said the only distractions were trips to Wal-Mart, but she needed to be with her boy. I encouraged her.

A few weeks before she left the company, we happened to be standing in the same space in a vestibule outside our office building, waiting for the rain to let up. We'd been avoiding each other, but this time there was no place else to go. It was evening and she was smoking an American Spirit. She wore flats and didn't seem so much taller than I.

"If somehow we could be together, would you want that now?" I asked, fiddling with the handle of my black umbrella. I had to work up the courage to ask.

She looked down, shaking her head slightly.

"I have no idea, darlin'," she replied, her voice echoing off the high-ceilinged portico. "I couldn't make a commitment to you or anyone. I just want to be with my son. I'm in no shape for a relationship."

That exchange brought closure to me. She was right, of course. I had my family and she had hers—the same situation we had started with.

Once she left, I missed being able to tell her about an article I'd seen about the new Carl Jung biography, discuss the movie "Junebug," about a young man from the south who couldn't go home again, or see the red message light on my office phone and listen to her rambling voicemails, her breath interrupted by long drags on a cigarette.

I stashed the artwork she had given me in a safety deposit box at Chase bank. It was precious to me, her tangible creations of affection. And as time passed, I recognized that instead of creating the truth as I wish it were I could simply tell the truth—I loved Josh, yet had been deeply in love with this woman. My relationship with her and the sexuality we expressed dropped a drawbridge for me to walk over, to access intimacy and recognize I had the capacity within me. With Erica's help, I transcended the chaotic thinking that had hammered me, that split me in two, and the need to pretend to be two people. Slowly, I stitched myself together and began looking for answers within. I had come out to myself, accepting that my sexuality could be fluid, that whoever I felt attracted to was okay. I was learning to love what was different about me, and to understand that no one could define what that was except myself. In fact, I didn't need to define it at all. It could just be.

CHAPTER 14

It was that same May that Josh and I sat across from each other in a wooden booth with chintz cushions at our favorite Irish pub in Malverne, a few towns from our home, near the art house movie theatre. I remembered when we had sat in a similar booth at Molly Malone's, another Irish pub, near our apartment on 23rd Street in Manhattan. That was nearly twenty-three years ago, when we discussed the prospect of getting married.

This time, we were circling back to each other, tentatively at first, enjoying our shared jokes and renewed comfort. We had been to the movies and as we sat down, Josh told me he had a high PH level that night. I chuckled. PH level meant Popcorn Hog and I expected he'd be shoveling buttered kernels into his mouth. I loved the "in" family jokes that made us smile, the ones no one outside us would find funny.

"You loved two things very deeply," he said, as the waitress transferred our Heinekens onto the table from her tray. "You loved her and me."

How I so appreciated those words! He validated the dilemma I had found myself in, without judgment. He accurately described what I had felt for nearly three years. He made it okay to talk about it, dissect it, and traverse a bumpy road that eventually led back to us. Only months before, so sure I was leaving him, he had written me a poem in a Valentine's Day card:

Roses are Red
Violets are Blue
It's not quite that simple
And neither are you.

You may take a sabbatical
Or just lay down low
Perhaps you can travel
And never pass "Go."

Wherever you Journey
Wherever you Roam
My heart will be with you
So please take it slow.

Now we were sitting together, holding hands.

"Do you think we can be resolved?" I asked.

"We'll work it out. Everything, my dear, can be worked out."

He uttered the phrase he had said to me so many times in our marriage; the words I wanted to hear! Words of comfort and reassurance I had come to rely on.

I didn't know what power had allowed us to alchemize the turmoil into a measure of tolerance and forgiveness. We were resilient when it came to our shared love. We loved our love. That night, the "us" made an appearance even if it had only been based on the phrase, "you loved two things very deeply," to which I could say, "Yes, you understand. Thank you."

Yet I couldn't pretend that everything was fine, nor could I suppress my deepest needs. Our refreshed marriage was far from perfect, of course, and Josh was hardly putting in any hours into his law practice and continuing to chase unexplained international money deals.

Within days, he approached me in our office, on the second floor of our house. "I'm gonna have to declare bankruptcy if this doesn't work," Josh said pointing Countrywide Bank's mortgage papers at my chest. The word bankruptcy terrified me. Josh had said the word in past years and I shooed it away. The word tasted bitter and salty in my mouth, a particle to spit out—a failure too abysmal to reconcile. Only desperate people without means declared bankruptcy. This didn't happen to a person like me. Maybe it happened to people who held up convenience stores, had their finances wiped out by medical emergencies, guys in corrugated boxes, or folks who knew they were headed there and didn't know how to stop it. Someone with knowledge of upcoming doom. Someone who'd let things go; someone who shrugged with indifference. But not me.

The house. He wanted to mortgage the house to cover his debts, the sum of which I didn't know and was afraid to ask.

"What do you mean?" I asked.

"We just have to hang in there until this thing happens." The thing he was referring to, of course, was the deal with the so-called illegitimate son that involved accessing gold certificates, though he had lately been talking about another arrangement with a financier in Croatia who needed a liver transplant and once he got it he could be moved to Switzerland to withdraw funds that Josh and his associates were going to manage. His commitment to this idea was so fierce that, as absurd as the circumstances sounded, I dared not laugh or question it lest I topple our still-precarious, newly resurrected marital bond.

It reminded me of the time when we were first married, living in Manhattan, and were approached by a wirey African-American man on the corner of Broome and West Broadway who flashed us a gold bar and said we could have it for $100. Josh and I looked at each other excitedly, our eyes locking, registering an unflinching willingness to gamble. Josh drew out his money clip, peeled off five twenties and handed it to the man quickly in exchange for the bar. We got home, scraped the surface of the bar with a box cutter, and realized we'd been had. I parked the "how could we be so stupid?" feeling somewhere inside myself and chalked it up as a life lesson to never again trust strangers offering riches.

"Where'd you find this bank?" I asked.

"Hector. He's a mortgage broker in Phoenix now."

"Really?"

I remembered our old friend Hector, someone we had known and loved since before we had married. Even though I knew Hector had been a one-time drug dealer and had even served prison time, I remembered him fondly as our dashing buddy, his body diminutive like a racehorse jockey. In the 80s, he wore ripped Sassoon jeans, Gucci loafers, and an expensive designer leather jacket with an off-center zipper; he was someone with big dreams that manifested in moves like purchasing and running a recording studio on Lafayette Street. I always loved the way he would fly into and out of our lives leaving the lingering scent of his "success is just on the horizon" attitude.

"Don't worry about it. Right now I gotta open up the cash flow," Josh said. He ran his hand over his shaven, bald head. I took the thick pile of documents, glanced at them, and placed them on my desk. Now, they rested on my side of the room.

A few days later as I sat at my desk writing and gazing at the neighbor's maple tree, Josh asked whether I had read the mortgage application. I shook my head.

"You know, there's not a lotta time to spare here," he declared circling the doorway. "We need to refinance, otherwise everything's coming to a halt."

The "t" in the word "halt" panged me. I was confused and afraid to say no to his request.

"Why only my name on it?"

"I told you. You got the better credit score and Hector says we'll get a better rate."

"What about you. Why are you off the hook?"

"I'm not. I told you."

He said, "I told you" each time with increasing irritation, like we were struggling, rung after rung, up a ladder and my questions slowed our ascent. I wanted to give him what he was asking for. After all, I could never repay him for his indulgence of my indiscretions.

"I'm responsible too," he said, like it was common knowledge. "Gonna put my initials everywhere you sign. I told you."

"And what about the amount? How much are we taking out?"

"We need four forty."

"Four-hundred and forty thousand dollars?" I was wide-eyed. We had a $140,000 mortgage and our house has been appraised for $650,000. We did well, having bought our home for $200,000 ten years before. It had tripled in value.

He looked at me, unapologetic. "We have no choice."

"Oh, but we always have a choice. Isn't that what you've been telling me?"

"I got these creditors on my back. And I don't think you wanna declare bankruptcy, right?"

"That's an awful lot of money," I answered.

"Let's just do this and get it over with."

The next night, I read on the Internet about these new mortgages: subprime mortgage products they were called. Seemed like banks were making lots of these loans in 2005. Banks would let you pay "interest only" or a reduced payment for a certain number of years before the payments increased. I read about flexible payment choices and how banks were no longer only offering rigid standard mortgages like they did in my parents' day. A lot more on the carousel than the thirty-year fixed. *The banks and mortgage companies understand us! They get us; they understand we need to be flexible with our payments.*

In the articles, I gleaned how anyone thinking about signing on to these mortgage "products" needed to exercise caution but I didn't believe their warnings were directed to me because Josh and I were educated. Josh was a lawyer who knew about contracts and real estate and would never let something bad happen. Even if he was angry about Claire and me, he loved me terribly and would protect me no matter what. "I'd cut off my arm for you," he had said. I'd come to rely on his trust, one that had been cemented early in our relationship.

Years before, I had traveled to Phoenix on my own. On my way home to JFK airport, the October weather had turned bitter. I hunkered down in my thin windbreaker to wait for the shuttle bus. Walking through the terminal, I spied him leaning against a wall with a grin and my winter coat over his arm. I had never felt so taken care of and grateful to have this man in my life. And from there the layers of trust and love nestled upon each other to create a foundation I thought I could dance upon.

The next day I called our Employee Assistance hotline at work to get a free consultation with a lawyer about the mortgage.

"I wouldn't sign it if I were you," he told me, his thick New York accent diminishing his credibility.

But I knew I was going to sign the mortgage. In fact it was never in question. This was something Josh and I were approaching together, in a barrel towards a waterfall.

We looked over the good-faith estimate, the following weekend. I tried to read every page but my eyes glossed over after a few paragraphs.

"I thought the idea was to pay off your mortgage," I whined.

Josh looked at the pages.

"It's fine," he said.

His words hold such currency.

The only page in readable print contained the monthly mortgage payment—that was only $1,547, very affordable. Countrywide was willing to refinance our mortgage at an adjustable rate for five years.

"That's just what we need," said Josh. "Within five years we can refinance again. And by then, we'll have the money to pay this back."

Soon I was at Josh's law office conference room at six-thirty p.m. signing every page of the document with the closing agent, a jovial, heavyset woman somewhere around fifty in a tight jacket and skirt that fell well below her knee which I thought needed a hem. She looked like a *mamadelle*, an Italian word my mother used to say, which my sisters and I gleaned as "frumpy." You never want to look like a *mamadelle*.

She was friendly and I was polite, doing my best to follow directions and sign dutifully where she pointed on the page.

The new mortgage payment of $1,547, plus the cost of our real estate taxes, felt manageable.

✦

"I wonder what percentage of the bird population is crazy?" Josh asked as we drove over the Long Beach bridge a few days later.

I turned to look at him, delighted. His jokiness had returned.

"There must be one in a million who shoots up a post office," he quipped.

"Yeah, you have to believe some genes gone awry."

"Maybe that's why I see a lot of birds walking lately. Notice that?

In the road."

I laughed. He was right. I did see a lot of birds walking.

"Your mood have anything to do with the new mortgage maybe?"

"Whaddaya mean?"

"You're lighter…your mood."

"More cash, more Flash. Of course."

I felt good about agreeing to sign. I had helped improve his mood.

I didn't understand, however, how refinancing worked and didn't look closely at the list of creditors receiving pie-charted portions of the $440,000 mortgage we'd just taken out.

It broke down like this: Only $140,000 of the $440,000 mortgage we had just taken out covered the old mortgage we had held on our home. The remaining $300,000 was divvied up among various creditors. All but $7,000 (my credit card total, mostly home renovation expenses) was debt Josh had accumulated on credit cards and business lines of credit. He had run up a tab of $293,000! But, at the time, I hadn't looked closely or questioned how or why Josh's debt had gotten so high. Nor did I understand what "equity" meant or how important it was to maintain it. I later learned that equity referred to the difference between the value of the house and the loan. Of course the value of homes fluctuates, so a home worth $650,000 today could be worth a lot less as market values fall. When we took out the $440,000 loan, first we paid off the old mortgage of $140,000 and then used the remainder, $300,000, to pay off debt. The $300,000 was the "equity" (value) or money that we extracted. Most homeowners, however, never want to touch the equity so that when the mortgage is paid off (after 30 years, say) the value, and the home, belongs completely to the homeowner.

I never questioned closely where this enormous sum had vanished to or how much open credit Josh still had access to.

Actually, I'd given up trying to track his debt early in our marriage, when he had two business credit cards with balances of around $20,000 each. We had argued bitterly about the best way to handle those balances until we stopped discussing it. My approach was to pay the lines back, little by little, like a bill. He insisted it was best to pay everything out of the line then deposit all checks, so all income went to paying down the balance, thus reducing the interest. That way, we could have access to the credit again. Because the credit cards and lines of credit were business accounts that he paid out of his professional lawyer's checking account, I never saw the statements. And once I returned to full-time work in 1997, I scraped that responsibility off my plate.

After we refinanced, every month when I paid the sum with the handy mortgage coupon I didn't notice the uptick on the principal of the loan, $440,000. Instead of seeing the mortgage amount go down as was supposed to happen as a mortgage was paid, ours was going up, imperceptibly at first.

+

The mortgage mattered little, however, as the glorious Long Island summer emerged. We spruced up our beach cabana, a brightly painted, wooden hut, in a string of attached huts with showers and tin roofs at our luminous south shore beach. Josh built a redwood plank shower floor for our cabana while we spent Sundays barbecuing with our friends. In August, we lounged at poolside at the Universal Sheraton hotel in a Sherman Oaks, California, while attending the wedding of Josh's business associate Oscar. We ate sliced salami and drank cognac in a hotel suite with Alexei, another associate, who had a belly like a basketball and whose words were draped in a heavy Russian accent. At poolside, I watched Josh dive and swim effortlessly, a smooth crawl to my end where I sat with my legs dangling in the water. He emerged with a dimpled smile.

"Do you think I should dye my hair red?" He laughed.

"You don't have any left. It's too late for you," I joked.

I loved this man. This neurotic, over-involved-in-me guy.

At the end of that summer, Matthew left for college in Boston. I promised myself not to cry though my heart was in tatters as I said goodbye to my son on the sidewalk outside his Northeastern University dorm room. I marveled at Matthew, a combination of the two of us—his thick, dark, rock star hair cascading over his shoulders, his slight boyish frame scuttling about. He had my go-with-the-flow disposition and Josh's dexterity. I cried so much on the drive home that when we stopped at a restaurant for dinner and I continued crying at the table, Josh felt obliged to tell the waitress why I was so upset.

"Son. Dropped off at college."

"I know," she said, "At this time of year, when I see a middle-age woman in tears, I know it's drop-off day. You think you're crying now," she continued, looking at me. "Just wait till you get the bill. I got two in school at the same time."

We laughed but she was right.

We welcomed the extra bucks from the lowered cost of our mortgage to help handle Matthew's college costs—tuition, dorm, food, and spending money. Even though he had snagged a partial scholarship, his expenses ran well over $3,000 a month. Fortunately, we had college savings to draw from and Matthew, a music student, helped manage costs by working in the college mailroom. Getting that mortgage felt like a godsend.

We ushered in the holidays that season as we always did, looking forward to spending the celebrations with our family and friends. That year, our friends Hal and Annie visited for Thanksgiving weekend. Early Saturday evening, as our happy hour began, Josh, with Hal at his side, marched into the yard with the electric chainsaw to cut cords of wood from a downed oak tree Josh had retrieved from a tree removal company working on our block. He and Hal were chopping wood, an activity Josh loved. I don't know if he was indulging a manly lumberjack fantasy, but he loved working out his body no matter the season. At intervals, Josh came into the house, his face flushed and sweat dripping, his oversized Sorel boots tracking dirt onto the floor. He darted over to the liquor cabinet and downed shots of Patron as he tossed the cut logs into the living room fireplace.

"They'll never take me alive," he snorted with a devilish grin and a theatrical smack of his lips after downing each shot. Then, he pulled his safety goggles back down over his eyes.

Annie, a newly minted aesthetician, gave me a facial in my bedroom, my dark hair headbanded with a floral bandanna, as I lay at the foot of the bed. The cucumber and avocado astringent Annie applied felt cool on my pores and smelled pleasing like an exotic vegetable salad. I heard the buzz saw over the tinny, New Age music Annie was playing. The scent of the fireplace added to the home-for-the-holidays feeling, but when I went downstairs I noticed the flames swirled manically, high into the flue. There were too many logs but Josh kept feeding the fire.

"Josh," we laughed. "Crazier than ever." We watched Josh and Hal from the window revving the motor of the chain saw and laughing. They seemed so entertained by the vrooom as Josh sliced the stack of logs. We never thought to admit that shots of Patron paired with chainsaw operation could be a bad idea.

Josh, Matthew, Adam, and I loved our extended family celebrations, like Christmas Day at my sister Laura's with the cousins, nieces, and nephews enjoying our traditional antipasto and lasagna dinner. At Josh's sister Wendy's apartment, our family gathered for Hanukkah latkes, brisket, and jelly doughnuts as Wendy and her booming teacher voice directed the teenage nieces, nephews, and her daughter to the living room floor to play the annual Happy Hanukkah bingo game. It reminded me of when I was a kid and my family played card games, like Michigan rummy, together. Wendy designed the game herself, as she might create a lesson plan for her students, using Hanukkah symbols like *dreidels, gelt,* and Maccabee shields to occupy the little squares on the playing boards. Only she could get us to play something pretty corny, which the kids enjoyed with unusual gusto for teenagers, sitting on the carpet falling into each other giggling and shoving until Wendy strode in in her "Bubbie's Kitchen" apron and yelled good-naturedly to "knock it off." When the kids were younger she'd invited the cousins for sleepovers, the only adult brave enough to tolerate the playful rowdiness of all five. "If you don't behave," she'd say, "I'm shipping ya home, so don't make me call your parents!" Wendy was formidable and we felt so lucky to have such a loving extended family.

CHAPTER 15

One year later, the following December, I sat nestled in the middle seat of the Long Island Railroad between two heavy-set commuters, including a woman reading the paperback, *The Namesake*. I was returning from work and we were facing west, that is, backwards, not the direction the train was going in, bundled in our winter coats, me in my chocolate brown Shearling with the fur lining, heavy as a lead blanket. My phone vibrated. I could just about make out Matthew's name scrolling across the tiny window of my flip phone without my glasses. I debated answering, mindful of cell phone etiquette on a crowded train.

"Dad got arrested!" Matthew blurted. He was home from college for the holiday break. Sweat beaded on my brow as I got a dirty look from the *Namesake* reader.

My mind leapt to FBI agents. Maybe they were back. Once, a few years earlier two middle-age guys in loose-in-the-ass jeans and "Members Only" jackets, came to our house on a sunny Saturday asking Josh if he had any contact with Khalill, a Lebanese small-business client Josh had known for years. I had never liked Khalill, someone who visited us often when we lived in Brooklyn and invited us to his hip East Village gourmet pizza restaurant. I saw him as a "taker," someone who never paid Josh yet always asked for free legal advice.

Josh told the FBI agents he hadn't seen Khalill in months and they left waving good-bye to me on the porch.

"Dad hit Mike's car," Matthew told me.

"Mike who?"

"The guy across the street."

"What? Where is Dad now?"

"At the police station." Matthew said, giving me the facts, urgency in his voice.

I anxiously pulled onto our block and turning into our driveway, I saw Mike, the neighbor, in front of his house directly across the street. I got out and inspected the rear of our Voyager, which had a fresh dent. I forced myself to cross the street, not knowing what kind of reception I'd get from Mike, a tall, late-fifties, gray-haired fireman with a bushy mustache and glasses. Mike babied his car—that I knew. He drove a beast—a red Durango with a predatory grill of silver teeth and gleaming side-steps he kept spit-clean. I walked over, heart thumping.

Shit. This was the same guy who yelled at my kids, when they were younger, if they played football in the street and if the ball bounced anywhere near his car. Other times he'd come out and scream at the boys if they were noisy, playing in the street during the afternoon, because he was trying to sleep. I knew it was better to face him in the moment than not. My therapist Erica's voice echoed, "What are you going to do about this? How are you going to step up?"

"Hey, Mike."

"I had no idea it was Josh," he said excitedly. "I wish he had told me." His tone was apologetic. "I heard a noise and came out. Had a dent in my car and someone drove away. So I called the police. Once I called them I couldn't cancel it," he shrugged. "By the time Josh got back and told me, the police were on their way."

"I'm sorry, Mike. Of course we'll pay for any damage," I said, my resentment growing.

Mike waved me away. He seemed genuinely upset though I still wasn't clear about the details of the arrest.

When I walked in the house, Matthew got up from watching a History Channel show about drugs in America, called "Hooked." We hugged each other quickly. I searched his face for some clue to what had happened and only saw a nervous, crooked smile.

"Dad hit Mike's car backing out of the driveway to drive Adam to practice. Then after he got home, the police came."

"So, Dad came into the house, then the police came? Did he do anything when he came in?"

"He drank something," Matthew said, pointing to the liquor cabinet. I walked past the TV, then swung open the two doors of the cabinet.

"Which bottle?"

Matthew got up and pointed to the bottle of Patron, with the chunky screw-off cap. There was little tequila left in the bottle.

"Then I heard some commotion and went to the door. I saw the cop cars with the lights on."

Then Matthew told me more: from the porch he watched his father walk in front of our house, back and forth about four times, before the police officers announced they were arresting him for driving under the influence. They let Josh go into the front seat of the Voyager, parked in the driveway, and get something. Then the cops beckoned to Matthew to join them on the sidewalk where he was instructed to cup his hands while his father emptied his pockets of keys, money, wallet, and Swiss army knife. They then pushed Josh against the car, handcuffed him, and led him to the back seat of the squad car and drove away. Drunk driving. My heart sank, not for Josh. But for my gentle son forced to assist with his father's arrest.

"Yup. Dad was pissed," Matthew said.

"Was there a crowd?" I asked, thinking of the lighted reindeer on our neighbors' lawns twinkling like an audience, laughing at the sideshow.

Suddenly, I heard someone at the door and in walked Adam, face flushed, now sixteen and almost six feet tall, in his black nylon workout pants with the zip-off legs and expensive basketball shoes. He'd gotten a ride from a friend.

"Is Dad in jail?" he asked, out of breath.

"How'd you know?" I said.

"Cause when he hit Mike's car, I told him to go back. It was crazy, Mom. I don't know why he didn't stop." *A sixteen-year-old know better.*

"Why didn't he go back?" I asked.

"He said I'd be late for practice and he'd take care of it later."

"Was he drinking?"

"Yeah, of course," Adam said, irritation in his voice.

"What do you mean, of course?"

"Mom, Dad drinks everyday!" he sputtered. The little boy who had clamped his lips together to keep from speaking out of turn in first grade had become my truth-teller. I thought immediately of the big red plastic party cups Josh was always cradling and his frequent trips to the liquor cabinet. I thought about the chain saw and nearly empty bottle of Patron. "He never smelled of booze!" I wanted to protest. He didn't have that ugly, bulbous red nose, veiny corpuscles, or rheumy eyes! I'd never found vodka bottles stashed in the basement!

But the words "Dad drinks everyday" stung. My face reddened. I looked down as my shame of denial snaked through me like warm, slow-moving liquid with the impulse to cover up almost eclipsing my willingness to admit I hadn't known. Yet with Adam's words I captured evidence—someone else's testimony that forced me to recognize it was real. I felt ashamed and responsible for believing Josh's drinking was within the range of "social." Yet I also felt vindicated, like some evidence was being shown to justify my suspicion that there was something desperately wrong. I was disgusted that my teenage son, with alcohol abuse rampant in the high school, was spending every afternoon with a drunk father. That he was in the car with a drunk. I remembered instantly those car accidents Josh had had, and wondered whether his falling asleep at the wheel had been the results of drugs or alcohol. I sighed in disgust at myself for not having protected my own kids.

Ten minutes later Josh slammed the front door. The three of us, lined up against the kitchen counter, looked up startled. We stole glances at each other, then at Josh. I didn't understand how he had gotten home but it felt like he was interrupting our plot to figure out our next moves. I had been about to call the police station to find out where he'd been locked up. I wanted the rescue. I was relieved and disappointed that he was home.

"What the hell happened?" I demanded.

"You wanna know what happened?" he screamed. "That bastard across the street called the cops!," Spit flew as he raged. *Always someone else's fault.*

"Dad, I told you to stop!" Adam said.

Josh flailed his arms, breath heaving from anger and a sprint, no doubt, from the police station. He was wearing just a white t-shirt and jeans with the temperature just above freezing. The bandage covering the scar of a fatty cyst removed the week before near his clavicle stood prominently on his chest like a badge. He didn't appear unsteady or inebriated and I sidled up to him to smell his breath, which wasn't easy because he was whirling around.

Confirmed. Alcohol.

He recoiled.

"I am not drunk," he shrieked as he caught on. He kicked his leather moccasins off his feet. "I could've lost my law license," he said with an uptick in his voice listing the grievances. "I could've served jail time. They wouldn't even let me come in the house and get my jacket. Plus they kept me sitting in the back of the police car for 20 minutes while people getting off the train walked by. I'm gonna sue those fuckers. They had no right to arrest me." He looked like he was going to cry. "Gonna start an action against them. I hate this town. Small-minded idiots."

We stood silent for a moment.

It was rare for Josh to rage like this and I hesitated saying anything remembering the "parabola of emotion" theory I'd once read about in a parenting book. Once the tantrum takes hold it's best not to interrupt because it only fuels the person's reaction. The last time I'd seen him remotely like this was at his office when he and I had the chicken tikka masala lunch and he was pacing and holding his head in his hands over me and Claire.

"So what are you doing home?" I said softly.

"Oh, sorry to disappoint."

"Come on. What happened?"

"They let me go," he said calmly, head down. "They had to. They had no right to arrest me."

He explained that they held him in a cell until the sergeant came and then released him because the cops had not observed him driving.

"So, he comes in, this big idiot," said Josh, "and says, 'this is your lucky day.' Well, it's not his lucky day cause I'm gonna sue his ass."

The police had only encountered Josh after he had parked our mini van in the driveway and he was inside our house. So, technically, they had no right to arrest because they hadn't seen him driving. I feared Josh's name would appear in the Crime Watch section of the local newspaper.

The kids and I drove to a Touch of Italy, our favorite pizzeria, to pick up dinner. They both came with me, which was unusual. Most times, they didn't like to leave the comfort of the TV or video game if they didn't have to. Their coming with me felt oddly symbolic, like they were siding with me or maybe felt safer. The mood in the car was buoyant. Despite my shakiness, I was excited about our discussion—what had happened to their father, how scary it was, how embarrassing. There was something oddly genuine about our conversation, like the three of us were solidly together. Plus, for me, their dad was now the suspect. No longer me. I was now the responsible parent with no secrets.

Josh's name never appeared in the local newspaper and no charges were ever pressed. He got a summons for leaving the scene of an accident and in return he dropped the lawsuit he had begun against the town police. While Josh felt justice had been done with his release and exoneration, I felt he had received a pass, a lucky break, "Broken Luck," perhaps.

But soon I made another discovery.

The following week, Josh's dad, Mel, confided that Josh had borrowed $10,000. Mel and I had started to speak often about Josh's behavior. We were concerned he was giving his law practice over to work on the international finance deals, that his drinking was noticeably interfering in our family's life, and that he hadn't been the same since September 11, 2001. Josh told his dad he needed the money for personal business expenses. He did not get specific. Of course, Mel had no idea we had refinanced the house, draining $300,000 of the equity to help Josh pay off debt. I was startled at Mel's revelation, which started me to create a mental catalog of the disturbing pieces of Josh's behavior. I didn't understand why Josh wouldn't just go into our joint savings account and take the money or ask me for it. His secretiveness alarmed me. Mel had asked me not to say anything to Josh.

"I needed money," he said when I confronted him that night. "Yeah, I got those creditors off my back, but I need money to live until these deals happen."

Again, with the deals.

"Do you have any idea how expensive it is to run our lives?" he asked.

"Josh," I snorted, "you need to stop with these crazy deals and get back to lawyering. I don't get it. Stop this. Get a job. This can't continue."

He shook his head.

"And tomorrow we're going to DA—Debtor's Anonymous," I added.

In 1992, a friend in AA recovery had told me about a twelve-step group for debtors. Back then when Josh had high balances on his credit cards, I mentioned it to him. He shrugged it off and I didn't go because I didn't believe I had a debt problem. But I'd never forgotten about the program. After Mel told me about my husband borrowing from him, I hurried to the Internet and found a beginner's meeting at a nearby church that began at nine a.m. on Saturday, the next day. Josh agreed. I was surprised but relieved that he was so willing.

"I'll go anywhere with you," he later said.

✦

We found the Saturday nine a.m. beginner's meeting of Debtor's Anonymous by walking through a dark hallway and down the polished Catholic school stairs. The dingy, cement floor in the church basement was full of puddles from umbrellas and snow boots. The morning was overcast and the windowless room was damp. A white Formica counter and sink were tucked at the back of the small room but no coffee was percolating as I had hoped. I'd heard about coffee somehow being important in those twelve-step meetings. Josh and I sat on cold, brown metal folding chairs side by side in the circle along with the other "debtors"—six men and two women including me, and a leader. I was angry for the mess he was making with our money, for not telling me about the cash he'd borrowed from his father, for having to be here. Josh looked angry, too, disdain cascading off him.

People seemed to know each other, chatting happily and I wondered how anyone could look so carefree if he or she had to be in this room.

"Please join me in the Serenity Prayer," said the leader, Henry, a frail octogenarian. His hands were veiny, thin, and his skin opaque. He wore his gray, wispy strands of hair pulled back neatly into a ponytail. His voice was breathy but there was a softness and sincerity that made me listen to him.

People stood in the circle and held hands. "God, grant me the serenity to accept the things I cannot change; courage to change the things I can; and wisdom to know the difference," everyone recited. I mumbled my way through the prayer, having heard it somewhere but not knowing it well. One of the directors at my office had hung a plaque outside her office with the prayer etched next to a hands raised in prayer. Josh didn't recite anything. Then everyone introduced themselves.

"First, let's read the twelve steps," said Henry, the leader. He passed around a sheet with the *12 Promises of Debtor's Anonymous*, which claimed that if you "practice the program" you will be released from hiding and denial into a world of abundance and prosperity. I figured those words were designed to make everyone feel better because sitting in that room was no badge of success.

People shared about their jobs and being "under-earners." Almost everyone thanked God for his and her prosperity, with one man raising his hands to the ceiling and exalting "thank you, God" every time he said anything. One woman talked about "time debting" and I guessed that meant being late. I had never heard these expressions before but I mentally directed everything I was hearing to Josh. I hoped he was listening. I was fixated on his getting it: let go of the secrets, admit his powerlessness, and embrace the help in the room. That would be our ticket to peace. As I thought about it, Josh and I had been in the grips of a pain fever for so long that it started to feel normal. Chaos and hurt had become companions to our marriage.

We left the meeting and in the parking lot with our "beginner's packet," I searched Josh's face for some evidence that he thought DA was worthwhile but I was afraid to ask. As a joiner of groups, I was willing to come back, as everyone insisted at the end of the meeting. I knew we needed help. He shrugged when I asked how he liked it. He picked at his nails.

"I don't know," he said. "How is a group of people with a bunch of platitudes gonna help me? They keep saying 'it's not about the money.' Ha. That's a good one. I gotta make this deal happen. Is there a room to help me do that?"

I exhaled exasperation.

"Look don't start getting pissy because I'm not jumping on your bandwagon," he said. "I said I'd go. And I'm here. Isn't that enough?"

A week and a half later, we spent Christmas Day with my family at my sister Laura's house. We had gathered as we did every year in the living room of my sister's cathedral-ceilinged Levitt home filled with a sparkling eight-foot Christmas tree, dozens of gift boxes, crumpled wrapping paper, riding toys, Santa and snow globes, and our traditional three-course dinner of antipasto, lasagna, and roast beef. I always thought of my parents on Christmas, both now deceased, my dad's death now three years earlier, because the holiday meant so much to them. Growing up in the Depression, my mother's family was too poor to afford Christmas gifts. She had told us if she got an orange it meant a lot. So, though she was frugal the rest of the year, she saved up in a Christmas club savings account to afford piles of gifts for me and my sisters. My mother loved giving us those gifts, her eyes shining with the anticipation of our reactions. She warned us every year that "this was a bad year for Santa," to playfully dispel our expectations. But it was never a bad year for Santa because my mom had squirreled away savings for gifts for me: from the Chatty Cathy doll to the Charlie McCarthy ventriloquist dummy to the Beatles White Album to a generous check when I became an adult.

On Christmas Day, Josh wore his Santa Claus suspenders and Rudolph snapback cap, which looked like he was wearing a stuffed animal on his head. And his Ray-Bans. He was still wearing his sunglasses all the time, indoors and out. He always loved to wear props whether it was a blond Beatles wig he'd come across in the attic or a Lone Ranger mask with an elastic string and cut-outs for the eyes—something he had once worn throughout Thanksgiving dinner.

As we drove home that night, Josh suddenly misjudged a turn and drove straight onto oncoming traffic of the six-lane road. We were alone in the car; the boys had left earlier, getting a ride from their cousins.

"What are you doing?" I screamed. Josh quickly corrected the car around the divider.

"Let me drive or let me out," I demanded.

"No! I'm driving. I'm fine," he responded.

"Let me drive!"

"You want out? Fine." He slowed the car but didn't stop. I thought instantly of the DUI and his arrest.

"You want out of the marriage, too? That's fine."

I said nothing, to avoid fueling his behavior into spiteful recklessness.

As we sat in the car, I caught the whiff of liquor. Once, as a twelve-year-old, I had gone with my older cousin Sylvia to her boyfriend's house, excited to be brought along. I was enamored with the lives of my older cousins and whenever they deigned to take me somewhere I was ecstatic. The living room of her boyfriend Dutch's house was part of the basement of a row house in Bensonhurst, Brooklyn. The room was dimly lit with indoor/outdoor carpeting and dark wood furniture. It was hot indoors, no air conditioning.

Dutch's father was listening to Perry Como on the stereo and insisted I dance with him. I protested politely—at twelve the only dancing I was doing was in front of the mirror in my bedroom to determine if I had any "rhythm," but he yanked me to the floor—me too polite to say no. With his face close to mine I smelled liquor but couldn't identify the powerful odor, which smelled dangerous and ugly. He was stumbling drunk. I inhaled that odor with his every exhale, labored and thick. As I grew up, I made the connection between that scent and alcohol.

Josh and I made it home, lugging Christmas packages and paper plates filled with leftovers. I couldn't deny that Josh had a drinking problem. Yet I still found it hard to believe my husband was a drunk. There was no slurring, unsteadiness, blacking out, or self-pity. He was no Jack Lemmon in *Days of Wine and Roses*, swearing not to drink then going on a bender and hiding bottles in the greenhouse.

CHAPTER 16

I'd been meaning to call Edward, my financial advisor, for days. I kept looking at the reminder in my daybook. Once a year I looked over our investments—mostly mutual funds held in our IRA accounts and an annuity set up when Matthew was a baby. Where were those statements? Had American Express gone paperless but forgotten to tell me? When I asked Josh if he'd seen the statements or how to access them online, he said he was waiting for American Express to send the PIN. But it was taking an awfully long time.

It was a gray, damp January morning, right after New Year's, 2007. I was at work. Edward answered the phone and after we exchanged holiday greetings, I asked why I hadn't received the statements.

"Better ask your husband," was his terse reply. "Then, get yourself a good lawyer, accountant, and private eye."

I was stunned. The best lawyer I knew was Josh. How could I possibly turn to another? And a private detective? Really?

I spun around in my swivel chair, heart pounding, tears welling up. My throat constricted into "sheep woman" voice—shaky and high-pitched—if I opened my mouth. I was afraid to speak, reluctant to let Edward know the depth of my upset.

I stared out the window at the unyielding Empire State Building, close enough to touch, unwavering as a stern parent.

"What?" I asked, hearing the words but my brain not connecting the meaning. "He did what? Cleared out his IRA account?"

My hands shook.

"When? Why?," I babbled. The office air vent suddenly got quiet as if it were eavesdropping.

He must be in trouble, I thought frantically, as Edward ticked off the dates the money had been withdrawn.

"November 17, $7,500. December 6, $20,000."

I thought of what Josh had told me about the men who came to his office looking for $200,000. I could never understand why Josh would have to pay someone else's debt but that must be it. *What the hell had gone wrong? What did this mean for the twenty-fifth wedding anniversary trip to Sorrento?*

"I'm sorry," Edward said over and over. "Remember, I called you in November, around Thanksgiving? Asked if everything was all right?"

Edward explained that he couldn't call me but kept hoping I would call him. Edward wasn't permitted to report my spouse's activity. His apologies seemed excessive since he hadn't done anything wrong. But the tone of his sympathy poked at my veneer of denial. This must be serious if he keeps apologizing.

First, the DUI, then $10,000 Josh had borrowed a month earlier from his dad. And, of course, the refinanced mortgage to the tune of almost a half million dollars. Now this.

If you wanted to get my full attention, you've got it now.

Was this the impact my affair had had on Josh? I was dazed: who was this man I had been married to for twenty-five years? My attorney-spouse. Father of my boys. Why was he lying to me?

I recalled Edward's words of two years ago as I sat across from him in his office blinking back tears: "Tell your husband to get a job." We had just re-mortgaged the house. Edward snarled about Josh, sparing no patience for what he perceived as excessive spending and trickling income.

"Where's the money going?" Edward asked on the phone. "Drugs? Some place else?"

I knew the money was going into the "international deals," especially funding related to the so-called "illegitimate son." The story was too farfetched to reveal to Edward right then.

Josh would have to pay a ten percent penalty upon withdrawing funds from his IRA account prematurely. This didn't escape me in that moment either. I knew about protecting retirement accounts, all those articles saying never to touch your IRA funds. Yet, our taxes hadn't been filed for the last three years, even though money had been withdrawn from my paycheck and Josh claimed he was paying quarterly. He kept telling he was going to file our taxes the following weekend for years, but that time never came. Somehow I thought he'd magically tend to this so I didn't consider it for more than a passing thought.

Edward offered to help me in any way he could, and when we got off the phone I was trembling.

A few minutes later, the phone rang. I hesitated, composing myself quickly. Luckily, it was my sister, Laura, not a work-related call.

"What's wrong?" she asked immediately.

"It's Josh."

"Is he okay?"

"He's in trouble."

I explained in tears what Edward had told me.

"Listen to me," she said, "today, right now, go to the bank and withdraw all the money that's in both names." I nodded. I needed instructions. I felt like someone dear had died. I was numb, confused, and rubbery. Something irretrievable had vanished, something more than cash.

At lunchtime I went to the bank. I cried, explaining my situation to the woman manager who gave me a tissue, squeezed my hand, and told me us women had to stick together. She was divorced. She understood.

I waited two days to confront Josh about what I knew. Partly I was procrastinating, afraid of what I might hear, fearful of the confrontation, and luxuriating for one more day in the fantasy of being taken care of. I longed to hear his statement, "we'll work it out," the phrase I'd heard so often over the years, and I wanted badly to hear him say it and believe it; yet I knew those words were an empty currency as the truth began to unravel.

Upon arriving home the day I spoke to Edward, I was impassive, despite the dread that churned through me. After dinner, I went to the second floor of our house to the office Josh and I shared. We'd added the room in the renovation and it embraced a beautiful eyebrow window that exposed the night sky. We had our own desks at opposite sides of the room. Josh's was cluttered with a twenty-inch monitor, a fax machine and scanner, piles of papers, a mountain of unopened mail, yellow post-it notes stuck everywhere, fortune cookie slips, Crazy Glue, blank CDs, and nail clippers strewn about. Over his desk, hung a cork bulletin board with photos of Adam scoring a goal, Matthew perched on a stool singing and playing guitar, and one of Josh and his Filipino client taken in federal prison in front of a faux landscape. Nearby stood his tawny mahogany credenza stuffed with client folders and stacks of paper documents.

I looked through the window, seething and frightened, hoping to get a game plan. How was I to sort through everything to get a complete financial picture? I had wanted to start looking through our financial papers before Josh suspected I knew he was secretly squirreling away money. I sat on the carpet wiping tears because I couldn't call him in and say, "Hey, let's tackle this." I got up and stood in the middle of the room, staring, overwhelmed, until I turned and walked out.

The next night, we sat at the kitchen table his mother had hand-painted with a whimsical design of blues, burgundy, and golds. The earth colors in our house. Adam was out at a friend's.

"I know," I said. I emphasized the word "know," trying to be direct so we wouldn't have to play the game of him denying and saying he had no idea what I was talking about, followed by us arguing about whether he knew what I was about to say rather than discussing the matter.

"I know you emptied your IRA and the college annuity."

He slumped.

"I'm tapped out," he said.

Josh wore a blue work shirt, a shade that matched his expressive eyes. The one he wore so often that Adam once asked if he was ever going to put on another. But I didn't mind that shirt; the blue matched the accent color in the lovingly painted table. It all seemed connected. Even though his mother, whom I loved dearly, had died eight years before, it was as if she was sitting with us.

He cast his eyes downward.

"Are you in trouble?"

He shook his head and looked away.

"So?" I asked.

"Simple. I needed cash." He got up and circled the kitchen.

"For what?" I demanded.

"For what?" He chortled. "What do you think keeps this place going?"

I cast an incredulous glance. "Why didn't you just come to me?"

A look of shame crept over him then he stopped and looked at me. "I thought I could replace the money before you found out. Jesus," he sighed, "I've been carrying this for months."

I felt a flash of anger as I thought of the lyrics to the rock song "The Weight" by The Band, "…and you put the load right on me."

"Edward told me to get a lawyer, accountant, and private eye." I looked at him for assurance, combing my fingers through my dark hair.

"Yeah, that's just what we need, a private eye."

"Well, why don't you start from the beginning so I can decide whether we do."

"Told you. I'm tapped out. There's not a lot to tell."

"What does that mean?"

"I don't have anything to give you," he snapped. "That's why I had to use my IRA money. Do you think I wanted to? I had no choice. I. Have. No. Money."

"Wait a minute. You were working. I saw you at the computer every day."

"Yes, I've been working…with Oscar and the clients to make this deal happen. I told him! I'm done with him if he doesn't come up with the access codes."

I stared at him. "No, no. No more. Stop. This is crazy. No more money to these guys. Where's the forty grand we gave that crazy client for his defense? Huh, where?"

We had taken money out of our home equity line to bankroll part of his client's attorney's fees. Josh insisted we would get it back when the client was released, which never happened. Instead, his client received a twelve-year federal prison sentence.

"And no more money to Skye," I added. Skye was the client's wife in the Philippines. I had seen an email from Josh promising her he would send money, a discovery that incensed me. "Please," I insisted.

"Like I told you, when the funds come in we'll be fine. Don't worry."

"Look. We can sell the house if we have to. I just need you to be honest with me."

He looked at me blankly.

"Honesty? You wanna talk about honesty," he spat.

"And you need to get a job," I added.

"What are you, my mother?" he barked. "Trust me. Everything's gonna be okay."

I naively believed this conversation would reveal all, he would show me the books, and we'd fix it. As days went on, however, he grew defensive and reluctant as I demanded to know where the dollars had gone. He claimed not to know. I might as well have been speaking another language when I asked where receipts, statements, and online accounts were. And when I asked about money to pay upcoming February bills, he laughed.

"I. Am. Tapped. Out!" he repeated one night in our bedroom. He enunciated each word with his voice raised and shook his head. Sitting on the bed, I stared absently at the dream catcher he had hung on the windowsill. "What part don't you understand?"

But I didn't understand. How could he have one month been supplying money to run the household then suddenly stop? I couldn't pay all our bills on my salary.

"What are you talking about?" I demanded. "There's got to be something!"

He shook his head with a you-just-don't-get-it expression, turned his back, and walked away.

I lay on the floor of my bedroom crying softly so Adam wouldn't hear, swinging from terror to narrow-eyed anger over having made this discovery without any warning from the person who claimed to love me.

"I trusted you!" I shrieked that night, stomping from our bedroom to the bathroom and pacing the upstairs hallway. I knew Adam was only down the hall and I wanted to shield him from the argument but I couldn't. I was outraged and frustrated at Josh's impenetrable wall. He was telling me the truth—he had no income or expectation of earning—yet I viewed his response as a barricade to the solution I wanted: fix the finances and bail us out of this mess. We had never had a night like that before, even in the angriest moments over my relationship with Claire. I wondered if this was retribution. Was this what I deserved?

Josh moved into Matthew's room and I thought yes, I don't want this stranger near me. I didn't want to soothe his up-all-night anxiety or watch him pacing the bedroom, wonder what he's up to in the bathroom for forty-five minutes, tolerate his sweating through his t-shirt, and calm him during his middle-of-the-night whimpering spurred by a nightmare.

The next day at work I told my boss that my husband was in financial distress and had secretly emptied accounts.

"Well, you don't have to worry about your job," she assured me. She couldn't have said anything more comforting.

"You go and take a day off if you need to. Get your stuff in order."

And I did. But the job of excavating our finances proved formidable. It would take months to plow through the documents that summarized our lives.

✦

On the first day of what I came to call Uncovering Our Hidden Financial Life, I sat at the dining room table, surrounded by the finance folders I had carried from our office: files containing documents related to the mortgage, real estate taxes, income taxes, insurances, education, and living expenses. I had never assembled these papers in one place before. Josh had gone into Manhattan for the day; I was sure he was making himself scarce to escape the line of fire, as he knew the task I'd set for myself that day.

I lifted the scariest folder first, the mortgage, with a pounding heart: *God, grant me the serenity to accept the things I cannot change.* I had learned in DA to bookend a difficult task by saying the serenity prayer before and after—to ask my Higher Power for help. I was learning to strive for clarity—getting the numbers on the page—no matter how frightening the tallies would be. I knew how to add and subtract, I told myself, something DA'ers claimed is all it took, along with courage and a shift in behavior, to become financially solvent, which meant having no debt.

I held the statement from our mortgage company, Countrywide Home Loans, which displayed my name. Despite what Josh told me about his sharing the responsibility for the mortgage, I recognized I was the one legally required to pay. Painful as it was to accept my foolishness at saying yes to signing onto a new loan, I gained a moment of clarity: I understood what was real.

The statement described our mortgage as a thirty-year conventional jumbo pay option adjustable rate (ARM) which meant the term of the loan had been reset at thirty years; that means despite having paid the mortgage for ten years, we were starting over. The pay options allowed us to pay in one of four ways: principal and interest, fifteen-year amortized payment, minimum payment, and interest-only payment. Since we refinanced in May 2005, almost two years earlier, we had been paying the minimum amount of $1,500 a month on a $440,000 loan. Even seeing the $440,000 figure, once again and up close, made me cringe since our old mortgage amount had been a reasonable $140,000. As I read the fine print, I confirmed my suspicion that the loan amount was increasing, not decreasing as one would think; the interest was being added to the principal loan amount by about a whopping $1,500 a month.

"God help us," I uttered, realizing that in two years the mortgage amount had already risen from $440,000 to $470,000. From that day on, watching $1,500 get added to the mortgage every month was like viewing the hotel furnace in the movie The Shining, with Jack Nicholson, expanding and expanding, ready to blow. I felt frantic to locate the shut-off valve.

I pulled the original mortgage documents, the one I signed with the mamadelle, eighty pages, dense, and full of legal language with no paragraph breaks. There were all kinds of breakdowns, columns, ratios, and few straightforward figures. Yup, those were my initials on each page.

I scoured through the closing documents, hands shaking, to take a closeup look at where the nearly $300,000 of equity (the difference between the $440,000 mortgage and our original $140,000 loan) had gone:

$140,000: Washington Mutual bank, old mortgage

$120,000: Chase bank, equity line (which Josh had been living off)

$49,200: Josh's credit card, MNBA American Bank

$45,750: Josh's credit card, MNBA American Bank

$24,500: Josh's credit card, Chase Manhattan Bank

$24,500: Josh's credit card, Chase Manhattan Bank

$7,400: Janet credit card, American Express
                (home remodeling expenses)

$6,600: Josh's credit card, Capital One Bank

$2,775: Josh's credit card, American Express

$2,033: Josh's business line of credit, Chase Manhattan Bank

$1,585: Josh's credit card, Citizen's

$1,530: Josh's credit card, CitiFinancial

$409: Josh's credit card, Old Navy

$388: Josh's credit card, American Express

$283: Josh's credit card, Dell Financial

$227: Josh's credit card, Amex

$42: Janet credit card, Gap

A total debt of $427,222! It was shocking but at least I had clarity. My husband's spendthrift ways had gone into perverse overdrive. Worse was that he had no intention of admitting it. Looking at the payoffs, I realized the list did not include additional debt Josh owed. I knew this because he mentioned the payoff had not covered his total debt. But to find out amounts and creditors I would need to excavate further.

In the meantime, I had to stymie the bleeding from our ugly mortgage. In going through the mortgage folder I found a letter addressed to "Dear Valued Customer" from Countrywide titled, *Significant Payment Increase Alert, October 2006.* That was only a few months ago. The letter explained the four "pay option" features and cautioned that my monthly minimum payment could increase significantly.

It was almost time for dinner. The sun had just set on a frigid February day when I dialed Countrywide.

After obediently following the cheery prompts—"For Loans, press three; say or press your account number; due to unusually call high volume, you are being put on hold but your call is very important to us, and will be answered in the order in which it was received"—I was finally speaking to a human being.

"Hello my name is Paul and how can I help you today?" asked the uber-polite customer service rep.

I explained to Paul about the "Dear Valued Customer" letter.

"I'm afraid my payment is about to rise," I said. Paul put me on hold where I heard a booming baritone pitch Countrywide's "products." It was approaching five-thirty and I hadn't prepared anything yet for dinner. Adam had basketball practice at eight and I had to feed the boy before he played. My stomach was growling too.

"Oh my. You're not in a very good loan," said Paul with astonishing honesty. "It looks like you have been current in your payments so we can offer you a refinance," he added with delight.

I breathed.

"I can offer you a fixed ten-year ARM at six-point-three-seven-five percent, no points."

Is that good?

"With a monthly payment of $2,530. Or a thirty-year fixed at six-point-five percent no points with a payment of $3,010.

That is without our $900 a month cost for real estate taxes. The feeling of now-familiar dread was roiling.

"Are there are any fees?"

Paul put me on hold.

"Mom, when are we eating?" Adam intoned from the den. The voices of ESPN Sportscenter's announcers blared.

"I see here your mortgage broker tacked on a three-year pre-payment penalty," said Paul calmly. "So it will cost you $15,000 to terminate this loan and get into a new one."

"What?" The blood rose to my temples.

"What?" I asked again.

"There's a prepayment penalty…" Paul hesitated. "I'm afraid you're not in a very good loan," he repeated. Paul's second acknowledgment of the severity of my finance-wrecking loan turned some screw in me.

Now I wept on the phone to Paul, who kept talking but I didn't hear what he was saying. I got the feeling he was trying to make me feel better but I couldn't hear him.

"We can add this $15,000 to the principal and see if you qualify for a $480,000 loan but I'd have to do the figures on that. Maybe $500,000 to cover closing costs."

It didn't matter. I was a puddle. Hector, our friend, the mortgage broker. How could he? I remembered asking Josh about a prepayment penalty and believing that there wasn't any. And I couldn't stop weeping. Even without working the figures I knew I didn't want to borrow money to pay off money I owed and that I'd lose another $15,000 if we sold. Salty tears wetting my papers. I eked out a barely audible "thank you" to Paul.

"Thank you for calling Countrywide," said Paul.

I sobbed, head on the counter. The kind of crying I would only do alone. Adam jumped up from the den.

"Mom, what's wrong?" I waved him away, shaking my head. I didn't want him to think anyone died.

"It's the mortgage."

He stared at me from a distance then came over and put his hand on my shoulder. He patted me, "It's okay, Mom."

In an instant my weeping gave way to rage and I flew into the dining room and tore through the mortgage folder looking for evidence of the pre-payment penalty. I found it buried in the folder. The page felt scorching as I handled it.

Email from Hector to Josh:

Buddy, oh, buddy, please let me add a prepayment penalty. Help me out with a bigger commission.

I threw the papers like a frisbee. It felt so unsatisfying. My eyes stung. My anger had nowhere to go, like a demon that wanted to hurt me. It felt like a building had fallen on me and I was buried beneath the rubble. I wanted to dig my way out but I only had a bent spoon.

"Did you know about this prepayment penalty?" I asked Josh as he hung up his coat when he got home that night. I approached him by the front door.

"What are you talking about?" he responded. Edge in his voice.

"Prepayment penalty. Can't sell or refinance unless we pay an additional fifteen grand. Do you know what this means?"

He shrugged. "Yeah, and?"

"Your fucking friend Hector," I screamed close to his face. "Your approval on the prepayment. Why don't you just serve us up, you bastard?"

"So what's another fifteen thousand dollars? Just tack it on to another thirty years. Why are you being so dramatic?"

"So that's your answer? Just borrow more money to pay off more debt? Why do I keep thinking you're part of the solution? What's wrong with me?" My fists were poised like a prize fighter's, under my chin, but I was shaking them at myself.

"You need to get over your anger," he said. "You're making yourself miserable."

✦

A few days later, a letter arrived, addressed to my husband and me, from our homeowner's insurance company: Declaration of Cancellation for Non-Payment. The premiums had not been paid and the company was no longer insuring our home. I was dumbfounded and angry beyond words. How in the world did my husband not pay this? There must have been warnings from the company. Then I thought of the heap of unopened mail in the office.

On the heels of this letter, another arrived from Countrywide:

Our system does not show that you maintain acceptable insurance coverage on your property. If we do not receive your verification and continuous insurance coverage the fire insurance coverage on your property will be obtained by Countrywide.

It ended by saying:

In the event of a claim, all payments under this coverage will be made to Countrywide and not to you. An affiliate of Countrywide Home Loans may receive a commission or other compensation if insurance is obtained by Countrywide.

In other words, if there is a fire and Countrywide has obtained the insurance on the house, they, not us, will be paid. And they receive a commission to boot. I was getting good at reading fine print.

Instead of calling the broker we'd been using for years, I found a new, local broker who reinstated the homeowners and gave me handsome quotes on the car insurance too. I signed us up for a homeowner's policy that costs $850 less a year than the premium I had taken out to cover the lapsed policy. I did the same with the car insurance. I switched us out of a policy with insurance giant AIG, where the premiums were running over $3,000 a year, to a policy costing $1,600.

On the second day of Uncovering Our Hidden Financial Life, I was in the home office. Insurance papers were everywhere: life, car, disability, and homeowner's. Having moved from the precipice of the lapsing homeowner's and inflated car insurance premiums, I needed to review the life insurance policies—a challenge to decipher because we held five policies from three different companies. The paperwork was so confusing that I couldn't tell the difference between the policies, premiums, and receipts. As I pawed through the folders, I felt my irritation rise: *Josh should be taking care of this.* If it were another time and not so serious, I might have ignored it out of disgust.

Then, I spotted a letter.

Dear Valued Customer: As you probably know, your term life insurance has now lapsed. However, we have made special arrangements with the plan insurer to extend the reinstatement period for fifteen more days only.

I looked closely at the folder and saw cancellation and reinstatement notices littering the file. I realized how many times we came close to losing our life insurance.

On the third and final day of uncovering, I started at night. The moon was high, visible through the eyebrow window. I recited the serenity prayer before I began, feeling like a surgeon, scrubbed, sterile, and about to cut. The printer spit out pages of my Equifax credit reports. In scouring the office I found a "privacy assist" document from Josh's bank that contained his credit report. Someone recommended I pull credit reports for our children but I didn't have the stomach.

I willed myself courage to read both credit reports.

First, my credit report:

0 potentially negative

21 accounts in good standing

I scanned the page. There's the old mortgage, now with a zero balance, like visiting an old friend in the grave. The car payments, old credit card balances. My eyes were afraid to scroll down. But thankfully there was nothing threatening.

Next, Josh's reports from all three reporting agencies: eight pages of accounts on Equifax alone.

Listed under factors that make your score higher:

You currently have a total of $142,125 available credit.

Below that, listed under factors that make your score lower:

You currently owe $122,368 on your revolving accounts.

Over $120,000 still owed!

I reeled like I'd been punched, and then the slow drip of defeat blanketed me. After having squeezed $300,000 of equity out of our home to pay down his debt, my husband still owed over $120,000. And could still borrow $148,000! I didn't know which was more ludicrous: the money he owed or the amount he could still access. I shook my head in disbelief, which gave way to a surge of panic, then tears.

"Breathe." I said trying to talk myself down. "They're only numbers."

Then I saw an entry: Bank of America, revolving balance: $50,176 with a limit of $51,500 and a "J" next to it, meaning "joint." What?

How could that be? I hadn't signed on to any joint business account. The monthly payments were over $900 a month and because payments were overdue, we owed $1,800.

I cross-checked my credit report, looking at the balance history and caught my breath once again. There it was. A $50,000 line of credit. The debt was mine, too.

"He ran up fifty grand in debt we now both owe," I said to no one, "and I never spent a dime of it."

Where did this account come from? I had never seen any credit card statements and I didn't remember signing on as a co-signer.

Forgery?

My face turned crimson.

Later that night, I asked Josh about the credit line.

"Remember when the conference call a few years ago at your office?" he asked. "And the bank was checking employment and he asked if you agreed to be on the line?"

I leaned against the kitchen counter, looking at Josh and peering through the sliding glass doors to our deck.

"I remember the call but not agreeing to anything."

"Well, you did."

"I thought he was asking me about my salary and years of work."

"Yeah, that's the call. I was converting from an MBNA credit line to a Bank of America credit card."

"But don't you have to sign something to be a co-signer?"

"Guess not."

By the time I found MoneyGrams paid to Asian addresses, forms naming Josh custodian of our boys' accounts, receipts showing he had paid our real estate taxes by credit card, $5,000 borrowed against the life insurance annuity, a $7,000 payment to a business associate, $3,500 cash advances, $585 on Benedetti Custom Shoes, $150 bills to Village Liquors, bills of $800 and $1,100 paid to Sprint Wireless (not our carrier), pawn shop receipts for the sale of his Rolexes, and late fees that amounted to thousands, it was time to get a lawyer.

CHAPTER 17

I lay in bed watching the blue-black sky of morning creep through the top of the window. I had an appointment with Bob Southard, a divorce attorney, that day. I didn't want my marriage to be over and as I watched the dawn approach, tears trickled onto my pillow. I wished I could arrest the dark and stop the daylight from appearing.

In the vestibule of the lawyer's office, Peggy, Bob's paralegal, greeted me. She was chipper and petite as a toy poodle with dark corkscrew curls and a mouth too big for her pixie face. Peggy told me how she ended a thirty-year marriage which oddly made me feel better. She handed me a badly photocopied "Statement of Client's Rights and Responsibilities" to sign. She spoke so intimately, touching my arm, I wondered if I'd met her before. She escorted me to Bob's office and I waited for him to get off the phone. The office was cluttered in the way I'd seen so many lawyer's offices—manila folders piled high, a carousel of rubber stamps, photos of the family at the son's bar mitzvah.

"Look, you got all the liability and you don't even own the asset," Bob said to me, referring to the house. He was heavy, balding, lawyer-looking, and unflinching. I nodded, feeling foolish for letting this happen.

"And tomorrow," Bob continued," go pay your taxes." I started to ask if I could do that and he interrupted.

"You file separately. You must. Freeze or cancel any joint accounts. Freeze credit cards. Title search the house then get him to sign the house over to you. File the FAFSA for college aid. Use a P.O. box for your mail. Put a lock on your phone."

After I told Bob about never having used the business line of credit and not having signed anything, he said, "Get the original application from Bank of America to see whether he forged your name."

I looked up from my notes.

"He didn't forge my name."

"You'd be surprised," Bob responded.

After two hours, Bob walked me out and I scribbled a check for $500. He wanted a $7,500 retainer to start, $250 an hour, $150 an hour for Peggy, and any other negotiating charged by the hour. I thought of what Josh could be earning.

✦

The following Sunday, Josh proposed a solution—that we tap into a home equity line to clear up the debt. I "puhhed" him away, cold-shoulder, and the house became eerily quiet. The pendulum in the antique wall clock—a wedding present —no longer swung because neither of us would wind it. We said little, avoiding each other. The TV was low, Adam scarce, meals silent. I darted out every weekday at seven-thirty in the morning, glad to be gone from our funeral home. I couldn't stop thinking of the line from the Erica Jong's book *Fear of Flying:*

There is no loneliness like the loneliness of a dead marriage.

Email, February 20, 2007:

Janet:

I want to remind you of my request to you. There is only one credit card that is joint obligation. It is at $51,500 and the interest rate is 20+%. There is no late payment history and I have been making all the payments until now.

I propose:

A home equity line of $100K.

I sign full responsibility for it and make the payments.

From the proceeds I will pay off the BOA joint credit card and close the account.

I will give you $10,000 from the proceeds which you can hold as security should I default. (This will be enough to cover approximately one year of payments.)

If you agree I will sign over the house and you can retain all the equity.

I need an answer from you by Friday. If you do not agree I will take other action I would rather avoid.

Even if your assessment of my actions and the consequences to YOU and your premonition of doom are correct (which they most assuredly are not) your premature decision to go it alone and terminate our relationship will significantly increase the economic holocaust you so wrongly believe is inevitable.

I truly regret and am very saddened and disappointed that you have permitted your anger and fear to cloud your judgment.

This change of heart is fueled by your self-righteous indignation at my excessive borrowing (you claim you had no idea about, right?) and the advice you obtain based on misconceptions and theories that you hold onto because they feed your justification. Justification that you unilaterally terminated our twenty-five-year marriage, treated me like I've never contributed a fucking thing to this family and more to the point, never will again. And your termination of our joint accounts and demands for HOUSE, SEPARATION AGREEMENT, all done so mean spiritedly to the very family you are trying to protect from me the "Dangerous" one.

I will not be bullied Janet. Even I have my limits. I will protect myself and stand up for what I believe is right and true, just like I have tried to do my whole life. I wish you well.

Josh

I did not dismiss the email as crazy, but neither did I agree.

✦

"This new credit card is great," I overheard Josh say on the phone that week as I approached our home office. I could tell he was talking to his associate Oscar in California. He leaned back in his chair, hands behind his head, headset perched on his dome. He straightened up when I came in.

We locked eyes when he hung up.

"If you continue along this path," I said, "you will lose everything you love." I searched his face for remorse but saw steel.

Soon, however, my anger dissolved into melancholy. I wanted us to be us again. I couldn't hang onto the ire. I'd never been good at holding grudges—maybe my father's "assume the best" attitude was too much to outmaneuver. I wondered: is it me? Maybe I was just not being compassionate enough. Not understanding enough. Maybe I *was* complicit. I missed him, my bedrock of love. He reminded me many times that I spent money too. Maybe he was right.

So when he asked if he could have $10,000 from the cash I had set aside, I countered with $5,000 and was talked up to $7,500. I walked through the doors of Citibank like a dutiful wife and plucked a cashier's check made out to him. I couldn't wait to hand him the check. I was excited, adrenaline pumping, I wanted to see the love in his eyes. I wanted to feel normal. He thanked me and even though I assumed a posture that appeared slightly annoyed, my heart sang.

At my therapist Erica's midtown office, the Kandinsky painting was hypnotic. I fessed to Erica about the $7,500.

"It was a lot of money, several thousand," I said looking for reaction to how bad this was. "You know he doesn't have any money. And he gave me a promissory note."

"Do you consider this a slip?" she asked, using AA language for a relapse.

"I dunno," I replied. "This is how we always treated each other: if one of us needed something we gave it," I explained. "But if I keep this up, I'm gonna run out of money. And I told him all we needed was a few thousand dollars income a month to salvage everything. I've explained this to him and still no job."

"There's not much you can do to make anyone, especially an alcoholic, do something."

I winced. The word "alcoholic."

"You know, he has the capacity to harm me," I said with a flash of insight.

"No," replied Erica. "You have the capacity to harm you."

I absorbed the blow of that remark and let it sink in. In fact, I'd never forgotten it. She was right. I was the only one who could harm me. I had choices and the ability to protect myself if I believed so.

"What do I have to do?"

"Abstain from discussing anything money-related with him," she advised. "Don't allude, intimate, blame, expect, hope, or get mad. Money, and how you handle it, is your business."

Just then I got another glimmer of something: Josh was not going to fix this! Even with the lure of the $7,500.

"You mean it's up to me?"

She nodded. Kindness in her eyes.

"You mean, I need to be the only person I can rely on?"

I reached for a tissue from the Kleenex box on the table to my right.

"I'm not sad," I said. "Just frustrated. Why do I have to clean up this mess? Why does he get off the hook?"

"You're taking care of yourself and your kids. That's your business," she answered leaning forward and clutching the arms of her black office chair.

"I'm trusting you," I said, playful threat in my voice.

"The well is dry. You can keep going back but it's dry."

My resentment swallowed me. Josh had lured me to the ledge and left me there. But I tiptoed out there willingly. Didn't I?

"Consider going to Al-Anon, for families of alcoholics," said Erica right before she leaned forward and grabbed her large green appointment book, the signal that time was up.

✦

It was a Thursday afternoon at a midtown Al-Anon meeting. I entered the room tentatively and sat in the back in one of the stackable chairs. The depressive energy in the room exhausted me and I didn't know whether to stay. I was angry that I even needed to be there. *I'm not the one with the problem. Why do I have to go to a program?*

A man, who I later learned was Ernest, looked thin and sickly. He was the leader, poised to start, holding typewritten sheets in a plastic sleeve. A woman sitting next to him on the couch dozed. Seating was arranged in a U-shape, with dusty, cheap-looking couches on two sides.

I justified my being there because of Josh's DUI arrest and his continued relationship with Smirnoff and those big red party cups. Plus, Erica
called him an alcoholic, so it must be true.

As the meeting began, people, mostly women, filtered in and recited the twelve steps of Al-Anon, similar to the DA twelve steps, and read
from a small, hardcover book called *Courage to Change.*

"Well," I began, fishing for a powerful indictment when asked at
the end of the meeting to share, "my husband was arrested in December for a DUI." I told the group—whose complete attention I commanded—about Josh's car accidents when he had the children in the
car. How his son had to witness his father's arrest. I enjoyed holding
court for my three minutes, convinced my situation was worse than
anything the room had ever heard. I wanted support from my fellow
"al-anonics," as they called themselves, that I was right and that Josh
needed to wake up and fix his life.

I didn't get the support I expected in Al-Anon—sympathy and acknowledgement that I was right—but over the weeks, I heard wisdom
and advice: to keep the focus on myself, attend six other meetings, don't
make any major decisions for six months, and to keep coming back. It
was sobering to hear that I needed to keep the focus on myself. That I
could unhinge from the alcoholic. I kept going back to meetings and
heard talk of "not taking anyone else's inventory" and the "qualifier,"
which meant the alcoholic. These folks were serene and grounded and
I wanted some of that.

I avoided telling Josh about Al-Anon, certain he would be angry
with me and the implication that he was an alcoholic. I pictured myself
telling him he was an alcoholic and saw us both laughing at the absur-
dity and then hugging him and hearing him say, "Everything's going
to be okay." Maybe the problem was me: I wasn't forgiving and loving
enough.

On the train to work in the mornings, I read through the Al-Anon
pamphlets which offered such a hopeful tone. As I read the one titled,
So You Love an Alcoholic, I spotted my problem on the page:

Sometimes a crisis—the loss of a job, accident, or arrest—can convince the alcoholic of the need for help. Coddling and overprotection at such time will not be helpful. The crisis may be necessary to recover. Do nothing to prevent such a crisis from happening—don't cover bad checks, pay overdue bills, or go to the boss with excuses. The suffering you are trying to ease by such actions may be the very thing needed to bring the alcoholic to a realization of the seriousness of the situation."

✦

A pang of remorse stabbed me. The $7,500.

It all sounded easy but even backing away from him in my small ways—like not involving him in bill paying or dropping the conversation about how he needed to get a job—detaching, they called it in Al-Anon—felt bristly. It took all my resolve not to retreat to the comfort of us, or some fantasized version of us, the us where all was forgiven and I could love him unconditionally.

The HBO special, *Drug Addiction in America*, aired in March 2007.

"I wanna watch something," I said snatching the remote from the coffee table. Most nights, Josh planted himself in front of the TV, watching cop dramas: *NCIS, Law and Order* reruns, or *Cold Case*, shows with elaborate plots that culminated with the slick criminal slipping on an insignificant detail that resulted in the pieces falling into place just in time for the cops to arrest the suspect.

We took our usual positions on our sectional sofa with the burgundy brushed cotton fabric: Josh to my left, my stockinged feet on the oak coffee table.

I'd been waiting for the show all week, excited by the hope that somehow my husband and I could break the wall that prohibited us from talking about his alcoholic and erratic behavior. Here was the intermediary.

"How can we comprehend a person who can't stop doing something despite catastrophic consequences?" asked Dr. Nora Volkow, the director of the National Institute on Drug Abuse. I listened intently, wanting desperately to understand why Josh couldn't leave behind his crazy attempts to make money through business deals he couldn't explain. I thought about the time he had been chopping cords of wood in the garage and barged in through the sliding glass doors holding the chain saw like a madman to cop a shot of tequila: the look on his face, ruddy and firey.

Now I wanted to understand how the person I'd loved could act so recklessly and devolve into someone who was bankrupting us.

Josh had recently told Adam and me he had won the Texas Hold 'Em Million Dollar Hand scratch-off lottery ticket. He strolled into the house brandishing the ticket confidently.

"I met these two young women on the train. Ooh la la!" He sashayed. "I gave 'em two crisp $100 bills since I'm a millionaire."

I turned off my attention, detached from listening lest I get pulled back into his insane thinking. Adam ripped the ticket from his father's hand and peered at it.

"Don't know what you're talking about Dad. That's not a straight flush!"

His father waved him away.

"Oh yeah?" said Adam, his voice reaching a pitch. "It's a spade. Oh my God! Get your glasses. You need a black club for a straight flush!"

On the HBO documentary that week, Dr. Volkow, so compelling with perfectly chosen words and delightful Spanish accent, explained how addiction was a disease of the brain and how, through frequent substance use, drugs actually modified the brain. I watched feeling tremendous empathy for the alcoholics and drug addicts interviewed and their parents and family because I sensed that no one would choose this. Substance users were caught in an ugly trap.

"I understand how this could happen to a person," I finally said. I was looking for the right words to prod Josh to open up about the drinking. I didn't want to argue with him. I wanted the show to open our communication about the proverbial elephant in the living room. Josh sat, stonily silent.

We watched the show over the next few nights. I learned about relapse and treatment options that made me feel hope. We watched a whole episode about a young couple who tried a new drug, Suboxone, for heroin withdrawal. I wanted them to succeed because they had struggled so. And treatment was so expensive or not available. One alcoholic woman in her fifties, looking drained and drawn, said grimly, "I've missed out on so much…" she hesitated, "because of this problem."

As much as I was learning to detach from Josh, there was some business we had to take care of together. The FAFSA form—Federal Assistance for Financial Student Aid—which we had to file to get considered for aid for Matthew's tuition at Northeastern, was due March 1. The previous year, 2006, we filed the form at the midnight deadline arguing and railing against the government for making the form difficult to fill out. It was not the sort of form, with its cryptic instructions, you wanted to leave for the last minute. Since the deadline for FAFSA came before the income tax deadline of April 15th, income could be estimated. So, filing the FAFSA is like a pre-income-tax filing.

"Just put down your income," I said when we came to the line that asked for "father's income." I'd been waiting for this opportunity to find out what his income had been once and for all since he wouldn't divulge. We hadn't filed our taxes, as I'd told the divorce lawyer, though I'd had the taxes withheld from my paycheck and Josh claimed to be paying quarterly.

I had believed Josh's failure to file our taxes was a case of procrastination but as we clawed our way through the FAFSA form, it became apparent he had no idea what to include in "father's income," no documentation, no record of income, no ledger. But he did have his list of business expenses. He was pulling numbers from the air and foisting his discomfort on me by lunging with statements like, "what's your problem?" whenever I asked where he was getting those numbers. I knew this method of discerning income didn't make sense. After all, I'd learned something simple in DA: money management is about addition, subtraction, and attention.

Through the filing of the 2006 FAFSA form, I gained more evidence to detach from Josh, recalling the urgency of the divorce lawyer telling me to file my taxes separately. And thinking again about the separation agreement. I felt gravely sad right then because I recognized my husband's untrustworthiness—not only in his word, but in his ability to set us on a right path. Josh shook his head when I said to please put down a number for father's income.

"I don't know," he said with irritation.

"What do you mean?" My patience drained.

Josh shook his head and sighed heavily. His body looked tight as a taut guitar string ready to snap. He toggled between the form and the worksheet while I stood over his right shoulder bending toward the computer monitor, red reading glasses on, squinting to read the figures. I noticed the back of his neck, chafed from shaving. I pondered for a moment, trying to remember when he had shaved off his ponytail. I couldn't remember.

"Here, just put this down," he said, finally, standing up from the leather chair and letting me sit. His income, after business expenses were deducted, was below $25,000. And while I was surprised at how little the amount was, when I looked at what he'd tallied, it looked possible and explained why he'd had incurred so much debt the previous year, even with the income from the withdrawn IRA funds.

Though relieved to finish filing the FAFSA form, I was furious at his refusal to get a job while I was attending DA meetings regularly, poring over our day-to-day expenses, and working on a plan towards solvency. It was the last time I would file the FAFSA form with him.

"Well, if you wanted to get my attention and punish me for Claire," I spat, "you've succeeded. Congratulations."

He looked at me.

"Please. Stop making it about you. No one is punishing you, except yourself."

After finishing the FAFSA form, I made an appointment with Marge, the tax preparer, to file my taxes. Josh and I had visited her office before when she tried to log his expenses and income but had to stop because he couldn't supply all the numbers.

I begged Josh to come and handle the taxes with me. He refused, telling me I'd be filing a fraudulent return. Even though I had grown to believe I was responsible for handling my own taxes as a grown-up woman, I was scared and teary at my appointment with Marge. Filing my taxes on my own was a bold step.

"You have the perfect right to file separately," Marge assured me.

Yet we couldn't understand what Josh meant when he said I'd be filing a fraudulent return. Her manner was gentle, yet focused, and together we completed three years of taxes—as "married, filing separately."

I continued to attend DA meetings, now on Tuesday nights, by myself as Josh's participation in the Saturday meeting dwindled. A second-floor classroom of a parochial school was where I began to admit my powerlessness over debt, examined my fear about money—not having it, earning it, deserving it, losing it—and recognized my belief that someone would always take care of me. I shared about being the youngest in my family who learned to rely on others—the Prince Charming—to rescue me and ensure my happiness.

I became friendly with a retired couple in their late sixties, Angelo and Barbara, who had been involved in the program for years. When I asked about their day-to-day spending, they told me they used the "envelope system."

"If there's no money in the Dinners Out envelope, we don't go," explained Angelo, a dark-haired man with an intense gaze. "We don't argue. The envelope tells us what we can and cannot do. I used to spend money I didn't have because I wanted to treat Barbara. Now the envelopes tell us." Barbara nodded.

"Did it improve your marriage?" I asked.

"Definitely," Barbara agreed.

I had learned of the envelope system from my mother. As a kid, I'd see her dip into the big black suede pocketbook she stashed on the top shelf of her bedroom closet, a secret place. There, she kept important papers and her envelopes with spending cash. But, as an adult, I felt way too sophisticated to use such an old-school system. Besides my husband was an attorney who managed money, property, trusts, and estates. So we had no system except overspending.

The next time I saw Angelo and Barbara, I approached them to help me with a pressure relief meeting—a PRM—whereby a person new to the DA program asked two others, preferably a man and woman, to meet and go over "the numbers," and come up with action steps. I'd been "keeping my numbers," writing every cent I'd spent for the last four months on a small, spiral-bound note pad. Josh had started to do it, too, until he stopped attending, declaring his money situation unlike anyone else's—too far gone, he claimed. I didn't agree, but I was learning I had no control over his choices.

Angelo and Barbara agreed to work with me. I was excited to meet and had no reluctance to show them my financials. Barbara gave me a "pre-pressure meeting questionnaire," to fill out.

What Brought You to DA? If you are in a couple, list your resentments, attitudes, or feelings regarding money and your partner.

Mostly I am furious at him for having been so reckless and irresponsible as to put us (the family) into such a precarious financial situation. After the initial shock of discovering the extent of the debt, I have continued to be extremely vigilant about my actions regarding money. I am angry and disappointed in myself for having gone along (denied) the problem.

Of course I didn't tell Angelo and Barbara about how my attention for three years had been diverted to Claire and about my suspicion that Josh's recklessness had been propelled by his desperation to win me back. I continued in my questionnaire response:

Now, however, I have been awakened. So I have separated our money and am keeping us going by carefully paying out the necessities and sticking to a strict spending plan. At first, I didn't think I could handle everything—I was obsessed with watching my account online—but I'm recognizing that the world didn't end. No creditors are knocking and I haven't been late with any payments… and no debting, a day at a time."

There was also a place on the form for expenses, income, debts, and assets, not unlike standard "assets and liabilities" forms I'd tried to fill out in the past. This time, I completed it out based on my income and the figures I had secured from Uncovering My Hidden Financial Life.

That spring, I attended the annual "DA Share-a-Day," a whole Saturday devoted to speakers, workshops, and twelve-step meetings about debt and money. I found a workshop on spreadsheets, something I'd heard people say was the next step after creating a spending plan—what

Angelo and Barbara were helping me do. In the spreadsheet workshop, the presenter, a sixty-ish woman sporting just-from-the-hairdresser lacquered piles of frosted hair and a jangle of bracelets, passed around her worksheet protected in a plastic sleeve. She appeared blasé while I eyed the page hungrily and marveled that she'd balanced her income and spending to the penny. It took me many months to perfect a system for myself, and later realized the frustration I'd felt was steeped in the belief I could master this in a day. This exercise brought home one of my favorite DA slogans: "Progress, Not Perfection."

I met Angelo and Barbara at the library where we secured a little corner with comfortable couches. We spoke in hushed tones. Barbara had created "Janet's Spending Plan," in her fluid teacherly penmanship, which included categories for such expenses as cable, clothing, and groceries and three categories Barbara insisted were necessary: Vacation/son; Vacation/weekends; Vacation/long-term. I wanted to knock these categories off but my duo insisted that depriving myself was not the answer. "Just start an envelope. It's a placeholder," they said, "even if you only put five dollars in it." They insisted I keep "Vacation/son" so I could visit Matthew at school.

My action steps were to cut my spending to bridge the difference between income and expenses, investigate mortgage options, monitor the credit reports, and write down every dollar I spent. I met with Angelo and Barbara once a month for the rest of the year. Having the support of these two people so generous with their time gave me the confidence to believe I was on the right track to becoming solvent. They offered me tremendous relief.

In April, my Unitarian congregation had a service auction, an event in which congregants offered services to the highest bidder, with proceeds going to the church. I bid $100, the lowest I could, to meet with Jennifer, a certified financial planner for an hour. I had hoped Jennifer could offer more general planning than my partners in DA, a bigger picture approach to what I needed to get solvent and not depend financially on Josh. She welcomed me into her home office, then sat behind a large cherry wood desk as she pushed aside the files piled high to make room for my papers.

I showed Jennifer the spending plan I had developed with Angelo and Barbara and list of assets and liabilities I had been working on. I explained about Josh's unwillingness to drop his rainbow-chasing quest that had now shifted to a businessman in Croatia. Josh was fixated on arranging for an ambulance to wend its way through the Swiss Alps to deliver the Croatian, suffering from liver disease, to the conference room table. The tale was so preposterous that it left me devoid of empathy for any of these supposed parties. At the end of the story, Jennifer looked pained.

"Listen," she said, "I had no idea you were going through this. I want you to come back as many times as you need. It's not going to cost you a dime. Just come back."

She emphasized "come back," as if she were a doctor and I a patient she was convincing to have an unpleasant but necessary procedure. I gushed my gratitude and added Jennifer to my team. I was realizing something: people will help you when you take steps to help yourself. I acquainted her with the rest of the facts and in a quick assessment she recommended an appraisal of the house, a deep look at our life insurance policies, and a review of our real estate taxes.

Then I showed her the letter from the previous fall, addressed to me, from Countrywide Mortgage with the heading *Significant Payment Increase Alert,* stating how the mortgage balance (what I owed) would be going up when it reached 103 percent of the original loan amount next spring, in about one year. The mortgage balance had already risen $30,000 from $440,000 (the original mortgage amount) to $470,000. This meant, as evidenced by a chart in the letter, that my payments would rise from $1,521 per month, the minimum option I was paying, to $3,622 per month—an increase of $2,101 or 138 percent.

Looking at the letter with Jennifer, I felt the familiar dread coat my insides, only this time it seemed worse and scarier because looking at it with another person who understood its meaning made it real. I couldn't minimize its seriousness or imagine a fantasy of someone saving me. I looked away from the letter fighting tears.

"Well, the good news is you're not under water on the house," she said, and I knew that meant owing more than what the property was valued at. Even with the mortgage balance rising, the house was still valued around $650,000, the "fair market value."

"You gotta consider unloading the house," she said, looking directly at me, an expression of sympathy on her face.

I looked back at her squarely, despite my tears and embarrassment. She handed me the box of Kleenex. I had thought a lot about selling but was afraid to let the idea breathe, as I might have to act on it.

I sobbed softly. "I know, I know. I love my house. Can't imagine not living there."

I thought about my beloved home where we had hosted Thanksgiving every year, those silly construction-paper place cards Josh and I had hand-drawn and placed on everyone's plate year after year. My home with the "good bones," as the engineer had described it when we moved in. The light-filled kitchen with stainless steel stovetop we splurged on. The house where our boys had grown, built snow forts in the backyard, plunged hands into cement to make the handprints that greeted me every day at the walkway. My home was where we'd hosted countless parties dimming the lights to dance party CDs, so much so that my niece once exclaimed, "they move the furniture!" We'd brought the house along from its ugly duckling status to a lovely, comfortable home. I'd kept a "house journal," that included before and after pictures taken every time any work had been done. In the journal, I pasted paint swatches and wrote dates for repairs and renovations, large and small such as the installation of decorative tiles with the turtle and other animal motifs above the fireplace. I thought about my parents, who had scrimped their whole lives just to leave me some money and how I had invested their sweat into my house. I remembered thinking how much they would've approved, since the renovation was completely financed by them. Our home sheltered the love in my life.

"Adam is almost out of high school. And Matthew knows of the circumstances," I whispered. I'd driven round-trip to Boston to visit Matthew at college in one day, 220 miles, to let him know of our financial distress and that I had visited a lawyer. After lunch, Matthew and I walked along Boylston Street in a slow plod, my son's sadness showing through his disappointed eyes and gripping good-bye embrace.

"So you'll downsize earlier than you would have liked," Jennifer said gently. "Get ready, emotionally, to sell next spring. Have a garage sale, go on E-bay, throw stuff out. You need to do it this summer and fall."

We figured the following spring would be the time to sell not only to avert the ballooning of the mortgage but because the three-year prepayment penalty would be removed and spring was the best selling season. It also gave me a year, which felt far away. Plus, I'd have to get Josh to sign the house over to me, or agree to sell it since, though I owned the mortgage, the house belonged to both us. As I walked out into the crisp, thawing winter air outside Jennifer's house, I let a bubble of relief swim through me. I was crestfallen over the prospect of selling my home but hungry for steps to resolve the mess. And Jennifer's pragmatism gave me the focus I needed.

An eager student, I devoured information about debt recovery—DA pamphlets, web sites, books like *Currency of Hope,* and Jerry Mundis's *How to Get Out of Debt, Stay Out of Debt, and Live Prosperously*, a paperback regaled by our group. I familiarized myself with investing, started reading the business section of the *Times*, and reviewed the prospectuses associated with my 401K.

About this time, I recruited Josh's sister, Wendy, to join me at DA, after she confessed to trouble with back taxes and credit cards. She was about to pay a financial adviser when I mentioned she could try DA for free. I confided in her about our financial situation, mindful to not disparage her brother.

"You don't need to tell me anything about my cockamamie brother," Wendy said, flouncing her reddish brown hair away from her shoulder. "I love him, but we all know he's a nut!"

I told Wendy about the jumbo mortgage and how Josh had drained all the equity, trusting her confidence. And soon Wendy sat next to me in the fellowship circle, getting there early, saving me a seat, taking notes eagerly in her small spiral notebook like the efficient teacher she was, sometimes throwing me a wide-eyed look when someone recounted an economic horror story. She became secretary at the monthly business meetings. And I really looked forward to seeing her every Tuesday to catch up on how her daughter Jamie, Matthew's age and the same-year college student, was getting on.

One night that spring, I was working on my laptop in the dining room while Josh watched a crime drama on television. I could see into the den from where I sat but I couldn't see him; he was hidden by the kitchen counter. I heard the drone of the tube. I walked into the kitchen to get a drink of water and saw Josh pointing the remote at the TV but he looked like he was sleeping, eyes closed, torso erect, jaw slack. An odd expression. I called his name tepidly, then louder. No answer. No movement.

"What in the world do you have to be tired about?" I said. *I'm up at six a.m. every day to catch a train, while you rise whenever you want.*

"Hey!" I said walking towards him now, loud.

His arm was extended, in a freeze frame, holding the remote as if he were handing it to someone.

I should snap a photo of you, to show you what you look like. All of a sudden a memory from 1982 slapped me. *My God, he looks like Jesse.*

Our friend, Jesse, a sax player, known in our circle for his abuse of *Dilaudid*, an opiate. Jesse, a rich boy—a trust funder—who lived with his brother and rarely left his apartment on West 77th Street.

"What are you doing?" I shook him now. He opened his eyes slowly, unstartled.

"Whatsa problem?"

I stared at him.

"Get out of here," I spewed, wanting the sight of him to go away, upstairs.

He shuffled upstairs, no argument.

My mind raced: He's jonesing! Nodding out! On horse, the works, junk, smack, H. Every cliché raining. Those hours locked in the bathroom! My desperation to fix our finances, huddled over the laptop, not wanting to see the truth about Josh's addiction.

My husband was a fucking drug addict.

As I watched him walk upstairs, my eyes narrowed. I was pissed off but self-satisfied in my anger and righteousness as I heard his steps above.

Heroin? Methadone? Something I didn't even know existed?

Heroin! So inner-city. How? Cocaine I could fathom for my high-wired husband. But heroin? A narcoleptic substance of jazz musicians and clinic-goers?

Then I recalled the time Josh "fell asleep" talking to our friend at the country club hoe-down and that string of car accidents. I grimaced in shame when I thought of our children in the car and then the shame was replaced by a surge that propelled me to open and slam-shut the sliding glass doors to the deck, where I stood in the cool, clear night and thought of the *Times* op-ed about the problem of lawyers and heroin use, penned by an attorney, that our friend had given us some years back which I'd refused to read until I saw the clipping in a reading folder in her bathroom and how I'd gingerly scanned it while sitting on the toilet. When I read the piece, about the pervasiveness and dangers of casual heroin use among lawyers, instead of feeling alarmed, I dismissed it with a crazy pride for my husband having traversed the reckless drug use from our 80s party days so well. *That was then. Now he's fine, just fine,* I told myself.

And even if he dabbled in drug use, he could handle it, I believed. I conferred this honor to him like a distorted badge of accomplishment and held onto a full, ripe indignation hitched to a refusal to believe he could be an addict.

That night, I said nothing about the nodding out, too scared to give it voice and still so willing to side with my self-doubt. But after that evening, I couldn't lie to myself. I remembered what a friend had once said about Josh when I confided my guilt over my relationship with Claire: "He's got a lover too," she said. "Only his doesn't have a pulse."

I didn't say anything to him about the nodding out, sticking to my Al-Anonic attempts to detach, though on some level still not wanting to believe it was true. But I knew his misuse of alcohol and drugs were not mine to manage. It was his business. My job was to take care of me and my sons and to remember that when it came to my husband's addictions I could remember the three C's: I didn't Create it, couldn't Cure it, and couldn't Control it.

Our twenty-fifth wedding anniversary was coming at the end of

April. I'd cancelled our trip to Sorrento, Italy, when I discovered the heap of financial detritus, much to Josh's irritation ("Why are you cancelling the trip? You have to punish both of us?").

I wanted an anniversary dinner despite the tension and mistrust hovering between us. I remembered my parents' and aunts' and uncles' twenty-fifth wedding anniversaries. They were considered milestones and celebrated in catering halls, VFW lodges, and Knights of Columbus rooms, decorated with brightly colored crepe paper, and Jimmy Roselli, the Italian crooner, pouring out of the speakers, always with dancing and booze. My Aunt Martha wore a bright blue sash and my Uncle Tony a crown with "*25!!*" printed on it.

One of our nieces had given Josh a gift certificate to a favorite restaurant, the Belgium Waterzooi, in nearby Garden City, as a thank you for gratis legal work he had done. He and I sat across from each other at the white-table clothed, dimly lit table, a cask iron bowl of *moules*, the restaurant's specialty, between us. We were stiff and careful, looking for some oasis of conversation to climb onto, until I didn't care.

"You're an addict," I blurted, the words spilling.

"Just admit it," I sneered.

Josh smiled.

"Nonsense and you know it." The waiter lifted the wine bottle from the silver bucket, and refreshed our goblets, dabbing the bottle's bottom with a red napkin.

"No, I happen to know you're an addict," I asserted, feeling like an actor, saying something I didn't really think I had evidence for. People make things up all the time and say them, but I could never do that comfortably. I didn't even like pranks, because it involved pretending. It always felt cruel and I could never bring myself to do it.

"Nodding out," I said slowly and deliberately leaning towards him, over the bowl of mussels, smelling the garlic and wine, noting how many were left. Even though I wasn't sure whether to believe what I was saying, I stuck to my position.

"You are a liar, stealer, and drug addict." My voice rang out louder than I'd intended. It felt good. I stood up. His wrinkled brow deepened and I sensed he was afraid, despite the elfish smirk that deepened his dimples. His classic nervous grin.

"Sit down, please," annoyance in his voice.

"I will not!"

"Then, fine, stand up. Finish your dinner standing."

"Fuck you."

"Happy anniversary to you too, my dear."

I shook, my face hot.

"And the house...you stole our fucking home! I'll never forgive you."

I waved the waiter over and signaled for the check. He brought the bill and I threw down cash and the gift certificate. Josh stared at me.

"Fuck you." I marched out of the restaurant, climbed into our car, and sped home. Good. Let him find his own way even if he has to walk.

✦

Two months later, as I walked into the glass-enclosed entry to the Skidmore College cafeteria, my phone vibrated. I'd just finished a poetry class at one of my favorite writing conferences, hosted by the International Women's Writing Guild. I was luxuriating in a respite from the months of anxiety of digging through our frightening finances. I flipped open my phone. Adam.

"Mom?"

It was early for him to be calling at eleven-thirty a.m. He didn't usually rise until after noon.

"What's the matter?"

"I don't know where Dad is."

Oh God, another arrest.

"What do you mean?" I asked.

"I've been here by myself."

"What?" I repeated. "Where are you? Why didn't you call me?"

"Home."

"Where the hell is he now? Did he say anything?"

"Nope."

"Are you okay?"

"Yeah. It's okay. I can take care of myself, you know."

At seventeen, Adam was old enough to look after himself but I worried he might jump on the chance to throw a keg party. It was the end of June and the summer kick-off between his junior and senior year in high school had begun. Final exams were over and high schoolers were celebrating all over town with surreptitious drinking and God knows what. The police had already been called one night in early spring when Josh and I were out and Adam had invited too many kids over who had stashed beers in the bushes. All the kids cleared out and he got off with a warning but I was nervous about substances he or any of his friends might be using. Even though Josh had been having his own bout with substances, we were clear with Adam about no drinking, ever. In fact, since the incident we stayed home or nearby in the evenings, especially weekends, to keep our eye on things.

"No parties! Okay?"

"Calm down. There's no one here."

"I can't believe he left you alone!" I seethed. "Don't worry. I'll be home this afternoon."

I can't believe I have to leave the conference! Another thing to add to my list of resentments.

I had been feeling so cared for by the women of this conference, by their embrace two nights ago when I had read an essay, not the safe piece about my son and our enjoying music together but the raw, risky one about my sexuality, in the auditorium before 200 attendees. I was thrilled by their applause, and later renewed by their accolades at the after-party where I danced with the elegant sound healer who led sessions invoking our spirits to resonate with song in the baroque chapel, and I wanted oh-so-much to be healed and feel free, released, as I had when I sprinted around the circle of women at daybreak on the morning of the summer solstice, fast like my fifth-grade self winning the fifty-yard dash, waving a rainbow-colored streamer. "You looked so happy," said my friend Hadley watching from the sidelines. So happy.

Only a few minutes after hanging up, my phone vibrated. Josh. His voice grim and shakey.

"I'm getting ready to leave the hospital." He paused. "I've been at

South Nassau Hospital, detoxing."

"From what?" I asked.

"Methadone."

When I heard the word "methadone," I conjured the image of lem-on-lime Gatorade-colored liquid in little plastic pill cups. But I never saw anything like that around our home. I wondered if it was a pill or something he kept in the little cold cream jar I had found and stashed in my closet. Maybe that's why he was always angry if the kids went into his closet. I knew methadone was a replacement for heroin, something addicts took to get weaned. When we lived in Manhattan I used to walk past a methadone clinic around the corner from our apartment. I would have never noticed it except that a friend pointed it out. I walked quickly passed the patrons—a disheveled, unrooted-looking bunch of guys loitering in front.

Methadone? Not surprised. I felt relieved to know where he was and a flash of vindication about the heroin, connecting the dots after the nodding out in front of the TV. But I was still steaming about Adam being left alone so I stayed silent not wanting to blurt something I'd regret—about his irresponsibility or how stunned I was he had taken this step on his own or how hurt I'd felt that he had waited for me to leave town and hadn't come to me.

The secrets. Always finding out after the fact. I was upset that he had named the drug, methadone—the interloper in our lives. I didn't know how to feel gratitude about the enormous step he had just taken. He must have sensed my irritation because a long silence ensued.

"How could you leave your son alone?" I poked, unable to resist. I went with the thing I felt entitled to say.

"I got a prescription for Suboxone," Josh said, "remember from the HBO show?"

Wow. He was really listening to that episode.

We had heard about this miracle drug for opiate addicts on the documentary on addiction. Suboxone, a medication approved for treatment of opiate dependence, a prescription that makes withdrawal palatable and possible.

"I'm getting clean, Janet," he said.

CHAPTER 18

Josh and I sat at the edge of the shore on red sand chairs on a brilliant July day. The fringed beach umbrella staked in the sand protected us from the unforgiving sun and I overheard an older man, just arriving at the beach, admonish his wife, "Grace, you don't have to tell me where to put the chairs. We've been coming here for thirty years." Josh and I smiled and shook our heads with an amused, "do we sound like that?" look. Seagulls hovered and the piping plovers rustled in the nesting area nearby.

"I never stopped doing it," Josh explained. The "it" being heroin with a sidekick of methadone. He was explaining his addiction to me, coming clean, as I'd asked him to do.

"At the very least," he said, "I owe you an explanation."

His addiction specialist, Dr. Wasser, prescribed 8 mg of Suboxone, along with 50 mg of amitriptyline, an anti-depressant. He could stay on Suboxone indefinitely.

"You know, I did heroin for, like, twenty-five years, on and off. Picked up methadone about five years ago, right after September 11th."

Hearing about the long-term drug use surprised me but mostly I felt irresponsible for never recognizing the extent of his problem.

"Why then?" I asked.

"It was available and I was just so used to drugging. I didn't want to feel anything, after that day."

I felt a wash of pity for him, remembering how devastated he was after the World Trade Center attack: about the loss of our friends, our city, our innocence, our lives shattered by his post-traumatic stress. It was as if he wore the city's collective grief. And I had shown indiffer-

ence to his suffering. I was drawn to Claire; she was a thing of beauty
I couldn't turn from, the antidote to my crumbling life. I could tell
from his knitted brow he was about to cry. His Ray-Bans, which he
had worn so often, even inside the house for years, didn't hide much
anymore.

"Getting off Suboxone, shouldn't be too hard," he said. "I'm on a
low level. It'll be easy."

I didn't believe him. I'd become so used to his minimizing, that I
dismissed what he was saying. Typical. Just like all the financial deals that
were going to rectify everything. All of them, which were about to cost
us our house, were no big deal.

We sat like we were listening for something. The surf was gentle. I
wanted him to keep talking.

"And remember when I had the DUI? Before they took me down
to the station I asked the cops to let me lock up my car? I had cocaine
in my pocket and I ate it. I pretended I was looking for my insurance
card."

I was astounded, alarmed, even a little amused by his never-ending
willingness to collude with his own self-destruction and my need to
find it comical as a shield to my own denial. No wonder he was raging
that night and pacing furiously.

As he opened up to me, I thought that we deserved this—the
whole falling down the financial well. Our arrogance of thinking we
could spew cash like a dispenser without any consequences, living like
we were entitled to it.

Even though I had felt the effects of his addiction—from the over-
drawn accounts to the mountains of debt to the nodding out to the
law practice that no longer existed—I still found it hard to believe this
had happened. This would have been the perfect opportunity for me
to step back into my anesthetic of denial. Everything's fine, just fine.
He was getting clean. And while I would have loved to hitch myself
to the dreaminess of hope and roll around in a magical thinking haze,
I had fortunately had enough recovery to realize that his steps towards
sobriety didn't mean our troubles were over. Awareness, Acceptance,

Action. I heard the slogan mentioned in Al-Anon. I wanted to aware.
I had to be.

Days later, I settled into the black leather chair in Erica's office.

I was excited to report to Erica about Josh's detox. Like I was giving my teacher a progress report on a successful assignment.

"That's encouraging," she said tepidly. I expected fanfare.

"That's it? Don't you think this is a turning point?"

"Do you?"

"Yes! If he gets sober, then he can work again, maybe build up his
practice, and we can maintain the house, and fix this craziness. He's
going to work two or three days a week for our friend Gary. He can
help me. I've told him this is salvageable. He just needs to bring in two
or three thousand a month."

"His recovery is great," answered Erica. "Great for him. That he's
taking a job with Gary's firm is great. But," and she paused, "What does
this have to do with you? Your recovery is for you."

She was sticking a pin in my balloon!

"Every time you go to the well, remember it's bankrupt. He can't
help you. He has a disease."

"Oh, that disease thing again," I said. "Sometimes I'm sick of hearing it."

"Well, let me ask you this: What do you know to be true?"

I stopped to consider, breaking my gaze and looking at the gray
wall behind her. Irritation fading.

"And, trust yourself," she added.

"My husband had a drug habit. That enormous mortgage is in my
name. I can't afford to support the household. And yeah, the liquor
cabinet is stocked and he's still filling those big red cups with vodka."

"Hope and dependence on someone else can be powerful."

I shook my head knowing I could get hooked on the hope. That
was my drug.

"And another thing," I added. "Is his recovery real? He won't go
to AA and didn't go to any kind of twenty-eight-day rehab. Aren't you
supposed to do those things if you're serious?"

"Everyone has his own road."

I nodded.

"I hate the solitary road."

"We're all on it. Every one of us."

✦

"It isn't pretty," I said bluntly to Jennifer, the financial planner from my church who had been meeting with me for the last few months. I was about to hand her a page detailing Josh's debts when her six-year-old son, Miles, crawled into the room on his belly like an infantryman.

"What is it now?" she asked him. While they had an exchange about where his clean bathing suit was, I got another chance to peruse the numbers.

The night before I came to Jennifer's office, I begged Josh to sit with me and break down the current debt. In the spirit of his recovery, I believed, and things looking hopeful between us because he was now under the care of Dr. Wasser, he agreed but only if I promised not to freak out, as he put it. I recited the serenity prayer in my head over and over to comply: "God grant me the serenity to accept the things I cannot change..." The debt levels scared the hell out of me. But my sobriety was taking the form of courage to face what was real and I wanted to believe he was facing it and being honest with me too.

The debt was worse than I had thought. It was now July 2007, and earlier in the year when I had gone through the credit reports, I discovered Josh owed closer to $200,000, about $70,000 more than I had thought.

"It's the American way," he exclaimed, attempting to minimize this calamity. He said his debt was like the government deficit: he owed a lot and could still borrow more.

And he was right: we mirrored the masses of Americans who had no idea they were heading down the slope of economic catastrophe into a pit of surprise, disdain, and blame. We were heralding the country's day of reckoning soon to be upon everyone in 2008.

I had been alarmed not only by the impossible-to-pay-back

$200,000, but the ridiculous sum of $148,000 he could still borrow. I was also concerned that he had not filed his taxes, though my lessons in detachment reminded me to take care of me. My tax returns were up to date, having been filed separately, an act that took blind courage.

"What's this beach club?," Jennifer asked as she looked over my spending plan. "You really need this?" She looked at me and I glanced back with a grim look. "College expenses, yes. Beach cabana? C'mon."

Of course, she was right, but every time I had to eliminate something it stoked my resentment.

"I know, I know. I have choices. I'm doing it for myself and my kids."

She glanced at the page and her eyes widened. I knew she'd scanned the $200,000 figure of Josh's debts.

I reminded her, "This debt is on top of the $470,000 mortgage, $300,000 of which was used to cover his debt. Plus, there are business lines that somehow were not on the credit report. And he owes money to people."

"All I care about is what's joint. And all I see is the $50,000 Bank of America line."

"That's right. Oh, and the Hilton Club time share."

"How much is that?"

"Twenty-two grand."

"Tell me again how this happened?"

"Well, first I didn't have a handle on the numbers since he never showed me his attorney's account, which he paid a lot of our bills out of. Then, he was supposed to be very rich by now, after investing in the international deals, and those business associates with all kinds of potential."

I heard myself. It sounded ridiculous.

"There's only going forward," she said. "It's amazing what you've handled. I've seen women come in here with situations like yours and they're paralyzed. He'll probably have to declare bankruptcy so you've gotta keep separating yourself financially."

She glanced back at the page.

"I see the mortgage is up to $470,000. Are you cleaning out the attic and getting ready to sell the house next spring?"

"Yes. Just had a garage sale."

My meeting with Jennifer spurred me to scour through the office later that day to look again at the credit reports to make sure I hadn't missed anything.

I rifled through the red folders sandwiched together in the small bookshelf by Josh's desk. I pulled the Bank of America folder and saw something new: a personalized report for Josh on the state of his credit from Bank of America. I scanned it, noticing nothing out of the ordinary except annoying charges like one $400 payment to National Public Radio. I was all for supporting favorite foundations, but not when you couldn't pay your mortgage.

Suddenly, I froze. Payments for airline tickets: $1,003 payment to Aeroflot Russian Airlines, another payment of $730 to American Airlines for a ticket to Dallas, a $1,013 payment for an American Airlines ticket to Buenos Aires. He hadn't made those trips. I couldn't imagine what they were for until I realized he must've bought those tickets for someone else and pocketed the cash. A creeping disbelief quickly gave way to a fury that raced through my body like an arson fire. It upset me so that the next day I called Bob Southard, the divorce lawyer I had seen earlier, to start drawing up the separation agreement. I didn't care if Josh dogged me around the house as he'd done with my first visit to Bob, lecturing about wasting money on legal representation. I had a right to be represented.

"What did I do that deserves your treatment of me?" Josh screamed that night in our kitchen when I told him I was going back to the lawyer.

"What are these insane charges?" I said, waving the credit card statements.

He ranted at me until I got close to his face. Eyes fierce.

"I'm not afraid of you," I said. "Try to bully me. I'm not afraid of you."

I flew out of the house, jumped into the minivan, and drove to a side street, blocks from my house. I called my friend Amanda, who had seen Josh nodding out at the country club hoe down.

"Good for you for standing your ground!" she declared.

"And leaving the house before it escalated," I added.

I felt a strange calmness, like something had shifted in me.

The next day I sent Josh an email:

Dear Josh,

Want to know what I'm so angry about? What I feel betrayed about? Let me tell you! Letting the debt get so out of hand that you emptied accounts. Disease or desperation? My attempts to intercede through the years to gain clarity— my attempts to look at the figures—what's coming in and out; do the taxes; set up Quickbooks; suggestions to reconcile your checking accounts; pay debts like a bill—all were met with harsh response and I would withdraw, always knowing in the back of my mind that this was not good, that it would come to a head one day, but I had a false, very false, sense of security since my little corner of the world was ok. I so much wanted to believe that everything was okay, when I knew it wasn't.

You continued to invest in the "deal" after I expressly said "no more." The $40K for your client's defense out of our home equity line? I said ok. I so wanted to be supportive, believe in you, plus I knew I couldn't stop you on some level and I felt way too guilty over things that had happened with Claire to risk a confrontation. You treated that $40K like it was nothing. It left us in a heartbeat with a feigned attempt (words really, promising to sue to get it back). Do you know how long it takes to pay back $40K?!! I knew there were credit lines. I remember them being at $20K and $25K and reaching a limit and I felt powerless to do anything about it: after all, it was your business line. You knew what you were doing; you're a lawyer, help other people with this very sort of thing.

Then of course the decision to borrow $300K against the house. Where in the world did that number come from? How? Where? Buying shoes for the kids? But again I felt guilty and responsible. I said ok. My name? Ok? It makes sense if I have the higher credit score. Even feeling proud that I had the higher credit score, smug. So I said yes, where do I sign? Trusting, trusting. Even signing the page with the prepayment penalty. No problem, buddy, you said to Hector when he asked if he could add the prepayment penalty to get a higher *commission, let me just serve up my wife and kids because this mortgage will free up the cash flow.*

I knew this mortgage couldn't signal anything good but again I didn't do my homework or refuse as I'm sure I would've been rebuked loudly by you and convinced it was all going to be fine because the money's coming. I wanted to believe it, too, that it would bail us out. Until the IRA emptying and the annuity emptying. When I asked how much it was you said: I don't know, maybe it was $20K; it's gone, you said. The very annuity we opened in our apartment in Brooklyn with Steiger, was that his name? It would be cashed in when our two-and half-year-old was ready for college. So far away, my God. Eons, the vagueness of the response—maybe $20K, like it was chump change. And you added, 'I financed it.'

The night I called Countrywide, in the days of the unraveling, finally, me picking my head up, out of the hole, finally, saying Wait a minute, this is not right, finally, finally, listening to that voice inside, siding with myself for once, calling Countrywide to find out that we can't be put into a new mortgage and yeah, "you're right, this is not a great loan for you," said the customer service guy. I cried on the phone. Wept. Another tidal wave of reality.

When I told you, you said, "What's $15K?" Like it was nothing. The minimization of this financial disaster is too much. What's my "I" message to you? I am furious to be put in a situation like this. I trusted you and when I came to you with my I messages of fear, anxiety, out of my mind I heard, "It's all not going to matter." Another platitude, disconnect from what's real. A mortgage that's eating up $1,000/month of our equity. This is real. These numbers are in black and white. Not some solution that you're counting on halfway around the world. And the kicker, just when I finally, finally get to the bottom of this mess, you say, "I'm tapped out. No more money. I can't give you any. I don't have any."

Wait.

How is this possible? Aren't you earning anything? No money to run the household? Finally, a light bulb for me. I can't count on him!! Hello!! It's you baby girl. Figure it out. It's a house of cards, honey. No, this isn't getting fixed by someone else. It's up to you!"

xxxooo

Janet

✦

It was bedtime, a humid August night, the air conditioning flowing freely over our bed. I walked into the room and saw Josh hunched over, on his side of the bed, head down, looking at the carpet. I thought, at first, he was fixing something he was holding but he was crying, shoulders shaking.

"If it wasn't for the kids, I'd kill myself."

I rubbed his back, told him soothingly how much he meant to us, but he nudged me away. His tears sounded like a death knoll, signaling the end of something. "Please tell me what's wrong," I begged.

Barely audible, frightened, desperate he told me, finally.

"I need money. Those guys are back. They want money otherwise they're going to hurt me."

I knew what guys he meant.

"What guys?" I asked.

"Remember the money my client owed those guys?"

"Yes, I do. $200,000. But I still don't understand what that has to do with you."

"I gave 'em money from time to time." He paused. He breathed a stuttered inhale like a toddler who'd been crying too much. "I thought it was enough to keep them away. Now, they want another $15,000. If you could come up with $20,000 you'll be saving me."

"Oh, I see. Fifteen for them and five for you?"

I wanted to ask what they'd threatened to do to him, to see if there were holes in his story, but the possibilities, Tony Soprano-style, were too ugly to hear aloud. How did this Jewish guy from Long Island whose parents showered him with love get into such fucked-up shit?

"I won't ask you for another cent," he pleaded. "And we can add it to the settlement in the separation agreement when we sell the house."

I said nothing but felt a rush of fear. What if this was true and these guys come to our house?

The next day, I called Amanda to help me hash out a decision and we agreed. You can't let him get beat up by a bunch of goons. I gave him the twenty grand.

Early that fall, Adam and I, along with Amanda and her son, Tyler, took a road trip to Maryland and Virginia to visit colleges. I was concerned, of course, about financing Adam's tuition, since Josh had emptied the college annuity fund and Matthew was already in a private university. Somehow I had to straddle the prospect of giving Adam the same opportunities as his brother but stay realistic about what was affordable. And the tuition would have to be paid out of savings, my pocket, and student loans. I didn't factor Josh in the financial forecast. When it came to money, from here on out, I was on my own.

"You're coming to visit? I'm so excited!" responded Claire by email when I told her we'd be coming to her town, Harrisonburg, Virginia, to tour James Madison University, one of the schools on Tyler's list. Though we hadn't seen each other in more than two years, Claire and I emailed occasionally, her messages almost always about her predicament of living somewhere she hated, the small southern town she'd grown up in and had managed to get away from when she left for college. I was excited yet anxious to see her, afraid of poking the hornet's nest. With our romance over, emails were mostly recounts of our distress—she caught in the turmoil of a custody fight and I treading on shaky ground at home.

The day we arrived to stay overnight in a hotel near the university, one stop in a circuit of campuses we were covering, the four of us stopped by Claire's place, a sunny high-ceiling ground floor apartment in a white clapboard house. She greeted us at the door with a broad smile and enormous hugs.

"Thank the merciful Lord. Folks from New York!" she exclaimed greeting us with the same words she had in her email. Her southern accent was more pronounced than I'd ever heard it. I had always loved her voice with its smooth, relaxing cadence. She looked thinner, wistful, still beautiful though, her russet hair longer and wilder.

"I haven't had a good haircut since Paolo," she said when I commented. Jamil, now seven, with charcoal hair and eyes, resembled her. His delicate features, deep dimples, squirrel cheeks, and endless eyelashes were hers.

When ushered in, Adam and Tyler politely sat on the painted, white

floor within the gallery-like sparseness of her living room next to a pile
of dried hickory pods, the boys' hands and sneakers enormous in the
way that teenage boys possess, like the paws of St. Bernards. When she
asked who wanted to go to school at JMU, Tyler nodded.

"It's the Bible belt, ya know. You ready for that?" she asked.

Claire's gray-blue eyes danced and I remember why I'd fallen so
hard for her. We were there for hardly fifteen minutes when she directed us to her computer, scrolling through photos of her grandmother
she'd been Photoshopping. Her energy was infectious—she didn't seem
to notice that our boys had no interest in what she was showing. It was
her genuineness, maybe even her seeming inability to read the social
landscape, that I found endearing.

For our tour of the town, Claire and Jamil escorted us to the local
Wal-Mart to point out what she claimed was the only entertaining
thing to do in town—peruse the merchandise: bolts of green fabric
patterned with repeating yellow John Deere tractors.

"Can you believe this place?" she said, stretching out the word
believe.

Later, with Adam and Tyler staying overnight with friends on cam-
pus, Claire, Amanda, and I grabbed drinks at the Artful Dodger, Harrisonburg's closest thing to a gay bar.

We were enveloped in cozy, overstuffed armchairs drinking Bud-
weisers. Amanda, in the middle of our triangle, knew all about the romance Claire and I had shared a handful of years ago.

"I really don't fit in here," Claire said, something she had told me a
million times. "Where are the museums, the art world, the openness?"
She asked her arms wide and theatrical.

As we started to talk, it was hard to hear, with the ceilings high and
Joe Walsh on the sound system. So I drifted away from the conversation,
went to the bar and surveyed the décor: tasteful prints and paintings,
rugs, a homey feel.

When I got back I picked up the conversation: Claire talking ani-
matedly about a guy she had been dating who turned out to be in the
CIA, someone she wanted to break up with.

Well, well. A fine lesbian you turned out to be. After badgering me about my decision to stay married. Look at you now.

She spoke in hushed tones and all I could make out was that she was breaking up with him. I sat down and joined in the conversation and as I listened intently to help her come up with a solution to her break-up, I felt the old familiar dynamics take over: she needs me and I help her.

The more we drank, the more Claire and I moved closer to each other while Amanda drifted over to the bar. I saw her talking and laughing with two gay men. When the song, "Through the Fire," by Chaka Kahn played, Claire grabbed my hand and led me to the wide open dance floor, no one else on it. She wrapped her arms around my neck and led me in a slow dance. I could feel her pelvis. I trailed her long, tapered back with my hand but it didn't feel right. I felt stiff and sensed it wasn't me she was after but somebody. Some body. Maybe a piece of New York.

"Come back to my place," she purred. "Jamil is with my mother tonight."

I shook my head and slid my body away from hers. I walked back towards Amanda and she nodded, as if to say it's okay for you to do what you want.

"No," I said. "Let's go." I had no desire to bring any more chaos into my life.

Later, laying down on my hotel room bed, I picked up a call from Claire. She wanted to see me before I left the next morning. I thought she might want to know how I was. She had not asked me once. I met her at eight a.m. at Panera for coffee and she told me again in great detail about the boyfriend, asking what she should do.

On the drive home, the boys were sprawled in the back seat, with comforters, pillows, and smelly socks.

"How are you?" Amanda asked as I buckled into the driver's seat of her Explorer. She looked at me ready to offer comfort if I needed it. No, doubt, she'd wondered if my seeing Claire had opened the scab.

"I'm doing well. Glad I saw her," I answered. Amanda looked at me.

"I'm done," I added.

For the rest of the trip, we heard the following from the back seat: feigned snoring, shrieks of "you idiot!" and threats to pummel if "you don't move over, you big fat piece of crap."

"Imagine if we spoke to each other like that," I said to Amanda, as we chuckled over our sons: soon-to-be college-boys.

+

By Thanksgiving, Josh had been on Suboxone five months. He was seeing Dr. Wasser regularly and had begun treatment with a cognitive behavioral therapist, Eugene. Josh had started working for Gary, his long-time lawyer friend who handled the closing on our house and whom he had shared space with on Park Row in New York City in the early days.

"I'm getting off Suboxone," he announced one night. "I'm ready for the next step." He explained about Naltrexone, an opioid blocker that quells the craving for drugs like heroin. "Once you start, you have to increase the dosage before decreasing. But when you come off, you're off everything. I talked to Dr. Wasser. I'm ready."

"Where do you do this detox? Rehab, a clinic somewhere?"

"Here. Home. Over Thanksgiving weekend."

I laughed nervously.

"Is it like the movies? The addict going through cold turkey? You know, Frank Sinatra and the man with the golden arm?"

"I don't know what it will be like," he replied. "Dr. Wasser says I can do it in my own bedroom."

A few days later, at my request, Josh and I sat across from Dr. Wasser, a heavyset man who looked like actor John Goodman.

"Look," Dr. Wasser said, eyes on me, "this is a success case. He's doing incredibly well."

"But doesn't he have to go to a twenty-eight-day rehab or something?"

"Not necessarily," said Dr. Wasser, "I think Josh is managing this."

While the doctor's testimony swayed me, it sounded too easy. I wasn't convinced Josh was getting to the bottom of the problem. Without a twelve-step program like Narcotics Anonymous or AA, I couldn't imagine how he could stay sober. But since I was out of the business of managing his recovery, I agreed to support his detox at home, despite what I'd read online on the unsanctioned, addict self-help sites: *methadone withdrawal? Don't try this at home.*

Naltrexone is described as "part of a complete treatment plan for drug abuse" to be used by people who have been addicted to opiates and helps prevent substance abusers from taking these drugs again. It cannot be used by people currently taking opiates, only those who have stopped. According to the web site webmd.com:

Naltrexone belongs to a class of drugs known as 'opiate antagonists,' which works in the brain to prevent the good-feeling effects of opiate use effects (e.g., feelings of well-being, pain relief, etc).

It also decreases the desire to take opiates. Working with a health-care professional, such as Dr. Wasser, Josh, after having been weaned off methadone through the use of Suboxone, would start the regimen by first increasing his dose of Naltrexone for two days then decreasing.

Josh began on Thanksgiving Day gradually increasing his dose from Friday to Sunday. I checked on him often, tiptoeing into the darkened bedroom in the dreary, metallic November light. He didn't get out of bed and I heard nothing. Eating little, cocooned in blankets, his shivering shook the comforters. I didn't see writhing, moaning, or distress, just a lump of a body, covered to his ears. And at the end of four days he got up, dressed, and resumed his life. Later, he said it felt like the flu and that's how it appeared.

"I will not pick up again," he told me.

That year, Christmas Day was less about celebrating—as it had always been—and more about sobering—for all of us. We had just opened our gifts in the living room, a fire kindling in the fireplace, amidst just-opened gift boxes and crumpled piles of wrapping paper. The six-foot tall Christmas tree lent the pine aroma we loved at the holidays. Josh sat in the high-back chair he'd pulled over from the dining room table. He and I had spoken about the need for him to tell the truth about his drug addiction to Matthew and Adam.

"You're only as sick as your secrets," I reminded him, repeating the AA slogan—and what better gift to give his children than the truth.

"I'm so ashamed," he began as he recapped his four days of detox at the hospital and explained his illness during the Thanksgiving weekend. He told the boys who stopped darting around and sat down when they recognized the somber tone of the conversation.

"I never shot up," he explained, "only snorted heroin, methadone, some coke. Now I'm clean for the first time in years," he admitted, crying softly and stroking the GPS watch the boys had given him as a Hanukkah gift.

Matthew, now a junior in college, got up and patted his dad affectionately on the head, the closest thing to a hug he could muster. A few months later, Matthew released a CD of self-written songs, including one titled, "Can't Say I Blame You."

> *Pedal-steel guitar intro.*
> *You don't want to talk about it.*
> *You just wanna live without it.*
> *Can't say I blame you anymore.*
> *Hard years will come and go.*
> *Most times there's nothing to show.*
> *Can't say I blame you anymore.*
>
> *But there's nothing like a couple pills to ease you from the pain.*
> *And there's nothing like a couple drinks to make it go away.*
> *Just make this go away.*
> *I know we're not out of luck but goddamn I'd say we're stuck.*
> *Can't say I blame you anymore.*
>
> *True love is hard to find.*
> *Life can be so unkind.*
> *Can't say I blame you anymore.*

Despite the promise of sobriety, so much financial damage had been done. The house had to be sold, so in February 2008, the same month the separation agreement was filed, I called in a professional realtor to give us an assessment.

"This house shows beautifully," said Micki, our elegant real estate broker as I escorted her through the house on a sunny Saturday. Her dark hair cascaded over her shoulders. "It's deceivingly large." From the front it looked narrow, but once you got inside it was deep and high.

"We renovated the whole house, not four years ago," I emphasized. "Added a bedroom and full bath on the second floor and extended down here." I walked over and pointed to the archway between the kitchen and the den, where the house had previously ended.

"The counters are Silestone, you know, better than granite because you don't have to oil them." I swept my arm along the surface like a game show presenter.

"Custom cabinets," I added. "Watch this," I said as I pulled out the utensil drawer and let it close by itself with a whisper. Sun flooded through the east windows, even in the pale mid-winter light, and gave the heart of the house—where we'd celebrated so much of our lives—a warm, loving feel. I was lobbying for the "mint" description in the real estate listing.

We'd chosen Micki after Josh and I saw her at an open house showing nearby. Micki was warm, not pushy as some brokers could be, and had experience selling homes in the neighborhood. Josh called brokers "jokers," but not Micki. I was putting my precious home in her hands to pass over to someone else.

"Yup, it's too big for us now that my youngest is off to college in September," I said with cheer. Josh was sitting with us at the kitchen table, his eyeglass repair kit open, the little screwdriver laying nearby as he fingered the screws of my reading glasses. He said little, unusual for him, the king of banter. He wouldn't look at me. Even though he had made big strides in his recovery from drugs, the financial havoc he had created couldn't be undone. His law work with Gary appeared unpredictable—he would go into the office some days and not others and still I didn't see checks or regular pay. He balked at going to DA, one of the few things that kept me sane and focused.

Sale of the house had to be imminent. The monthly mortgage payment was set to rise in March to $3,400, almost $1,800 more than what we were paying. Our real estate taxes ran over $900 a month, plus the other expenses of maintaining our home in Nassau County, one of the highest-taxed counties in the country.

In the separation agreement, the value of the house was set at $650,000 with a mortgage balance of $470,000. The difference, or equity, was valued at $180,000. In our agreement, Josh would assume all responsibility for business debt including the Bank of America credit line, which had both names attached. I understood, through my attorney, that creditors don't care about separation or any kind of agreement people make between themselves. If creditors don't get paid they are coming after anyone whose name is on the account. Yet, I refused to overtly accept the BOA account into my hands until I had to. Feeling the injustice of being saddled with $50,000 of debt. which I had no hand in spending, I staunchly refused to ..car Josh of that obligation in writing. I was responsible for the mortgage on the Hilton vacation timeshare, which ran $286 a month. I owed him approximately $60,000 in lieu of equitable distribution (the money New York expects divorcing couples to split equally) since I had already given him $27,500. We agreed I would pay him $10,000 on the signing of the agreement and $22,500 upon the sale of the house. In exchange, all bank accounts were left to me as were my pension, IRA, and 401K. He agreed to pay child support of $1,200 a month plus forty percent of health care costs and forty percent of education expenses, though I would never see any of that cash.

I closed the front door and watched through the diaphanous curtain as Micki got into her black Mazda and scribbled notes. I hurried over to Josh before he could make his way down the basement stairs, grabbing his flannel elbow harder than I meant to. He spun around, a look of dread in his eyes.

"I will never forgive you."

I said it with no equivocation, though later regretted it, feeling like I had assigned myself to a position of hardness that felt unnatural. Though I was afraid he might pick up again, being clean of drugs for only two months, I wanted to hurt him. I wanted him to feel the depths of my pain.But he continued to disregard us and double-down on his finance deals despite our ricochet towards bankruptcy.

Journal entry from February 2008:

I need to sell my house pronto. Spent three days not sleeping and crying constantly. It's like I'm going through withdrawal from my drug, my husband.

It started with belief he could come with me when I move. Live with me there. I was optimistic, like, ok, this is bad but it's not the end of the world. It is terribly sad and shocking but doable. Let's cancel the separation agreement. We could start anew. Then over the weekend we talked about the separation agreement and he said he wanted the balance of the money I was to pay out to him ($32,500) to execute the agreement. He wanted it all upon signing!! I got so upset—all he wanted was more money. Did he know what that request did to me? "Why don't you get money for the plane ticket you bought? For all the MoneyGrams you sent?" I shouted. I stormed out of the house. I ran into Amanda and we went to Dunkin' Donuts. All day and all night I reeled. And slowly, through the night—not able to sleep, pacing, realizing—that he can't come with me. If he does, the problem follows me—worrying about whether or how he's going to contribute, whether he's clean and this nightmare continues. And I felt so bereft, so sad, so wanting my old life back. So wanting my sorrow to end. But mostly grieving my life and realizing it won't "be fine" no matter how much I want it to be. I told him in the night I'd give him the money but then he had to leave me alone—forever.

Whenever Micki, the realtor, had an appointment for a showing, I cleared out of the house. If I couldn't, I was as cheerful as a lottery winner. That's after vacuuming, spritzing the stainless appliances with W-D40, and clearing the toaster oven, CD player, and stray supermarket circulars off the counters to make it looked like no one lived there. I baked chocolate chip cookies to fill the air home with the scent of comfort. Sometimes I was out of breath when the doorbell rang so I'd compose myself then welcome the couple with a chumminess reserved for relatives I hadn't seen in a while.

"Yes, the custom-designed pillow cabinets close quietly and the garbage disposal switch is hidden here," I'd say, opening the hidden-away sponge drawer. Micki and I worked like a straight man/funny man team.

"You should see the house in the morning when the sunlight streams in," I'd say.

"Yes, bring your sunglasses!" Micki would quip.

And we'd laugh. And then I'd glance at the framed photo of Matthew, age three, cradling Adam, two months, atop the oak sideboard or I'd spy the hand-painted vegetable bin from my grandmother and think "that piece of furniture belongs in that spot and nowhere else."

✦

Two months later, a letter unexpectedly arrived, return receipt requested, from Countrywide Bank:

> *We are pleased to advise that you are eligible for a loan modification. Your monthly mortgage payment will be $2,164.00, effective May 2008. A modification fee of $99 must be paid for the modification to become effective.*

Included were a phone number to call, documents to sign, and a prepaid Fed-Ex envelope. Countrywide Bank was offering me a modification on the mortgage that was about to skyrocket in two months! Boom. A salve to my pain.

The new mortgage—based on paying interest only—would cost $530 more a month than we were currently paying on the minimum payment option, bringing the monthly mortgage payment to $2,164. The good news: this interest-only option would freeze the negative amortization and the loan balance would not go any higher. The prepayment penalty period would be over. Somehow I'd have to squeeze out the extra $529 a month and I was determined to do it even if it meant getting a second job. I stared at the letter, reading it over and over just to make sure I wasn't dreaming. I was selected! How decent of Countrywide.

I sat in the first-floor atrium of South Nassau Hospital, the same institution Josh visited to get clean of drugs, the struggling March sun warming my chair while I waited to take my friend Nicole home from shoulder surgery. The surgeon was repairing a bone spur, a "labral tear," caused by the physical therapy she'd received after her lumpectomy. I anticipated the buzz of the vibrating remote control bar the floor nurse had given me, nestled in the tight front pocket of my jeans, waiting for the signal that Nicole's procedure was over. The time gave me the chance to look at the paperwork sent by Countrywide. As of May 2008, I could start paying the modified payment.

I called Abdelinda Cruz, the modification representative listed on the letter, to say yes, count me in! When I finally reached her I wanted to kiss her through the phone.

"Yes, you qualify for a modification," Abdelinda's voice soft and forgiving. "You need to send a check for $99 and the notarized page."

Had Abdelinda picked me out herself from a pool of borrowers with good credit in a bad situation? It was like a Red Rover team I was being invited to and I was hearing Abdelinda's Southern California Latina inflection announcing, "Red Rover, Red Rover, we call Janet over," and I wanted to skip to the other side of the grassy playground because of this miracle, this gift landing in my cupped, open hands. I wanted to hug Abdelina and her hard Rs. She understood, being Latina, the love of family, bonds of deep attachment that don't appear on the customer copy of Countrywide's loan modification #122406. The affection of family who have your back when you mess up. She understood the sneakerhead teenage son who didn't want to leave his home, his bedroom with the Syracuse University pennant hung at the side of the loft bed built by his father and the burgundy mini blinds bent from tossing one too many Nerf basketballs, and the fluorescent camping lantern hung underneath the bed where flannel blankets and down pillows invite friends to sleep over and where his father hid sometimes, the shame paralyzing.

Had Countrywide seen the error of their ways? Were they an errant spouse too? Making amends for their greediness? Bringing the cleaved parts of my marriage and family together, reuniting us because we deserved a break amidst the steely financial world where intent had no place?

Now with our little boys as young men—one at Northeastern University and the other about to enter a Maryland college that fall—my family got a second chance. Countrywide threw a life preserver and I was grateful. And just like that, we were rescued, purged, forgiven of our sins. Our Higher Power so unpredictable and so merciful. I called Micki, the real estate broker. Take the house off the market! We changed our minds! We don't want to downsize anymore! My panic over the prospect of losing the house had dissolved and I let light and compassion for Josh seep in. Was this what it felt like to get a drug fix? To be desperate with need and then feel flooded with the warm, oozy feeling of well-being?

✦

The stale, humid air of our basement injected a laziness to the project Matthew and I were undertaking: he had agreed to record me in his home studio singing "Our Love Is Here to Stay," from the American songbook, a gift to Josh. This version, a duet by Louis Armstrong and Ella Fitzgerald, was one of my and Josh's favorites.

Matthew's ambitious little home studio, included a Tascam engineering board, speakers and amps, metal music stands, a keyboard, guitars, and a number of monitors that created foot-pedaled effects. When he was in high school and building up this studio, Matthew had local bands as recording clients. If the rest of the family was home when recording was in session, we were instructed not to use the bathroom because water running through the basement pipes would be picked up on the recording.

"Did you practice?" Matthew asked.

"Do I have to? I know the song."

Matthew sat at the computer authoritatively, his slender frame dressed in the black t-shirt uniform of musicians. He grunted a laugh.

"It's not that easy, you know."

He clicked on the track of Ella and Louis, their voices and styles blending effortlessly: "It's very clear...our love is here to stay..." I first heard standards like this Cole Porter song on Julius LaRosa's Make Believe Ballroom on WNEW radio in the 60s, a show my mother listened to daily. I became a lover of these songs from the 30s, 40s, and 50s and even Matthew and Adam knew many Louis and Ella duets.

Matthew dubbed my voice over Ella and Louis's. When he played the tracks of their singing to guide me while he recorded, I was surprised at how fast and up-tempo it was and how perfectly in synch Ella and Louis were. I didn't even have the words printed out and since Ella and Louis were providing different harmonies I had trouble finding a sweet spot. Ella's soprano was too high and Louis's baritone too low. I was a beat behind every note.

"Better let Ella handle this part," my son said when Ella sang the scat bridge.

Many attempts later, we got a sample good enough to edit.

As the country was about to be roiled in the collapse of Lehman Brothers, and Bear Stearns about to be bought by Merrill-Lynch, and Americans about to raise their heads in disbelief over the economic fire ignited by Wall Street's end-of-the-line hot potato game with no more hands eager to swap credit defaults for all those shaky mortgages, I handed my husband his gift—"Ella, Louis, and Janet," singing "Our Love Is Here to Stay" together on CD.

I beamed as Josh looked at the CD with surprise, then at my face, then at the CD. His eyes pooled with tears and I took the CD from his hand and I slipped it in the boom box sitting in a corner of the kitchen counter. As I declared in song that our love was here to stay, Josh turned his back and wept. I knew he cried easily—he couldn't watch the Miss America pageant dry-eyed and cried for days when Kentucky Derby winner Barbaro was euthanized. But his tears seemed to have no end—he continued weeping long after the boom box was switched off.

"I love you," I told him wanting him to understand that the mortgage modification and the prospect of keeping our house had given me renewed forgiveness. Cradling me into his arms, he smiled weakly. "I know you do."

CHAPTER 19

Journal entries from 2009:

January 20
Inauguration of Barack Obama. The swearing-in ceremony. Poet Elizabeth Alexander. Thrilling. We are united in hope and optimism. At last.

January 22
Clear blue September 11th cloudless sky, bitter cold, windy. Home from work at seven p.m. Josh asleep on the sofa, the long end of the sectional L; he's facing the back. He doesn't turn around when I come in. Wearing his gray-flannel p.j.s, long-sleeved, worn too many times, droopy, like his face, when I see it: drawn, colorless, stubbled.

January 25
Drive to Baltimore. Down and back in one day, over eight hours. Deliver Adam to his dorm, safe and sound. Josh too sick to come. His cough is vicious and he still hasn't gotten off the couch. On the return trip alone at night: Southern Jersey, just over the Delaware Memorial Bridge onto the Turnpike, Exit 3 to Camden, the road dark and scary. No turnpike lights, isolated, the Garmin doesn't register the route. Keep the course until I emerge and yes, on the right road. We watch a report on CBS's 60 Minutes about an ingredient in red wine that helps you live longer. "Please, no," Josh says.

March 14
Sitting at my writing desk, looking out the window at my favorite tree, a maple, the sun filtering behind it through the window onto my desk, my hands, my journal. Behind my tree, which I've claimed because I've been watching since

last summer, is another tree whose branches point up like a wide poplar. About a week ago, I visited the trees, looked up at them, and realized how patient they are. They wait. They don't complain. They stand patiently until something happens, until they bloom.

March 29:

I lift the lid of our office photocopier. I'm in a rush to copy a story I've been working on to take to Greenport, an hour and a half drive east, where I'm headed for the weekend with my writing friends Jessica and Hadley.

I remove a document lying on the glass. Page two is staring at me. It looks official. With all the paperwork I've perused in the last two years, I know to grab suspicious-looking documents immediately. This one looks scary and apparently had been faxed recently by Josh because the FAX button had been pushed.

I turn the page over. My eye goes immediately to the heading: Lawyer's Fund for Client Protection. It's a petition to the Bar Association fund to replace money.

Attorney Joshua took $45,000 in retainer and periodic legal fees. Loss estimated at $230,000. I blanch. Precise amount will be determined upon subpoenaed bank records.

What?

I don't even have to read the rest but I do, like I'm at the scene of someone else's bad accident and can't avert my eyes.

Attorney Joshua failed to answer repeated demands from this office. Further demands in person and in writing. Grievance Committee. Tenth Judicial District. Loss reported to District Attorney.

A petition to a Bar Association Fund. Did he want me to find this? Is that why he left it in the copier? What happened to all this money?

Freney.

I recognize the name of the client. Estate of Freney. For years, I'd heard this name. Like an old friend. How could such a lovely French surname now indicate such terribleness?

*The escrow. The escrow. The money attorneys hold in good keeping for their
clients. The enemy of every desperate addicted-to-something attorney.*

He is done. And so are we.

✦

My memory flashed to 2007, two years ago, when I had started
excavating our financials. I tore the room apart then, rifling through
Josh's lawyer files to satisfy my hunger for documents that would shed
light on the truth. I had found an escrow statement then, zero balance.
I shoved it back in the folder quickly like holding it in my fingers too
long would not let me deny that Josh's troubles were deep and frightening. Did I know then? Maybe that's why I wasn't surprised.

Walking slowly downstairs into the living room, I held the sheet of
paper ready to present. I showed it to him. He looked at me. Eyes alive
with fear.

"I did it," he confessed. "I did a very bad thing," he admitted sounding like a child who'd no longer wished to hide the truth.

"I'm not angry," I managed after a long pause. "Just so sad." The
words come out measured, clipped. He nodded.

The weight of my broken-heartedness made standing too hard so
I sat for a while, laying my head on the comforter with the Boynton
hippo, the boys' childhood duvet Josh had been sleeping on. Then Josh
carted his slumped body upstairs to his hiding space, the lair, as we
called it, beneath Adam's loft bed. I heard where the footsteps stopped.
He must be so glad I'm leaving for the weekend, I thought. *He doesn't have
to face me.* And my heart broke for him. In that moment, I understood
my husband's incessant sweating at night, the pacing, the crying, the
isolating. He didn't know where to go to purge the guilt.

And I thought of the victims—how awful. Their money was gone.
I wondered if they would get it back from the Bar Association fund.
I covered my face in my hands. How shameful to be associated with
such a thing.

On the way to pick up my friends at the train station for our drive to Greenport, I thought of the boys and the shame of this. I drove our mini van through flooded streets, splashing, leaving a wake. He will be dis-barred. I knew it. Will the clients get their money back from the fund? What are we going to tell people? Should I email the ethicist from *The New York Times* for advice? What do I tell people when they ask where he is? Josh's eighty-four-year-old dad, whose congestive heart failure was showing itself through the Coumadin clusters of bruises that shone on his translucent skin, his slow, halting shuffle, and bony chicken-wing arms? Always so proud of his son. And Josh's sister, Wendy, not long ago diagnosed with MDS, myelodysplastic syndrome, a pre-leukemic condition she'd been managing with blood transfusions. And my sons? However will we tell them? I shuddered. Our troubles had to be kept between Josh and me right now. We couldn't add to the family's worries. Besides, it was not the sort of news I wanted to share with anyone.

I thought of my sister Christine who told me once she couldn't listen to the car radio when her adult son had gotten a disciplinary warning from his company—with decisions to follow about the status of his job—because his laptop had been stolen from the company car. He hadn't followed the policy of taking the laptop with him at all times. Until her son was told he would keep his job, Christine kept the car radio off. I had wondered then: was she not allowing herself the small pleasure because she felt responsible too or imagined her action having bearing on the results?

I thought of my affair with Claire and believed for a moment that my turning away from Josh during his most vulnerable moments—his 9/11 post-traumatic stress—caused him to commit this theft. I knew I wasn't responsible for my husband's actions; nevertheless, the shame was visceral.

As I drove, I turned the radio off, mirroring Christine's behavior and my parents' habit of abruptly turning the radio off when our family car rolled through the cemetery gates to visit my grandparents' graves.

✦

Hadley, Jessica, and I arrived at the motel and found Greenport cold and rainy. The motel's sliding glass doors led to a grassy area dotted with crab grass and a beat-up wooden picnic table. The sky looked bruised and threatening. The horizon held a thick, eggplant-colored line like a border. My old life on one side, new life on the other.

Spasms of stomach pain and nausea kept me awake. I couldn't get out of the motel bed. I lay still under the tufted bedspread in the late afternoon, thick floor-length drapes, like those from a high school auditorium, sequestering me. Hadley and Jessica, to whom I said nothing about what had happened, were so kind. They brought chicken noodle soup to my room.

The next day Hadley, a grief counselor, wanted us to create collages around loss as she was trying out a bereavement workshop. I didn't feel like cutting out pictures from magazines to express my sadness but I did and, surprisingly, the heaviness lifted briefly. Purple was the overriding color in my collage. It reminded me of the threatening sky.

In the months that followed, Josh and I waited. We told no one. We didn't know when he would be prosecuted. The Bar Association, investigating him, had gone to the District Attorney, so it could be months before we heard. In the meantime, Josh had retained an attorney and grappled with the possibility of turning himself in.

In my everyday life, I lived, though subdued. Going to work, cooking, dinner, a movie. The prospect of my husband's arrest and prosecution consumed me. However, my feelings were ruled by thoughts that dribbled or sprung unexpectedly in waves, undulating, fierce, gripping. I feared he would be arrested at any moment, burly police officers knocking on the door, escorting him to a waiting police car, red lights spinning, carnival-like, announcing our nadir.

The worry—thick and gnarly—sat squarely on my chest most nights—between three and six a.m., the hellish witching hours when fear paralyzed me in my bed and recriminating thoughts taunted mercilessly—if only I had been a more loving and attentive wife, if only I had been more aware of his needs, if only I had not tolerated his habits, not been so selfish, a weakling to my thirst for Claire. I hallucinated a terrifying future—Josh, a gentle man, raped, beaten, even murdered, in prison and I wondered if his wit will be an asset or danger if he dared show it. Many nights, I wept silently in the dark. On the rare occasions I gave him unspoken permission to join me in our bed—and I was crying—he turned towards me spooning gingerly, space between us like logs in a fireplace allowing for circulation of air, rubbing my back lightly, tentatively, comforting me, whispering, "Everything's gonna be alright." If, at that moment, he was the source of my anguish I shrugged him off me and he retreated instantly. Other times I accepted the comfort, my need for the familiar trumping every other emotion.

My grief left little room for anger. I didn't have the energy for it. But when it did flare up it was about many things: his disinterest in joining a twelve-step group like Alcoholics Anonymous, for one. This lack of desire for recovery irked me. I urged him to join AA because a judge, I told him, would look more favorably if he were in recovery. All the while I knew I was committing a "slip," Al-Anon speak for my relapse, trying to force a solution and control his behavior. Even as I said the words I knew I was drunk with co-dependence, my wishing he would do what I wanted so he might reduce his jail time and I could be released from the pain of losing him.

Some days I grew excited. Holding the secret of my husband's impending prosecution. Knowing it would explode soon. Anticipating things would change, some crazy fear mixed with thrill, creating combustibility. And that Josh and I shared the secret produced unexpected intimacy. He had taken to being silent at times and jokingly told me he would answer questions by blinking, once for yes, twice for no. We were in the supermarket, one time, pushing a cart down the produce aisle, and heard Tom Petty's "The Waiting is the Hardest Part." We glanced at each other; he blinked once.

I felt so much grief for this man I loved who would be leaving us. Leaving us! I knew he would be going to prison—and part of me wanted him to go immediately and get it over with. The amount of money stolen was too much to be pardoned in this day of the Bernie Madoffs, the demon of all our economic woes, the embodiment of our blamelessness. So much easier to point a finger than look at our own participation. And always the thought: Did Josh commit this crime to stave off our own family's economic tsunami? Mostly, I wondered: Who is this man? How could I have trusted him so implicitly and how could he have propelled us into such disaster? How could he have stolen money from clients he loved and worked so hard for, often for next to no money? How could he have taken something that wasn't his? Our family code of going the extra mile, donating our time to good causes. He who had been so giving and kind—like the time he returned a wallet, he'd found in a taxi in Midtown, full of credit cards and cash. He tracked down the owner, a woman from Arizona, by following the trail of a hotel receipt and meeting with her to return it. After she flew home, she sent a small bell-shaped stone wind chime painted with cactus, which we'd hung on our front porch.

The depth of my confusion was endless.

And one spring weekend we painted our bedroom, a steel blue-gray, in anticipation of having to sell the house.

"You're the dainty paintee," he declared smiling.

Roller in hand, he swathed our bedroom ceiling with white paint while standing on a rickety step stool. He looked down at me while I plied a second coat on the wood trim along the floor.

"Look how delicately you paint."

+

That May, Josh announced, "My sister is going ahead with the transplant, the stem cells."

We had just sat down to dinner in the kitchen. So many announcements in this kitchen: my discovery of the emptied accounts; knowledge of his crime and investigation by the Bar Association, and now this.

I looked at him surprised.

"What?" he asked.

"I don't know. Just suddenly seems so serious."

"It is. I'm the donor," he added. "The bone marrow match."

I knew he had gotten tested but realizing what it meant was another thing.

"Is it okay? Considering your druggie past?" He sighed; then he got up and opened the refrigerator.

"It's been two years," he said. "I've been clean, you know."

"Well, except for the drinking." As soon as I said it, I wished I hadn't.

"Please don't start. I've been cleared as a donor."

"All right. All right." I said quickly. "You're brave. Isn't the procedure painful?

"I don't care. It's the least I can do."

+

Wendy's MDS, a blood cancer, had seemed contained to me, maybe because she had appeared healthy except for the blood transfusions, which she needed more frequently. Yet, Wendy had not missed work and rarely spoke about how she felt except to show me, on occasion, the swelling of her feet and legs which looked uncomfortable but not life threatening.

"Look at the shoes I have to wear," she intoned before Passover dinner as we stood peeling hard-boiled eggs. She lifted her Birkenstock besotted foot. Her commentary on the shoes was the worst complaint I'd heard.

"Sit down," I implored. "Do this at the table." I carried the bowl over and pulled out a kitchen chair.

"I'm fine, just fine," she joked. "Really, it's the shoes. You know me, I never met a shoe sale I didn't love."

"Wendy wants to do it this summer," Josh continued, "after she finishes teaching and Jamie's graduation."

Her only child Jamie was graduating from Ithaca College and Josh, the boys and I were looking forward to the weekend ceremony and celebration. Though the threat of Josh's arrest had been in the air for the last month, his days at home now held a new urgency. The threat of his incarceration was scary enough but now he needed to be free to save his sister's life.

That summer, with Wendy's procedure imminent, Josh was scheduled to have the hospital nurse inject him with Procrit, a medication
that increases red blood cell production. The same day we learned of
Wendy's procedure date, Josh got a call from his lawyer telling him the
assistant DA was eyeing his case.

But Wendy wasn't ready for Josh's preparation. She had a cold and
her doctors wouldn't start the process until she was healthy. Since they
would be replacing her blood with new cells, she would be too open
to infection, which her body would not be able to fight. We knew that
once the doctors began to replace her blood, she would be in isolation
while her body regenerated. I remembered when Lil, Josh's mother,
was sequestered in a low-lighted, noiseless, eerie isolation room during
her chemotherapy treatments at Mt. Sinai. I imagined it would be the
same for Wendy.

Wendy recovered easily from her cold while Josh and I waited for
confirmation of the dates he needed to be injected with Procrit. No
one, of course, except Josh and I knew he was awaiting prosecution,
and though he told me that any sentencing wouldn't happen quickly I
lived in anguish of his not being present to donate his stem cells. I loved
Wendy and her "get it done" attitude, girlish giggle, her booming voice
leaving messages for us on voicemail in her trademark Long Island accent, inquiring about a routine doctor's visit one of the boys may have
had or to find out about the appropriateness of a gift she wanted to get
someone.

I prayed daily, during my morning meditation, that the bone marrow transplant would release Wendy from the deleterious effects of her
disease and she could live without transfusions and the fear of MDS
transforming into leukemia.

I began reading Comfortable with Uncertainty by Pema Chodron, a
Buddhist nun who implores her readers to accept what is and not fight
the feelings no matter how painful. Accept the pain and work through
it. I carried the book with me as if I needed the certainty of the book

to remind me there was no certainty. It was, in fact, the pain of future loss I anticipated. I feared my husband leaving us and an unknown future for me and the boys. And now I added the very real fear that Wendy wouldn't get the bone marrow she desperately needed in time. During Wendy's illness, Josh's dad's health was failing as well. Mel's heart condition and appearance were troubling. His pallor was gray and his clothes hung on his frame. We were frightened about his prospects, too. Josh spent many days taking Mel to doctor visits, Mt. Sinai hospital, and rehab facilities.

Once Wendy got the go-ahead on her procedure, Josh arrived at North Shore Hospital the day of the procedure to extract bone marrow. His upper body lay at a forty-five degree angle on the chunky leather hospital recliner. Under different circumstances he could be getting a tooth extracted in that position but the harsh fluorescent lights, the scent of hospital disinfectant, and the air conditioning turned too high assured otherwise. He smiled, fingering a squishy ball in his right hand with both arms tethered to IV poles.

"My sister's getting back at me for all the rotten things I did to her when I was a kid," he joked with the nurses.

Blood, vivid red, flowed from a tube inserted into the vein in his right arm, then recycled into his body through a vein in his left arm. He made a joke about his veins being "good veins," and I shot him a scolding look. I didn't appreciate jokes about drug addiction. Because of the now prevalent use of this process, apheresis, Josh did not have to undergo the painful bone marrow transplant procedure I'd imagined, where the doctors extract fluid directly from the marrow in the spine or hip. Josh did the procedure wearing street clothes and was released at four p.m. the same day.

Wendy remained for two months in the oncology isolation unit at North Shore Hospital, just as we'd anticipated. We entered her room— filled with cards and balloons celebrating her second "birthday." We wore paper hospital gowns, masks, and latex gloves. After the initial chemotherapy and start of the infusion, we fully anticipated her restoration to health. But her blood count never went up as we had hoped and she developed fevers and kidney failure. Our lovely Wendy passed away in September, having just turned fifty-four years old.

Days later in our living room, Josh and I held each other weeping bitter tears as we watched the blackened *Yahrzeit* memorial candle, Star of David decorated, burn its last bit of red and blue flame. Our heads were down on the mantel of the fireplace, resting on folded, sleeveless arms. Josh gasped as the light extinguished and we were now tethered to Wendy, who now lived within us in the deepest flickering place where love and pain collected.

CHAPTER 20

"They're going to prosecute," my husband said.

Josh looked straight ahead at the TV as he spoke. It was Monday night and the television series *24* was on, Jack Bauer looking rugged and composed even though the whole city of bad guys was shooting at him.

I froze at the kitchen sink and spun around at Josh's news.

The word "prosecute" sliced through me, hatchet-like. I felt cleaved. I knew this was coming, yet his clipped words, attorney-like, made it real.

"I spoke to the lawyer today. I'm turning myself in. It will take a few days." Josh stood up, hands shoved deep into the pockets of his jeans. When he turned toward me his Paul Newman blue eyes were damp. His figure struck me, in that moment, as that of a prisoner, with his shaven head and his blue work shirt, now looking state-issued.

Outside, the leaves rustled in the warm October night. Earlier I'd gone up to the attic to take out the plastic Halloween bowl for the trick-or-treaters who would show up soon on the porch. Usually on Halloween night, I'd place a sign on the bowl filled with Snickers and Hershey's Kisses saying, *Take one please and leave the rest.* The honor system.

The boys, now both at college and too old for costumes and goblins, would have to hear the news of their dad's upcoming arraignment through a phone call. The thought of that call and the sadness and shame it would inflict on my two beautiful boys was almost too painful a thought to cradle. But, for me, there would be no more secrets, only forthright honesty and acceptance of what was. After waiting six months for the news of whether Josh would be prosecuted, I felt relief, even though the news was horrifying. It was like a fever had been spiking, starting with the discovery that Josh had emptied his IRA account almost three years ago, followed by my excavation of our chaotic finances, the investigation by the Bar Association, and the D.A. being informed of his illegal conduct. Wendy's death was the latest horrific uptick in the fever. Things would either explode or ride a wave back down.

+

A Class C felony charge, grand larceny, was introduced into Nassau County Superior Court (first district court) at the end of October. The District Attorney's office claimed that as a retained attorney, Josh had been negotiating claims, collecting assets, and paying federal, state, and income taxes on behalf of the Freney estate. After the IRS discovered Josh had not been paying the estate's taxes on time, the co-administrator and bank looked into the matter to find that the account had a four dollar balance. They charged Josh with having stolen the money and he could face up to fifteen years in prison. He had withdrawn the money little by little, just as he had done with his IRA and our sons' college annuity fund, with the intention of paying it back when the international deals he had been fiddling with came to fruition. I had let go of that foolish notion long ago but I knew that Josh, even on the day of prosecution, still clung to it like a leaky life raft.

On the day of arraignment, I waited on a long line outside to enter the District Court in Hempstead and go through the metal detector. Josh was already inside, having been driven over in a police vehicle after he turned himself in. The wind was blustery and the sun strong and I wore a brown and gold hounds tooth jacket with a teal blue silk scarf. No one was wearing a hounds tooth jacket except me. Others wore sneakers and jeans and flimsy cloth jackets. As I looked around, any class status I believed I'd owned had fallen away. The perceived "step-up" from my parents' working class status by virtue of marrying a lawyer, something my parents were impressed with, gave way with no fight from me. I was no better than anyone on this line. I didn't feel that begrudgingly; it was a fact—we were all equals here.

I spotted the attorneys—earnest, rushing, arms full of files and briefcases. Men in pressed suits and women in beige raincoats and pumps. They were laughing, unhesitating, thrusting forward to get on with their day, to get this court date over so they could scramble to their golf games, pilates, or, if they were associates, to make a dent in their sixty-hour weeks. I saw two young men—one dark-haired with peach-colored skin who reminded me of Adam—and I thought *there's my son if he'd graduated law school and was following in his father's shoes.* Tears welled up. No, that dream was over. I didn't own that anymore.

In the room marked Arraignment A, five court officers flanked Judge Donald Birnbaum's raised bench in the well. Josh stood with his lawyer Mark and pled not guilty, which, as Josh explained, is what you do at the arraignment to begin the negotiations. His posture was straight and I had noticed earlier how clear-eyed and perfunctory he was, knotting his tie after stepping into his suit pants and wingtips at home in the morning. I had seen him dress so many mornings in that gray Armani suit and vintage Jerry Garcia tie as he prepared for his court dates as the client attorney. Today he looked the same, but was a classified criminal.

Josh had been fingerprinted and mug-shot already in the District Attorney's office and at the police station where they completed the booking. The arraignment was quick, with the judge declaring a $20,000 bail bond. I was surprised at how anti-climactic it felt.

With the business card from Josh's lawyer Mark firmly in palm, I left the court and wended my way to a local storefront on a side street in a sorry part of town. It was three o'clock in the afternoon. I looked for the bail bondsman and when I spotted the garish red, white, and blue storefront signage I knew I'd found the place.

There's no place, except prison perhaps, to make you feel more like a criminal than the bail bondsmen's office. Even though the clerks were friendly and sported crew cuts and cheap suit jackets over Banlon shirts, the clientele remind you that you have fucked up badly because you are there, you are now one of them. Consider the tattooed, surly teenage son arguing with his parents as the mother, talon-like fingernails, threatens to haul off and smash him good.

My bail bond representative, a blond square-jawed handsome twenty-something guy, slipped off his jacket to reveal impressive arms and solid pecs you can rely on. He told me he was a former Marine and punctuated every sentence with "know what I mean?" Yes, you are loud and clear, sir. He explained that I pay him a percentage, about $1,400, of the $20,000 bond, which is non-refundable, their fee, and show proof of the collateral I am posting as surety. Why didn't Josh tell me I would need the deed to the house or that there would be a fee I should be prepared to pay? And two forms of ID and pay stubs and an electric bill to show proof of residence. That I needed to offer the house as collateral didn't even dawn on me while Josh was knotting his Jerry Garcia tie in the morning.

I rushed home and retrieved all the documents easily, especially pay stubs, because of my meticulous DA-inspired record-keeping. I put the $1,400 fee on my American Express card, breaking my credit card abstinence and knowing it would become another bill I would harbor resentment about paying. I dashed back to the court and filed the bail bond, so Josh could be released, snaking through the building to find the proper cashier, heels clicking on polished marble floors.

When we got home, Josh explained: the next step will be an offer of proof to the District Attorney, part of the negotiations, and finally the sentencing hearing which could take place in anywhere from six months to a year or two.

"Then I'll appear before the judge and he'll sentence me," he explained like he was talking about someone else. "We'll hope the judge will take our recommendation."

I nestled into his body, hugged him hard, and sobbed. "I've been holding that in all day," I said.

Then, Josh left to tell his father he was going to state prison.

Later that evening, my sister Laura called.

"Are you all right?" she asked without saying hello. I had been sitting at my desk in the home office when I picked up the phone. A small desk lamp emitted a low, intimate light. Her voice, breathy and full of anticipation, signaled to me that the news had spilled to the world.

"I just wanna know you're okay. Do you need me to come over?"

"Really, I'm fine. I've been living with this, you know." I steadied my voice to reassure her. "I've known for six months," I said, wanting her to appreciate my dutifulness.

"I saw it on Channel 12," she told me.

I froze. The local cable news station. I feared this would happen.

Soon the calls and texts poured in. I rushed downstairs, aware that news spreads quickly.

Josh's cousin Sandra called.

"Josh, what the hell?" she said. I heard her voice—high pitched, nearly shrieking—as he held the phone between us.

"It's a long story, Sandra," he replied to her rapid-fire string of questions. After his yes and no's, she ended the call with the reminder: "I'm here if you need anything."

Even if his family didn't understand, they did not abandon him.

"And that mug shot!" she exclaimed. "I didn't realize your ears were so big."

"We gotta call the boys," I said. They were both away at college. "They cannot hear this from someone else."

I had instinctively said "we," but was clear this was something he needed to do. I wondered if he had rehearsed what he would say in this moment but it didn't matter how it came out, just as long as they heard this news from their father.

"Tell them before the Yankee game starts," I added. Josh and the boys had been texting all week about the playoffs, with the Yankees ahead in the World Series.

And tell them white collar crime, I wanted to add so they would know that it wasn't robbery or assault or something violent. But instead I dashed outside to the porch. I couldn't protect my children anymore.

Though their feelings would run the gamut from hurt to disappointment to anger, our sons, in that moment, rallied to their father's side.

You're the man, Daddio. I love you no matter what, texted Adam.

And, the next day, Josh's cousin Sandra sent me a text: *I love you,*

Janet. I'm here.

The support of my family and friends meant everything.

A few days later, we heard from our neighbor about a rash of rob-beries. *Everyone will think it's Josh.* When I mentioned my concern to him, he confided those same thoughts.

The following weekend, I traveled with Laura and Christine and two of the cousins I'd grown up with to visit the wineries on the north fork of Long Island. The wineries were enjoying their high season, dec-orated with towers of cornstalks, pumpkins, hay bales, and string quar-tets inviting guests, like us, to sample wine and cheese tastings. We had planned this weekend for months and I was grateful to get away for a few days. Plus, it was a comfort to be with my family, who still doted on me, especially in these circumstances, just like they did when I was little, the youngest of the six girl cousins who had grown up together in the same two-family house in Brooklyn. That coming week, the local newspaper was due to come out with an article about Josh's arrest. We knew because a reporter had called, asking for a comment, which Josh declined to give. I was readying myself for the discomfort of knowing our neighbors, indeed the whole town, would know.

My phone buzzed—Amanda.

"Listen. I know you're away and I hate to bother you…"

I walked outside to a brick patio to get away from the din of noise in the winery's rotunda-like indoors.

"I want to give you a heads-up! There's a story about Josh on the local newspaper's website and it mentions Adam."

The color drained from my face.

"What?"

"Yes, I'm so sorry. I didn't know if I should tell you but then I asked myself if I'd want to know and yes, I would, so I dialed you."

"I'm glad you did. Thank you," I said politely.

"I'll read it to you: 'this is not the first run-in with the law for this family. In June, police had been called to the home and son Adam was issued a summons.'"

It was true. Josh and I had left Adam alone one weekend just after he had returned from college in June, finishing his freshman year. It was a few weeks before he left to be a counselor at the Adirondacks summer camp he had attended. We left for the weekend not thinking there would be any problem as he had already spent a year away at school. He had just turned nineteen, after all. We were not used to chaperoning anymore and didn't give it much thought when we left. Adam called us abashedly the next morning and told us about the summons he had gotten for underage drinking. We were angry but grateful no one had gotten hurt.

"What were you thinking?" I lectured my son, secretly worried about whether he was taking on his father's recklessness. I wondered if his dad's prosecution had rendered all positive child-rearing moot.

"I just invited a few kids and, I swear Mom, I was trying to keep everyone out. We were pushing people away."

The prospect of having my son now associated with his father's crime incensed me. Adam didn't deserve to be linked to a felony but I didn't know who to be angrier with—Josh, Adam, or the newspaper.

I dialed Josh, angry all over again, for putting us in this ugly situation. I asked him to rummage through our family phone book with the scribbled-in addresses and phone numbers I'd kept for years to look for the home number of Adam's friend from elementary school whose father owned the newspaper. I jotted down the number then steeled myself, mustering courage to ring the father to ask him to delete the paragraph about Adam in the print version of the newspaper due out that Thursday. It was a Saturday afternoon and I hoped he would be home. I knew he didn't have to honor my request, but being a former magazine editor myself I felt a kinship with him. Plus he and his wife had always been gracious people whom I liked very much.

I left a voicemail and surprisingly, the dad called me back. I asked for my favor.

"Hey," he responded, "I've told my kids many times, if you are in trouble with the law your name and photo will appear. I can't protect you."

"I don't disagree with you. But Adam has done nothing wrong in relation to his father's crime. And neither have I. I can hold my head up because I did not commit any crime and neither has my son. Affiliating him with his dad's charge is just unnecessary." I mustered up confidence to say what I believed.

"I can't guarantee anything," he said. "The editors make these decisions."

"I understand," I said.

I could never summon up the courage to read the article online. But when the tabloid came out that week, it didn't include Adam's name. The article, however, told the story of Josh's felony as described by the District Attorney's office with the sordid, though accurate, headline "Attorney Charged with Stealing from Dead Client." The feature occupied a quarter of the page and, yes, Josh's ears did look big in the mug shot.

I moved forward with fear as my sidekick. I was afraid of selling my house and not having a place to go, of keeping the house and running out of money, of people's judgments, of making mistakes, of getting sick from stress, of Josh's imagined prison life, of my boys' ability to cope, and a loneliness so dank and deep I feared I might never emerge. I woke up abruptly many nights, heart pounding, skin hot and prickly, and I tried to ride the sensation like a surfer on a mammoth Hawaiian wave, as Pema Chodron suggested.

One night I heard footsteps on the stairs leading to the bedroom and my heart leapt hoping it was Josh who would comfort me and then remembering our love was bankrupt, untrustworthy, and I couldn't keep going to the empty well and expecting it to be full. I knew he was suffering as was I but we could not soothe each other any more, even with the wounds of the loss of Wendy so fresh and our lives unraveling by the minute and I wondered if I'd imagined those footsteps. I pulled the sheet over my ear but the sound of my breathing disgusted me because maybe I didn't want to be alive.

Josh didn't speak of his fear but bundled himself on the couch in wool blankets and a Swiss ear-flap hat. He grew a bristly, unkempt beard. He smelled of alcohol. He hid in the "lair," under Adam's loft bed. He burrowed under blankets in his sweatshirt and drawstring pants like a sad homeless refugee trying to stay warm.

One night, after hours of crying in bed, I sat up. I was in a black and white movie, the bedroom a backdrop of shadows. It was right before Christmas and there was no Happy Hannukah bingo this year and all I could manage was the wreath from the Boy Scouts on the front door. I sat up. I saw the moon and a few stars through the top of the window. And suddenly I knew what I needed to do.

"No one is going to save you. Unload the house," I said aloud.

And the fever, at its peak, finally broke.

CHAPTER 21

The following Saturday in February, 2010, I ushered in Micki, the cheerful realtor, and we sat at the hand-painted kitchen table, where I signed the sales agreement. I didn't have to consult with anyone about the sale because I was the owner. Josh had conferred the house to me in an arms-length transaction where I paid the transfer tax two years earlier when we drew up the separation agreement. I had to sell the house, which I would never own outright, before it ate up what was left of my savings. Even with the mortgage modification, the loan had ballooned to an astronomic $483,000. The house was not "under water" yet. The idea of doing nothing and letting the home lapse into foreclosure, which could buy me a few years, was not something I could live with.

During 2010, millions of people across the United States were wringing their hands along with me as banks seized more than a million U.S. homes, hitting a new record. Only five years earlier, banks had taken over just 100,000 homes. A 2014 study published in the American Journal of Public Health linked the foreclosure crisis with an increase in suicide rates.

I wanted to get clean. Shower the financial crud off me and move out of the house before Josh's case skipped to the sentencing phase, when he would be unavailable to help me haul cartons of books or lift the top of the china cabinet, or break up the bed frames. I was not schlepping the contents of the house by myself.

Micki jotted notes as she and I walked through each room. I no longer had to pretend I was down-sizing nor did I feign delight in welcoming strangers who wanted no more than to see the inside of my closets. I was out to sell the house pronto and determined to do what it would take—lowering the price or giving away pieces of furniture so the house staged better—whatever Micki recommended. She became my partner, her eyes warm and caring. She never asked about Josh or why we were selling but we both knew.

I wouldn't be able to sell the house if there was a lien. I learned that a lien is like a clamp-down that makes all sales stop. The IRS might issue a lien on an asset, like a house, when someone owed the federal government back taxes.

My DA pressure relief partners reminded me about checking on liens before the house was listed and thank goodness my divorce lawyer had implored me to pay my income taxes separately. But Josh hadn't handled his taxes, despite the certified letters from the IRS I'd seen strewn about. He insisted that his tax attorney was on it but I didn't hear of any visits to the IRS office. (I later understood the reason he hadn't paid his taxes all those years: he was required to pay income tax on the funds he had pilfered and he couldn't very well claim the income from monies obtained from an act he had been hiding.)

Since my husband had lapsed on his credit card payments, the unrelenting phone calls from creditors gave way to summonses served at our door. Fierce-looking gentleman appeared on Saturday mornings. I could make out their figures through the lacey door curtain.

"Hey, it's for you," I called and he came downstairs and accepted the papers. He always said thank you to the process servers.

As the prospect of selling the house gained momentum, I was determined to stay focused on those finances that directly affected me: the mortgage, the joint Bank of America credit line (now at $38,000 with $890 per month payments), and our time share mortgage with a balance of $12,000. These three nagging debts hung around my neck. There were many other bills, like tuition and the cost of running the house, but these three became the triumvirate of solvency. If I could get these off my back, I could breathe and rebuild my financial life.

I had asked Josh to check at the county courthouse for any tax liens on our property.

"You know your way around the courthouse these days," I said. He texted me *luetuhm*, which I figured out meant, "love you even though you hate me." I texted back: *luetusm*—love you even though you screwed me. Sense of humor or no, I was relieved when he told me there were no liens on the property.

And an interesting thing happened as we exchanged texts that day. He messaged me saying he was at an AA meeting. *Well, there you go*, I said to myself. While I was encouraged by his step toward recovery it couldn't mean as much to me as it would have a year ago. And that was a good thing. His recovery was his business not mine. I'd learned that much in Al-Anon.

Micki thought the house would sell by April and indeed we got a serious offer in March by a couple in their thirties with a toddler. I was excited and not completely surprised because the home, described as "mint" in the ads, showed beautifully. The $100,000 renovation, only five years old, infused the house with a warm blend of vintage and contemporary, large high-ceiling open–space rooms coupled with restored moldings, parquet floors, glass doorknobs, and working tiled fireplace. It was the home I had always dreamed I would own.

When I met the buyers, the Sheldons, the wife, Kim, had told me how much her year-and-a-half-old daughter liked to sashay through the house. *Yup. It's big enough for that. Your daughter can sashay all she wants once you own it.*

I had dropped the price twice to get this offer and wanted desperately to close. I was anxious to check off the biggest item on my financial tickler list. Gary, our friend who managed the original closing fifteen years earlier and with whom Josh had been working, offered to handle the closing without charge. I added his generosity to a long string of assistance people had given me.

As we waited for the closing, which would happen in a few months, I continued my daily work-a-day routine: up at six fifteen a.m. to catch the seven thirty-five commuter train.

Since the beginning of the year, my work as editor at the non-profit had ramped up to include a multi-book project. My old boss, who had supported me, had left and I had been promoted to a manager position. The staff I had been promised never materialized and as a result I stumbled along, working long hours and diligently completing the planning and content of the series. Even with my troubles at home,

I never missed a day but things were not working out in this new position as I had hoped: I was working harder than ever but didn't seem to make progress toward completion of the books. Soon enough, I was told I would be shifted into a new role. At first I was relieved because I could feel the lack of progress in the project yet was helpless as to how to fix it. The new position, however, carried a twenty percent pay cut. Nearly $1,000 a month less in my take-home pay! I felt crushed. Most days, by mid-morning, no matter how hard I focused on my work and wore the mask of positivity, I found myself in the ladies room stifling sobs, spilling tears for every event that had happened: from my romance with Claire and the pain it caused; the tentacles of 9/11, the death of my vibrant sister-in-law Wendy, the parabolic rise of Josh's slavish addictions and desperate acts, and the loss of my home and everything I believed I could count on.

So many mornings I left the house with Josh asleep. His job had become waiting for his sentencing and he was exhausted from pacing and watching old movies into the wee hours. I found copies of emails, however, that pointed to his work with his posse of business associates. Emails that mentioned things I still had no familiarity with: bank trust agreements, surplus contribution agreements, confidentiality agreements, and bank swifts for private international investments. Plus, I'd found a record of fresh Western Union and MoneyGram wire transfers sent to such people as the wife of the Filipino client and other shady folks like Oscar. Over one six-month period in 2006, Josh had completed international money transfers totaling $72,000, with fees of $1,800. These payments not only stoked my fury but helped me recognize where all the money had gone. Though I believe he felt he was funding business prospects I knew Josh was lining the pockets of hucksters. His disease was deep; he was hooked on a classic get-rich-quick notion he couldn't dump—one that pulled him along and buried him. It was much easier to feel compassion when my husband had gotten into drug treatment because no one chooses addiction, but the fact remained: he had gambled our home and family, life together, hundreds of thousands of dollars, his livelihood, and now faced incarceration as a result of a scam. Not a penny ever materialized while my husband chased the dragon and the pipedream.

During the day, Josh looked after Mel, his dad, whose heart disease made it hard for him to walk from room to room. In and out of the hospital and rehabilitation, Josh's dad had once fallen in the bathroom when we were visiting the rehab facility. Seeing Mel on the tile floor was heartbreaking and frightening, his body brittle and helpless. The nurses scooped Josh's dad to the bed and viewing him so vulnerable made me realize how much I owed Mel, who had been my confidante at times and was such a kind, loving gentleman. I also recognized how much Mel needed Josh right now and wondered if the attention Josh was giving his father helped Josh stay sober. I hadn't seen him touch a drink in months.

At the end of April, the Sheldons, our home buyers, signed the contract. I was in the kitchen unpacking groceries—yogurts, a rotisserie chicken—smiling at the satisfaction of cleaning up some of this financial detritus, and wondering who I would be in my new life and where I would live. The very things that had given me such anguish became, momentarily, promising.

Josh bounced into the room.

"Hey listen. We may not have to sell the house." His body eager.

"We already sold it."

"Don't sign so fast," he said. "Wait a couple days. This guy is coming in from California."

"And what?" I ask crumpling plastic grocery bags. "Bringing a million dollars in a suitcase?"

"He says he's coming, bringing coordinates. Nothing like this has ever happened before. Don't you want to keep the house if you can?" By coordinates he meant location markers for secret bank codes.

I knew better than to even look at him. Two crabs in a bucket. One tries to pull the other back in if he tries to climb out.

"I'm signing," I said, "I'm ready to move on." And then my heart sunk. I walked away. That debting disease. Sad.

"Show me the jack post," I said changing the subject and proud that I remembered the name of the small wooden ballast we had installed to support a beam in the basement. Besides the permit for the new water heater, the jack post was one of the few items the buyers' engineer requested.

My conversations with the soon-to-be new owner, Kim, were pleasant as we discussed furniture the couple might be interested in buying. I had gathered all the appliance booklets, take-out menus, even my house journal to leave them as a moving-in gift. We had even left the sound system speakers mounted and wired throughout the downstairs as well as the audio component that controlled the speakers for each room, including the outdoor deck. Josh had labeled each knob: Kitchen, Dining Room, Living Room, Den, so you could hear the music in the room you wished. Music was such a part of our home I couldn't see tearing the speaker wires down when it was all ready for the new family.

Before we went downstairs to look at the post, Josh retrieved a Chapstick from his cubby, a series of little mail slots we had designed and labeled for each family member.

"My lips are chapped from kissing you," he joked as he applied the Chapstick over his plump lips. I couldn't help but smile. As I reached the bottom of the basement stairs, I noticed how much Josh had packed, boxes stacked and marked, and the empty floor space where bookshelves had been. *He's packing up his home too.* He must have felt unfathomable guilt.

In the meantime, Josh had conference dates, meetings with the judge, where he and his lawyer Mark negotiated his plea, all moving closer and closer to a sentencing hearing.

And, then, suddenly, boom! The revelation of another escrow account he had pilfered.

Freney was not the only client my husband had "borrowed" money from.

"The hits just keep on coming," I exclaimed when Josh told me.

Mark told Josh it could mean another surrender at the police station and I imagined it would result in additional news coverage and another story in the newspaper.

✦

Erica, my lovely therapist, ushered me into her office. She was warm and excited to see me.

"You're selling the house for a reason," she reminded me. "To put yourself on solid financial footing."

"I know these things somewhere in the recesses of my being, but hearing you say it makes it sound real."

"Well, you have good sense. You make good decisions."

I nodded a thank you. The same Kandinsky print I had been looking at for years behind Erica's head had not changed. It offered a consistent visual puzzle, just like the circumstances I discussed in that room. No answers, just lines, colors, and choices of interpretation.

"And why am I going to live with my sister?"

She smiled. "You know."

"To get on my feet?" I whispered.

My moving into someone else's house was almost too painful to say out loud. That Josh and I were moving out of our home, the family breaking up, and I going to live in a bedroom in my sister Christine and brother-in-law Roger's split level home was almost too deflating to bear. I was very grateful my sister had offered space to breathe, a break from the weight of the mortgage and house expenses, and a way for me to afford to keep Adam in college. The hardship letter I had written asking the college to lend support to my son in the face of his father's incarceration went nowhere as the financial aid office only made exceptions for job loss and death of a parent.

"And maybe this closes a chapter on your enabling behavior, too," Erica suggested. I loved when she stated her perceptions, not always making me work for it.

✦

"Cause it's witchcraft. That crazy witchcraft," my sister Laura and I sang, arms around each other's shoulders, at a cozy Italian restaurant on Newbury Street in Boston. It was the night before Matthew's graduation from Northeastern University, the middle of May.

Tipsy, my sisters and I liked to sing, the way we used to as kids when my father strummed guitar and we all sang old Italian love songs.

"'Witchcraft' just may be the greatest song ever written," I insisted, holding my goblet of wine up to our waiter, for a pour. "And although I know it's strictly taboo…"

"You say that about every song," Laura said.

"And my beautiful son," I gushed. Matthew looked over shyly, grinning an uncomfortable half smile, eyes pleading to stop.

We toasted to Matthew graduating early in his music program. He'd already completed three studio internships and had moved to Los Angeles to start a career as a recording engineer and singer/songwriter.

"Okay, everybody has to say one thing nice about Matthew," I insisted.

Everyone—Laura, Christine, Roger, and Josh—sighed a collective groan. Josh's dad was not well enough to make the trip and Adam had semester finals so he couldn't come.

"You've been groaning at my requests since forever," I slurred. I saw the waiter roll his eyes when our voices shrieked and I didn't care because there had been so little to celebrate and I was going to enjoy this night.

"Yesterday when we were having lunch at the diner," I said to Matthew. "I looked into your eyes—the brown and the blue—and remembered holding you as an infant.

"One eye blew this way; one eye blew that way," said Josh.

"Oh that joke again, the one-liner from the dais of over-told jokes," I groaned. "But, the intensity of that baby gaze," I said getting quickly back to the subject of my son.

Matthew squirmed. "Thank you, Mama. Love you."

"I love you, man," Josh said as he raised his Diet Pepsi in the direction of his son.

Christine chimed in and imitated Matthew, at age three, dictating to the adults that the Little Mermaid video be played over and over, from the beginning, from Ariel's solo on the rock. "Play it from the beginning…" she shrieked.

We ended the night with Matthew leaving to meet up with his college friends for a final goodbye as we walked back to the hotel in the warm spring air.

The graduation ceremony took place the next day, at the TD Garden, near the North End of Boston. Josh and I sat next to each other and I elbowed him, pointing to Matthew's name in the program, graduating cum laude. We smiled like idiots. It seemed such a cliché to be proud of a child on graduation day but as I watched the sea of graduates flow into the arena, I felt unabashed joy that Josh and I, sitting close together despite the hurt and disappointment, could watch our son achieve this milestone. And when Matthew's name was called, his mortarboarded head a dot on the landscape in a cavernous place, we all shouted and whistled. I was proud of my son and grateful, too, that the tuition payments for one kid were over. With no more private university tuition to pay, I felt lighter. And with the house expenses soon coming off my plate, I enjoyed, in that moment, one plump drop of freedom in my bucket.

I'd made a lunch reservation at an Italian *grotto* restaurant in the North End where the doors would be wide open to reveal hand-painted Venetian scenes, and tables would be clustered *a familia*. I chose the restaurant with care, wanting our lunch to be special and elegant. I'd saved cash in an envelope to treat everyone.

We walked along the serpentine cobblestone streets on our way to the restaurant, passing Italian bakeries with baba rhum cakes in the window.

"We have to check the separation agreement," I heard Josh say softly on his cell phone, "and speak to Antonia."

"What's going on?" I asked, suddenly very afraid.

He sighed.

"There's an IRS claim on the house," he answered, annoyed at me for asking.

"You said you checked at the courthouse in March!" I spat struggling to keep my voice down.

"Relax. I did. One was put on since," he whispered.

I grew quiet as I hauled my body uphill, trying to appear as if nothing was wrong. As my sisters remarked about the North End's style of row houses and how they reminded them of our grandmother's in Brooklyn, I smiled and added, "Yup. Could see Grandma Lucy leaning on a pillow on the windowsill."

My mind circled through the solutions—call Antonia, the tax attorney, tomorrow, appeal to the IRS, get this taken care of, somehow. I didn't fully understand how these things worked but knew I needed to fix this. And quickly: the buyers wouldn't hold on forever and mortgage commitments expire. I shook my head as I gave my husband the once-over.

"You have dug us into this well with your fucking recklessness," I muttered as I sidled up to him. He looked at me, pained.

The ride home in Josh's dad's Volvo sedan, which we had to borrow for the five-and a half hour trip because our mini van had ridden its final miles, was tight and airless. Five of us were jammed together and the Friday night traffic into New York City made the trip interminable. After we arrived home and Matthew dashed out of the house to meet up with friends, I let my rage off the leash, screaming at Josh for every sin he had committed. In AA, there's a saying: First it gets bad. Then it gets worse. Then it gets difficult. Then it gets real.

At eight thirty the next morning, a Saturday, I called Gary from our home office. The trees outside appeared tender in their new blooms and I noticed the spread of the maple's limbs reaching farther over the neighbor's garage.

"There isn't much I can tell you," Gary said. "We'll call Antonia but I think we have to give the buyers back their down payment. Don't think you're going to be able to sell this house. I'm really sorry."

"The Sheldons are coming today, you know. To measure. What do I do?"

"Nothing, yet. Until we talk to Antonia."

"Can't we call her today? I can't wait."

Late in the afternoon, Allen, the husband home buyer, climbed the stairs talking on his cell phone.

"I'm at the new house," he reported, phone trapped between his ear and shoulder. He cast his tape measure behind Josh's pine desk to measure the width of the room. He never looked at me.

Then it hit me: *it won't be my house much longer. I won't come home to this porch. I won't gaze at the sky through the eyebrow window. I won't wait for the burst of the weeping cherry. I won't be greeted by the word Chutzpah chiseled into the garden stone. I won't glance at the handprints of my children in cement. I won't put my key in the door and say I'm home.*

✦

"I've done everything and now the IRS is going to take it all?" I pleaded to Antonia, over the phone.

I was at my office, looking at the west side of Manhattan: weathered water towers squatting on rooftops, asserting themselves amidst the landscape of cement and steel.

Before Antonia agreed to represent me—to ask the IRS to release the lien and give me the ability to sell the house—I had written her a sprawling email recapping the events. I told her about the refinance and the negatively amortizing loan, the crushing debt, Josh's mug shot in the newspaper, the law practice he no longer had, his runaway business schemes, my taxes filed separately, Josh's drug problem, the big red cups of vodka, the kids in college, my DA buddies.

Spilling it to her felt good.

"I'm going to do everything I can for you," she responded.

My body loosened. I'd been carrying inside me the stress of these bundled events. A seasoned tax lawyer like Antonia understood the enormity of what had happened! She was sympathetic and prepared to stand in front of me—with her arsenal of knowledge and experience—to fight for what I deserved. She didn't even know me but recognized I deserved relief. The generosity of her spirit stemmed the depletion of mine. I could've easily traveled towards victimhood and self-pity, but she fueled me with fight.

"We're looking at three possibilities," she explained in her rapid-fire speech. I listened intently, jotting notes. "One: The IRS will take all the proceeds. Two: They'll take Josh's half. Or three: They'll let you have the total. I have no idea how they're going to rule. We file the petition, then we wait."

"We're not even looking at a lot of money," I said, "but I'd better come out with something." I wanted to add, "or my spirit will be crushed," but I was afraid I would cry if I said those words.

She gathered the exhibits, including our separation agreement, and summed up the details in her memo to the IRS:

Ms. Lombardi is currently in contract to sell her home out of dire financial necessity. Ms. Lombardi has been advised she does not have marketable title due to the federal tax lien against her husband. Therefore, she is unable to sell her home until the lien is released. Unfortunately, Ms. Lombardi is unable to maintain the home because of the harm caused by her husband, and is at the brink of foreclosure.

Mr. P, having betrayed his wife on many levels, had promised the world. Unfortunately, the emotional and financial position he had placed the family in is irreparable. The money from the sub-prime mortgage he had convinced his wife to co-sign was rapidly depleted by his investment in a business deal which never materialized and to feed his addiction. Since Mr. P was earning very little money and was secretive as to the source of his funds, his wife elected to file separately in order not to have any unknown tax liability. The fact that Mr. P's tax liabilities are preventing her from selling the house is an additional obstacle to his wife's ability to provide for herself and her family.

We, therefore, respectfully request that you provide us with documentation suitable to the Title Company which will allow the sale of the property and Ms. Lombardi the right to go forward without being punished for her husband's actions and provide for her family.

I prayed for the willingness to surrender. Let my Higher Power handle what I couldn't. Then I waited.

After sweating through thirty-one days, waiting for a ruling, Antonia called.

"Good thing your buyers got an extension on their mortgage commitment. The IRS is discharging the property from the tax lien."

"Thank God! And…am I coming out with any money?"

"They're taking the amount Josh would've had coming to him,

pending the sale of the house, according to the separation agreement."
I thought for a moment about the agreement and realized yes, I had
agreed he would get $22,500 of the sale proceeds in exchange for his
relinquishing any claim on my pension. That I had agreed to give him
even a penny from the sale ticked me off, but I followed a wise Al-
Anon slogan: "Look back, but don't stare."

I added up the numbers quickly in my head: The sale of the home
I loved and had supported for fifteen years, and whose value had tripled
to nearly $600,000 would net me a paltry $25,000. And I was grateful.
It would've broken me to come out with nothing. I said a prayer of
gratitude because with each dollar of debt leaving me, I shed a layer of
my troubles.

CHAPTER 22

Journal entry from May 27, 2010:

Josh left the house at six thirty a.m. to be arraigned on a second charge: A class D Felony, grand larceny. He was turning himself in. He dressed like he was going to court as an attorney—tailored brown pants and short-sleeve tan shirt. He smelled clean, fresh. He leaned over the bed and I hugged him goodbye.

Only days before, we had talked about this second charge. A second felony charge, he explained, would mean a longer prison sentence and more money to pay towards restitution.

"If I could come up with some money, my sentence might be reduced." He looked at me expectantly.

"Money from where?" I chuckled.

"You have money. Your 401K."

"No. I won't be touching that," I answered.

As with the first account, I asked about the clients whose estate he pilfered. I was afraid I might hear a familiar name and feel betrayed on their behalf. I had known many of my husband's clients by name—the Schramms, Taylors, and Giordanos, and felt a kinship even though I had never met them. I was relieved the client's name was not familiar to me.

"The escrow money had been slotted to pay taxes, like with Freney," he said. We faced each other on the couch, Josh looking down at his hands.

"What do you mean?"

"The money wasn't coming out of their pockets. It was going to the IRS."

"Is that supposed to make it okay?"

"It's not supposed to make it anything. It's the truth." He looked at me, clear eyed.

I winced.

"The truth? That went the way of your Truth cap, blown onto the railroad tracks."

"Yup. I guess the truth just floated away," he said.

I felt sanguine about this second felony charge—like being less anxious with a second baby. I feared the arrest would make the news and we'd have to deal with the exposure and shame once more. But even that felt manageable. As it turned out, the second arrest never went public.

As we inched toward the house closing—one month away—another obstacle arose: the removal of the $20,000 bail bond, which I had guaranteed using the house as collateral, on the day of Josh's arraignment—the day I visited the bail bondsman. We had used the house as collateral so we didn't have to come up with the $20,000 in cash. I had paid a $1,400 fee for the right. Now, to sell the house we had to have the bond removed. It would be considered another lien.

The bail bondsman would remove the bond—and give us a signed letter we could present at the closing—when the bond was replaced by cash or guaranteed by someone else's property.

I couldn't imagine who would put up their home for Josh's bail bond. The lien removal could be handled at the closing but we needed to have the money that day. And I was afraid that if we didn't have the $20,000 it would come out of the meager proceeds from the sale of the house.

"You're going to have to ask your father, Josh," I said.

"We'll handle it at closing," he replied.

I knew this would be a hard thing for Josh to ask his dad, not doing well in St. Francis heart hospital. We had been visiting regularly. His dad looked frail.

And thus began an argument between me and Josh, fueled by Gary, our friend and attorney, who agreed that it would be better to remove the bail bond lien before the closing.

Soon, Gary called me at work, mid-afternoon on a busy day. I was surrounded by emails, meeting requests, and deadlines.

"Did you tell Josh to call me?" he snorted.

"What are you talking about?"

"I swear, if he calls me again I won't handle this closing. You'll have to find someone else to take this case!"

"Wait a minute," I said. "Is this about the bail bond?"

"Of course! Josh's insisting it can be satisfied at the closing. And he accused me of telling the buyer's attorney that the second mortgage is a bail bond. Like I would tell the attorney that he's under prosecution."

"Well…"

"I didn't tell anybody your crazy husband is going to jail."

I groaned.

"Look, just calm down," I said. "Josh's dad has agreed to put up the money for the bond."

"I don't care. If Josh calls me one more time and tells me I'm a liar, I can't represent you. He can't get away with that." It sounded like a line from a B-grade western.

"All right Gary," I said. "Do what you gotta do."

I hung up. The thought of finding another attorney made me want to weep. I knew I couldn't use Josh as closing attorney, even though he was still a member of the Bar. I needed to find another lawyer, to make sure I was represented well and fully. I had learned that much. Yet the lines of trust and love and forgiveness were blurry. I wanted my husband at the closing. I couldn't shake thinking of him as a protector. I yearned to feel that we were still in this together, as a couple, a family who loved each other. I knew it would be the last thing we did together before we'd separate.

A few minutes later, my cell phone buzzed.

"Do you know how many closings I've done?" Josh asked.

I went into a nearby conference room and closed the door.

"The bond can be handled at the closing!," he yelled. "And Gary had no right to tell the buyer's attorney about my prosecution."

I shook my head, inhaling loudly.

He just wants to be right, to be the better lawyer. God, I didn't need these two idiots fighting.

"Please," I begged, "Let's just get this bail bond released."

"You'll sell your house," he barked.

We hung up and I dabbed my eyes with a crumpled up napkin I found in my pocket. The tears were not only from frustration but from a deeper recognition that my husband, even in these last months, wasn't protecting me. That love and comfort I'd grown to depend on were absent. There was no secure ground no matter how hard I kept looking for it.

When I got back to my desk, there was an email from Gary:

Sorry. I wouldn't just 'bail' on you. Of course, I'll handle the closing.

Over the next few weeks, we removed our furniture and belongings little by little. My sister Christine and I had cleaned out the attic—the dark, musty space with the chalet ceiling—that had been filled with old toys, sports trophies, ski clothes, books, boxes of old birthday cards, and the boys' artwork from pre-K to high school. In short, our past.

The attic air was thick as the June temperature sweltered and my sister and I rifled through the piles. Beads of sweat dotted my forehead and the back of my neck felt clammy. Christine was a task master and I needed that: If I'd held onto a piece of macaroni–glued artwork for more than a few moments, she'd hold open the black Hefty trash bag and gesture for me to toss it.

"They're only going to throw it away when you die," she directed.

I kept a few pieces such as a small Mother's Day quilt Adam had decorated in second grade. The teacher had sewn the quilt from assorted fabrics we had given her—Adam's outgrown baseball flannel pajamas and red-and-blue polka dot fabric from a Halloween costume Josh had made. Adam had Magic Markered the saying: *Happy Moter's Day!* I couldn't bear to part with it.

When we were done, the dusty floorboards were visible. The space looked empty and gloomy.

Between packing up the house and making arrangements to move, I started negotiating with the Bank of America to settle on payment of the outstanding $38,000 loan. I was hoping to settle for twenty-five cents on the dollar, making the payoff around $10,000.

I had gotten to this point of negotiation after some months of investigating why my name had been attached to Josh's credit line in the first place. First, I called and wrote Bank of America requesting that my name be taken off the account. I realized quickly they had no intention of releasing me just because I had asked. The proof from Bank of America that I was a co-signer was a ridiculous one-page computer print-out of their "comments record," and internal processing sheet, saying, in code:

the CCO stating OK to add COAPP, only 10K of addtnl rvlvng dbtI.

This meant nothing to me but it did seem to matter to the bank. They still claimed I was a co-signer.

"Look, I did some research," I said to Gary on the phone trying to enlist some help. "There's a New York state General Obligations Law and Federal Trade Commission rule that requires a co-signer to sign." I paused fumbling for the page I'd printed out from the Internet and read, "A contract describing the obligation to pay. Prior to signing, the co-signer must be given written disclosure, in at least ten-point type, explaining that the co-signer is agreeing to pay; the co-signer may be sued on the obligation; and the co-signer may be liable for fees."

"Yeah, and."

"I never signed anything. They called me at my office and I answered a couple of questions. I didn't know I was agreeing to be a co-signer."

"Well, get in line. You think BOA," Gary said with a mocking tone around the acronym, "is going to say, hey I'm sorry. You're off the hook. They want you more than ever. You're the only one who might pay them something."

"What should I do? Stop paying them so I can negotiate?"

"As opposed to what?"

"Suing them…for my never having signed any agreement to be a co-signer."

"Sue Bank of America? Know what that's going to cost? And more time and interest accruing on the money owed? Settle with them so I can stop seeing that damn BOA in the subject line from you."

I had spoken to a credit repair expert. He suggested I stop making payments to gain leverage if I wanted to make a settlement, meaning in a few months I would offer to pay a portion of the debt and they might forgive the rest. I knew this came with a tax liability, too, that I'd have to pay income taxes on the difference between the full amount of the debt and the agreed-upon payoff if Bank of America would agree.

Making a decision not to pay a bill in full scared me. I was intimidated by the power of the banks. Growing up, my parents wouldn't dream of not paying their bills. You keep things simple; you don't chew off more than you can pay; and you don't welch on your debts. It's a matter of integrity. Plus, it felt just plain wrong not to pay back your debts. On a practical level, I didn't want delinquent payments bringing down my credit score. Mostly, I felt afraid to make this decision on my own—without Josh and the blame I could cast onto him if it didn't work out. But I was willing. I could be afraid and still do it. As I heard someone say in an Al-Anon meeting, "I don't have to like the way it feels but I can do it anyway."

I designated BOA debt as tickler item number two on the list of the three financial headaches I needed to divest: the house, BOA credit line, and the Hilton hotel time share. The BOA credit line payments were $890 a month, almost twenty percent of my take-home pay. Josh had missed some payments which, of course, affected my credit, and now he wasn't paying at all. I was making all the payments—by cash at the teller window. So I stopped making payments.

Now, ready to settle, I needed Josh's help because he was the primary account holder. I didn't expect any money from him, since he had none, but I wanted him to negotiate with the bank. I had grown to handle all financial obligations on my own, breaking the dependence we'd shared. So relying on him even to do something as simple as call the bank and keep up the correspondence made me feel vulnerable. I didn't want to be disappointed or worse, angry and frustrated, if he didn't cooperate.

At around six thirty p.m., Josh sat in the office and I insisted he call the bank at that moment. Half-filled cardboard boxes sat in the corner of the room.

"Why do you want to do this now?" he asked. "Don't you have enough expenses with moving and Adam's tuition coming?"

I paused for a second, thinking he might be right. But then I remembered not to listen. I asked myself what I wanted to do.

"I want to get this over with," I replied. "I want to be debt-free."

He looked at me, puzzled.

"Call them."

"Suit yourself."

He dialed and put the phone on speaker.

We offered the bank $7,500 to settle and they wouldn't take anything less than twenty-five cents on the dollar, what I was willing to pay. The final settlement amounted to a little over $9,000, which I agreed to pay out in three installments. Even though I had never spent a penny running up this account I was happy to pay it because I wanted it all behind me. Another layer of relief washed over me as I checked off the payoff of the Bank of America credit line as the second accomplishment on my tickler list.

As we got ready to move out the middle of July, the same month we had moved in, the house felt large and echo-y, the only sound the whirr of Josh's power drill disassembling furniture and pulling anchor screws out of the wall. One evening, the Home Run Derby was on television. Over the years, I'd heard about this baseball competition from Josh and the boys, always chattering about it on the night before the All-Star game. The TV volume was low, Josh never even glancing at the screen as we shoveled framed photos and kitchen gadgets into cartons. The raspberry-colored couch I'd lain awake on during so many middle of the nights—obsessing, recounting events, trying to understand how and why things had gone so badly and always hoping to be called back to bed by Josh—sat and waited to be moved into a storage unit. We were not alone. Our pain and shame of borrowing too much reflected the new American landscape of unfolding economic failure, the shadow side of the American dream.

"Should we keep all these nutcrackers?" I said holding up a plastic bag filled with the silver nutcrackers my parents had enjoyed on Thanksgiving Day.

He looked like a ghost, tired, eyes rimmed with dark.

"Not unless you can fit me in one."

I chuckled, then started to cry.

"I'm sorry," I said.

"Why? What are you sorry about?"

"I don't know."

I looked around. The china cabinet was gone. I remembered the day we had bought the beautiful, brass drawer pulls from the funky hardware store on Magazine Street in New Orleans.

The olive-green living room sofa, we had inherited from Josh's parents' house, was gone, donated, and in its place stood the metal folding table littered with packing tape and bubble wrap. The stones from the garden – engraved with the words *Chutzpah* and *Imagine* – sat on the porch waiting for a new home somewhere as were the small smooth stones I'd collected from Shelter Island—the flattest stones and the oval pale-blue specimens I could find the day I walked the beach. And my acoustic guitar—a gift from my parents on my fifteenth birthday—retrieved from the curb three times, leaned against the wall.

Later, in my bedroom, I looked at the framed photo of the four of us at Splish Splash water park: Adam, a year old, and Matthew, four, our family so filled with promise. Josh had cleared off his collection of ephemera: paper items shoved into the frame of our bedroom mirror, the cover of the playbill from the Broadway show "Prelude to a Kiss," a handful of paper cranes, and photos of him and his dad. It was a strange place to store the bits of one's life and although the untidiness had irritated me from time to time the collection was an homage, a physical tag cloud to our lives, an altar, perhaps, and upon seeing it all cleared away I felt hollow.

By the end of the night, when I walked back into our bedroom, I saw Josh sitting cross-legged on our bed in Matthew's black graduation gown.

"You always did love props, you buffoon." I laughed.

He stood up slowly, the black gown swaying. As he left the room, he turned toward me. "Good night, students," he said.

The next day, I settled into my meditation cushion, as I had been doing for two years. I loved to gaze on the neighbor's maple tree and had even made a pencil sketch of its bare branches during the winter.

I was especially looking forward to seeing the tree that morning, to feel comforted by its lush, full summer leaves. As I got onto the floor, something didn't look right. I felt a little panicky at first until it hit me: the maple was gone. It had vanished. My eye kept circling the window looking for it. I put on my shoes and dashed around the corner and stood in front of the neighbor's house. The sight startled me. A mount of dirt and tire marks held the spot where the majestic tree had been.

Later that week, Josh called me at work. He sounded distraught and could hardly get his words out.

"My dad," he said, "My dad."

Josh's dad died that morning in St. Francis Hospital. Josh had been getting ready to visit him, as he did nearly every day, when he got the call. I felt sad we hadn't been at his bedside. For over thirty years, Josh's dad had been very loving to me; it had been only nine months since we lost Wendy.

Josh and I identified the body later that day. I had never seen Josh's dad without his glasses.

Another mournful service, two days of sitting shiva, and waiting. At least Josh's dad didn't have to witness his son, later that year, begin his long-awaited prison sentence.

✦

Micki, my real estate broker, arrived early at my house for the three p.m. walkthrough the day before closing. Josh had left to bring a carload to the local dump—the back of the station wagon piled high. Though we hadn't discussed his being at the walkthrough I was glad he was gone and sensed that his shame had kept him away.

A walkthrough gives the buyer the right to inspect the property, to make sure all the agreed-upon repairs—such as the jack post installed in the basement—were completed and met with their satisfaction.

The house was nearly empty but for two massive oak wall units in the living room, a smaller bookshelf and the desk in the office. The buyers had expressed interest in buying those pieces so we left them.

It was an exhausting feat—moving the contents of our four-bed-

room house to various places—the curb, the town dump, friends' base-
ments and attics, the rented storage unit, Josh's brother's house in upper
Westchester—where Josh would be living until his sentencing—and
my sister's home, where Adam and I were bound. Matthew had moved
to Los Angeles. When he came home for visits he would no longer be
sleeping in his old bedroom.

We had said goodbye to our neighbors with tears and promises to
visit. I even videoed Adam, in his white muscle t-shirt, interviewing
Beau, the three-year-old cherub-cheeked boy next door, and swinging
him in a seat Adam made with his arms.

Throughout the packing, I willed myself to go through the mo-
tions, to keep my river of sadness at bay. I was afraid that if I started to
cry I wouldn't stop. I promised myself a long indulgent sob when I got
to my sister's house but before that I would steel myself. And I found
I could.

In preparing for the walkthrough, I noticed the light in the upstairs
linen closet was out even after I replaced the bulb. We hadn't had any
problems with the electricity. Yet I needed to tell the buyers so nothing
would look like a cover-up.

Micki and I greeted Allen and Kim with their team of co-brokers,
Sybil and Frances, veterans in real estate sales, as they arrived. Kim, who
I had been waiting to hear back from about the sale of the furniture and
the dining room fixture, looked angry from the moment she entered.

In the living room, Allen and Kim inspected the windows, pushing
our white sheer curtains aside, peering into the fireplace, and looking
closely at the parquet floors. I thought about how naively Josh and I
had done our walkthrough—we hadn't even noticed the fourteen broken windows. Throughout the fifteen years of ownership, we had main-
tained our house meticulously, and just to make sure the walkthrough
went well, scrubbed every corner.

I pointed to our black multi-room audio component still wired to
the speakers and sitting on the floor in the corner.

"We're leaving the unit. Since it's already set up." I felt a lump in
my throat because I always loved the music in our home, the soul of us,
which so deeply saturated us, especially our musician son.

Kim thanked me with a nod, her lips pursed and tight.

"Are you still interested in buying the fixture?" I asked pointing to the dining room chandelier, which had a graceful curved iron frame. Kim stopped abruptly.

"Why would I pay you for a fixture included in our contract?" she asked. I backed away.

"The contract includes a fixture," I said, "but this is brand new and rather expensive. We're selling it for a fraction of what it cost."

"I'm not paying you a cent," she declared, her bulky body planted firmly.

I paused, glancing at Micki's quizzical expression.

No one said anything for a few moments. My face reddened.

"Look, if it really means that much, take it."

Kim's eyes were filled with fire as she turned towards me. "And I don't want your husband at the closing tomorrow. He's a convicted felon!"

I stumbled backwards almost not sure I'd heard the words correctly. Throughout the ordeal, no one had spoken to me that way.

"What does my husband have to do with you and this house?" I said now steaming.

"No one's been convicted of anything," Micki said.

"And I'll invite anyone I want to the closing." I added.

"And, you," Kim shrieked, turning to Micki, "you're an asshole! You never returned our emails. Is there something wrong with you?"

Micki's jaw fell and her eyes welled up.

Kim continued pointing into the family room. "I want those wall units removed today!"

"I thought you wanted them," I said, worried about how we were going to remove eight-foot solid oak units before the next morning.

"We want them out," Kim screamed.

Sybil and Frances approached Kim to calm her. She shrugged them off and told me she was calling her lawyer because the house was supposed to be "broom clean." She pushed the sliding glass doors and bolted out to the deck. Her husband ran after her.

Micki and I huddled with the two brokers. Micki explained she

had never received any emails from Kim or the brokers about the furniture or anything. I told them Kim hadn't returned my calls so I thought
they wanted the furniture. I saw Kim outside on her cell phone gesticulating wildly as her husband lingered near her.

Kim's about-face of harshness felt like a mystery until I realized
what had happened: someone must have told the Sheldons' lawyer that
the second mortgage, now lifted by the bail bondsman since Josh's dad
had posted cash to replace the house as collateral, was in fact a bail
bond. She must've done some research to conclude that he had been
prosecuted. And she was going to let me know what she thought of
that.

Kim slipped back into the house.

"I'll wait in the car," she sputtered.

As Allen and the brokers were getting ready to leave, we paused by
the front door.

"I've been nothing but respectful to you and your wife," I said.
"And I'd expect the same. Is this the kind of energy you want to bring
in your new home?"

"You know, it all has taken its toll," Allen said, "and it's taken a very
long time to close."

"It's only been four months," I reminded him. "And I have bent
over backwards to make this happen. Is this really the way you want to
leave it?"

He apologized.

"It's been stressful," he added.

"She really needs to get control of herself."

After they left, I turned to Micki who was crying now.

"Micki, this is not about us. We've done everything with courtesy
and respect. This is not about us."

The next day the closing took place at the bank's lawyer's office
and Kim did not come. Gary did not appear either; he sent one of his
associates. Earlier that morning, Gary told me on the phone that Kim
had called her lawyer the night before in tears apologizing for her behavior.

"If she really wanted to apologize, she could've called me," I said.

"Buying a house doesn't always bring out the best in people," Gary responded. And I had to agree.

The closing went easily. Josh and I, and Allen and his lawyer finished the proceeding quickly and cordially. We even joked during the process.

As we exited, Josh and I took the stairs together to the building's garage that opened onto a busy boulevard. Cars sped by, the late afternoon sun hovering. Our station wagon was filled high.

"You sure you gonna make it to Westchester?" I asked. "You can't see out the back window." The back tires were low from the weight.

He shrugged. He started to say something, then stopped. The air conditioning didn't work so Josh had taped a mini battery-operated fan onto the dashboard. I felt sad for him.

We looked at each other for a long minute with regret and longing, then hugged quickly, got into our cars, and drove in opposite directions. Two weeks later at the end of July, on my birthday, Josh pled guilty in county court to grand larceny in the second degree, a class C felony, and grand larceny in the third degree, a class D felony.

CHAPTER 23

Journal entry from July 2010:

I am in the thicket of some strange woods—dense with confusion. I am grabbing at any branch for relief but the pain distorts everything. I keep trying to feel better, do something differently, rage maybe to purge this feeling of unfairness. Then I remind myself… I won't feel better for a long, long time.

I felt relief from having sold the house. But the price for that assuagement was a mixture of incredulity at what had happened and a clutching to retrieve my life as I had known it. I longed for what had been, chaotic and uncontrollable as it was.

Adam and I moved into Christine's home, with two empty bedrooms, vacated by her grown sons. Chris and Roger's split level—a house style that populated so much of Long Island, the utilitarian upstairs/downstairs design—felt familiar and safe. Yet at times I felt infantilized as I cast myself back into the role of baby sister.

"We'll play games!" Christine said when I arrived, trying to put a positive spin on my bleakness which she could no doubt discern by my shrunken demeanor and listlessness. I woke up and went to sleep in tears but we only talked about the trauma when I came out of my room with puffy eyes.

She and my brother-in-law, Roger, whom I had known since age thirteen, seemed excited to have us. I was concerned, though, about my college son's habit of leaving a trail wherever he went. I called it Adam's wake. Lately, his wake included large tubs of protein powder and whey that sat on the kitchen counter ready for concocting elaborate, multi-ingredient protein shakes. His wake also included a dozen cartons of imported t-shirts that occupied the living room after he launched a t-shirt business. And there was the chin-up bar he'd installed in the doorway of his room. I wondered how long before they were tired of us. And though I dreaded his going back to school in late August, Adam's departure would restore order to my sister's home. Yet my family greeted Adam with hugs and their faces lit up when I came through the door. They added a cable box in my room so I could watch my own programs and helped me shuffle the furniture around to have a comfortable desk area. I stacked my precious books next to my nephew's high school yearbook and copies of *Hot Rod* magazine. Christine and Roger's endless generosity and kindness were beyond anything I'd felt I deserved.

I fell easily into their Friday night ritual of eating sesame crust pizza and joining them on outings like one to the feast at St. Rocco's Church. And though I enjoyed our time and jokes, grief was my companion. Every night when I walked home from the train station meandering around lawn sprinklers, I paused at their front door. My yearning for the familiar fit of the key in my own door robbed me of my breath for a few seconds. Then I gathered myself, turned the key, and stepped in with a smile.

A few weeks after separating, Josh had another shoulder surgery at a nearby hospital and needed to convalesce. He couldn't drive himself home from the procedure and I didn't have the heart to say no. Christine and Roger were agreeable to his staying that night before going back to Westchester.

I wanted to heal and move on in my life but I had no idea what that meant. Those words sounded plausible and sensible to anyone who knew me. If I looked for agreement to the idea of divorcing and moving on, I had plenty of support: people who heralded it, understood it, and told me I deserved it. But really, I wanted to recapture something, like when I was five years old and had left my cardigan at a friend's house around the corner. I ran back in a panic to get it, as if the sweater would evaporate if I didn't get there immediately. So I saw and talked to Josh regularly in an attempt to hold onto something, an impossible-to-guarantee assurance that someday things would be the way they were—in my idealized version anyway. In my sanitized memory of our marriage.

One night I met Josh and other friends at the Fishery, a local pub on a canal, where our friend Bruce's band was playing. When I got into my car at the end of the evening, I saw he had neatly placed Matthew's Yankees cap on the seat, his bluetooth device because I had lost mine, and the motion sickness sea bands we had always kept in our glove compartment because of Adam's car sickness. These little things carved a hole in my heart and restarted the cycle of grieving, questioning, and self-pity.

Finally, I noticed that when I saw Josh, I spent days recovering from the idea that we would be whole again—that when he came out of prison—we could be a family again. We could pick up as if nothing has happened. And it was this hope that was excruciating. This desire for retrieval was crushing me and soon I just wanted him to "go in," as he called it. The waiting for jail time to begin was tough and I, too, wanted to be released.

Soon, Josh told me he would be going in December 14, the day of his sentencing. He expected the judge to give him one to three years for two felony counts.

At Thanksgiving, Josh asked if he could spend the day with us: Adam, Matthew (home from Los Angeles), my family, and me.

"It's easier if I don't see you," I responded. "You can see the boys over the weekend, if you want."

I wondered if I was taking a hard stance to help myself or punish him. But I felt better with less contact and I just wanted him to go to prison already. It had started to feel like a tired story—would you believe, my husband is going to prison!—and I wanted my life to be about more than my husband's crime. I had blessings to be grateful for—two healthy sons, loving family and friends, a place to live for the time being, and my own good health. And I wanted to stop crying. All the crying while wearing my contact lenses had irritated my pupils; I'd gotten an eye infection from the tears, tissues, and rubbing. I was dying for a belly laugh. For days leading up to Thanksgiving, it took all my willpower not to call Josh and say, "I'm sorry, please come home." But I didn't.

✦

"I can't let go," I told Erica the following week in our session. She looked at me hard.

"It's takes years to get over a twenty-seven-year marriage! Especially with circumstances like yours. You really think you could heal like that?" She snapped her fingers.

"I want to feel better. I want to go on."

Erica shifted in her seat. She leaned closer.

"What's the conflict?"

I pulled a tissue from the Kleenex box.

"Well, I'm angry, furious. And hurt."

"At what?"

"Being left with a financial mess and not having any help with tuition or his debt or expenses. We lost our fucking house. And he gets off the hook!"

She was quiet.

"Yeah, he'll have no responsibilities in jail. He'll be able to read and not work and get fed."

She nodded.

"Your anger is healthy. For now, let's set the anger aside." She pointed her fingertips into her palm to indicate a place. "What else?"

I choked back a sob. "So sad that he's going away. He's leaving us. And I don't know how long he'll be gone. So I want to make it right. I want to forgive him and be loving to him. He is, after all, going to prison. How horrible."

"Ok, sadness is understandable. Who wouldn't be sad? But are you tamping down your feelings when you say you want to make it right?"

I thought about this for a minute.

"Yeah, there's a piece of denial that insists it's not so bad. I'm trying to erase the pain, feel better, by convincing myself it's not so bad."

"Ok, let's call that 'back pedaling' and set that in a separate box. What else?"

"Guilt," I said and counted on my fingers each guilty act, "Not recognizing the signs of his desperation, my infidelity, my self-righteous expectation he would take care of me, and my stupid blind trust."

I paused. Tears fell.

"Go on," Erica whispered. She looked teary, too.

"Love. We share a deep love. I can't help it. We had a world—our kids, our home, our friends. I keep thinking about the time we went to the pumpkin patch before we had kids. I was paying and he showed up at the check-out counter with a tiny painted pumpkin. 'This is the prettiest pumpkin,' he said. 'Like you. You're the prettiest pumpkin.' I probably would've forgotten that incident but we kept the 'prettiest pumpkin,' on the windowsill for years. It discolored and got hollow but I didn't throw it away. I can't stop thinking about it. Is that crazy?"

Erica shook her head.

"If he loved me so much," I continued, "why did he destroy us?"

Erica nodded. "He didn't do it to you. He's an addict. Remember, hate the disease but have compassion for the addict."

"I want to stop loving him but I can't. If I could just stop caring, I'd feel better."

"The anger and the love are warring," Erica said. "So, how about we put the love in a separate vessel, inside you, so you can honor it there."

I sobbed. It felt so right. Honor my love. Wow! I had permission to love him…and even celebrate that love.

I was invited to dinner at Josh's brother's a few days before he was to leave for prison and I said yes. Even though I was keeping my distance I couldn't imagine not going to my husband's farewell dinner. I wished our sons could be there, but they were where they were supposed to be. Matthew was in California, working as a recording engineer, and Adam at college in Maryland. They'd been in touch with their father. I kept thinking about them as little boys padding around in their pajamas upstairs at bedtime. And my heart broke. I could separate myself emotionally from Josh, decide whether I wanted to stay married, attached, but they couldn't. They had to sort out their feelings and make peace with their father. I couldn't do that for them.

It was a warm clear December night. The moon and stars lit up the dark road. It was the first time I drove to his brother's house by myself and it was tricky. They lived on an isolated foothill and the road signs were tough to read without streetlights. It was hot in the car, and unseasonably warm outside. I was sweating and thirsty and nervous about the dark road. The GPS directed me but it was still confusing. I was afraid to take my hands off the wheel to swig water from my bottle. I imagined a force, God, my Higher Power, the universe, directing me. Get to Lewis Road, make a left, and yes, I recognized the lake house, up Charring Road, mini mansions set back, their interior lights twinkling. All those families, safe, not driving alone. Letting go of the wheel, I punched Josh's number on my cell. "You're five minutes away," he told me. More lefts and rights, pitch-black sky. I saw their house in the distance through the bare trees and embraced the comfort of the familiar. I pulled into their driveway, stepped into the refreshing air, wishing I could linger outdoors.

Josh looked jaunty in his red Western-style shirt, jeans, and his Tony Lamas. We ate a delicious steak dinner with polite, witty conversation and no mention of Josh leaving for prison, which I was glad for. Later Josh handed me the baby Taylor guitar for Matthew to have and a Christmas gift for me tucked in a bag. He was clear-eyed and peaceful, like the night sky, a long way from the fibrillating, compulsive person nicknamed "Flash" from years ago.

I drove home confidently knowing there would be many long, dark roads for me to travel on my own.

✦

The day Josh went to state prison, an angry wind whipped the flag at the entrance to the county courthouse. I had considered skipping the sentencing since I had been keeping my distance from him lately, but I wanted to see him one last time and had hoped for some closure or at least relief from the parrying between love, grief, and disbelief.

I got lost traversing the court buildings—Josh had told me criminal court was the western-most building in the complex. And, as I asked people for directions to criminal court, I found myself exhibiting some weird swagger: *Yes, I'm headed to criminal court to see my husband. Yup, we're bad. No civil court for me.*

In my haste to arrive on time, however, my eyes welled up, not sure if it was the five-degree air assaulting my face or the deep sadness I'd been cultivating ever since I found that notice from the New York Bar Association in our home fax machine a year-and-a-half ago. I knew we were over then, but I still didn't really know what "over" meant. I could have sued for divorce by now but I didn't. I still felt love despite the position I was in—displaced, in debt, my family scattered. Yet I couldn't squash that love. I couldn't hate him no matter how hard I tried. But with the support of Erica I was learning to honor that love, while letting the anger and all the other feelings breathe. The one thing I was discovering was that when I felt compassion for Josh, I wasn't angry. Anger and compassion couldn't occupy the same space at the same time.

I thought of Josh as the crazy buffoon who made me laugh by wearing a frosted-color Beatles wig on his bald head or the guy who'd escorted our down-and-out friend Michael to the Department of Motor Vehicles to help him pay his back tickets. Could this be the same man spending the next few years in the harsh cement walls of prison? I had heard that state prison was worse than federal but I knew nothing about it, not even how "worse" could be defined. I did know he could be incarcerated anywhere in New York State including near the Canadian border, making weekend visits impossible.

I entered the building, emptied my pockets before going through the metal detector, then walked upstairs. I spied Josh sitting in a cheap, plastic chair at the end of the long, narrow waiting area. He cradled his smart phone, not wanting to lose contact with the world quite yet, I imagined.

As I approached, he stood up and spread his arms before his brother and all the people waiting outside the courtrooms.

"You came!" he exclaimed.

He held his arms wide like he used to when we were first married and I had asked how much he loved me. Now our eyes were moist. I knew it would be a long time before I'd see him on the streets again. Witnessing his joy at my appearance stoked that deep, undeniable love.

There it was, springing from a well, even in the face of all this ugliness.

As we waited, we joked about all the jobs he could do in jail. He liked to grill and brewed a mean cup of coffee so that could qualify him for kitchen duty. Or his status as laundry Nazi at home ("Take off those whites and throw them in the basket!") could translate well.

"Yup, I have a lot of potential," he said.

Heading into the courtroom, Josh handed his cell phone, leather belt, and tube of eczema cream, to his brother. He slipped off his gold wedding band—with our initials and wedding date inscribed on the inside, identical to mine—and slid it into my palm. I closed my hand tight.

Inside the courtroom, a sign, *In God We Trust,* hung over the judge's head. The courtroom was compact, not sprawling like TV courtrooms, filled with police officers, a stenographer, the clerk, the bailiffs, and white-shirted court officers. The harsh fluorescent was intimidating. My short-lived swagger from outside was replaced with the desire to sit up and behave.

"I tried a case in front of this judge eleven years ago," Josh whispered to me.

The room was too hot in the way government offices with ancient cast iron radiators can be. It was right before Christmas, and one of the clerks wore a tie with mini Christmas trees.

The courtroom with its air of indifference was spitting on everything I was—my goodness, my kindness, my soul. How did I end up here, married to this man, not having known what was going on? Yet I was here and couldn't help but think about Josh's guilt, his willingness to admit it, and the destructive power of addiction and its sidekick, denial.

When the court clerk called the case—the People vs. Joshua P.—my husband stepped up to the judge, who was holding his temple and looking down, reading. My heart thudded. Josh stood next to his lawyer and the assistant district attorney who had turned to me earlier with a gracious nod. I wondered if the somberness I sensed around the judge and his bench was due to Josh's having been an attorney with no previous record. Maybe the judge thought of him as one of their own, a family man like himself, who'd made a whopper of a mistake.

"Grand larceny in the second degree, Class C felony ($242,000). Grand larceny third degree, Class D ($125,000). The People recommend to incarcerate one and one-half to four years," said the Assistant District Attorney. When the court officer said the word "felony," I wished Josh had been sitting next to me because what came to mind was a perverse joke he and our niece, Jamie, had shared: she called him Felonious Unc—F.U.—a nickname he'd given himself. I would've turned to him and said, "Yup, Felonious Unc, that's you."

Then, Mark, Josh's lawyer, read a statement.

"My client was a citizen in good standing who became addicted to heroin and adapted a lifestyle as a heroin addict. He's a lawyer, husband, brother, and father. It saddens all of us to see such moral turpitude in such a fine man, whom I've known personally for many years. My client has made admissions to things he didn't have to. He's accepted responsibility and speaks to the willingness to commit to recovery. We ask the court to be consistent with one to three years."

Then Josh spoke. I watched the back of his head.

"I stand before you a new person, your honor. I've been carrying around this shame and guilt for all these years. I stopped drugs and drinking and feel like I'm embarking on a new journey. I'm relieved to be here today. I want to apologize to my clients, my wife, my sons, my brother, the rest of my family, our friends, and to the court. I hope someday I can be forgiven."

The judge granted the sentence in accordance with one to three years. I wondered if the sentencing had anything to do with Josh having given the court $80,000 in restitution, money he had inherited from his father. We had talked about it. I carried some resentment because I could've used that money to pay his debt and the boys' tuitions. Yet I understood. I didn't want him in jail any longer than he had to be and it was right for him to pay back his clients any money he could.

But what about me? I had received very little financial assistance. I was cleaning up the financial mess entirely on my own.

As the bailiff handcuffed him behind his back, Josh asked if he could walk hands free. The bailiff shook his head. Josh looked at me, smiled small and tight, as he walked through the caged-off area towards the door.

As I drove into the parking lot of the motor vehicle office about two miles from the courthouse to register Josh's dad's Volvo to me, I felt the car tug. I got out and saw the right front tire flat. I went into the DMV office, took care of getting new license plates, then called AAA. An hour later, the tow truck came driven by a young black guy, pants hanging low.

"You can go sit in the truck," he offered as he grabbed the tire iron out of his truck. "It's warm and clean. Go ahead." The temperature was well below freezing.

At first I said no, then climbed into the front seat of the cab, engine running. It was spotless and toasty. A sign lay on the dashboard: only one passenger could ride in the truck.

After he finished fixing the flat, putting the donut tire on, I asked if he wouldn't mind screwing the new plates on, which he did.

"It's been some day," I said as I handed him a tip. "My husband went to prison today."

He looked at me with sincere concern.

"I hope not for too long."

"Long enough. One to three," I bragged, like a pro.

This *was* a new beginning, as Josh had said. Maybe for me, too.

CHAPTER 24

The new beginning wasn't the clean break I had hoped for. I found myself still wrestling with what had happened. I lay awake at night in a bed alone trying to reconcile the accounts of the two columns I'd created—one for love and another for betrayal: in the love column would appear a memory: about a year after we met, 1980, Josh and I drove my dad's Chevy Impala, a ten-year-old beast of a car which we'd nicknamed the Love Bomb, a sedan that maneuvered slower than the Queen Mary. Making it up the winding dirt road to the house we'd rented was a questionable endeavor. It had rained and when Josh, driving, made the turn, the Love Bomb refused to go any farther. It slid back onto a log and wouldn't budge. It was well after midnight, no ambient light on the spooky, cricket-noisy road, and we were at least a mile to the house. We got out of the car and in the blindness inspected the Love Bomb. We looked at each other in the dark, and laughed.

We sloughed up the hill holding hands and roaring at our misfortune. That neither of us had gotten upset fueled my belief that we would always work things out; we would always be all right. Also, in the love column was the day we painted our bedroom before we put the house up for sale when he called me the "dainty paintee." I whitewashed the wood trim and windowsills so delicately, he said.

In the betrayal column, very long on the page, appeared such items as the $40,000 gouge into our home equity line of credit for the client's defense even though Josh wasn't even the attorney of record and we never received any money in repayment. Of course, that we no longer owned the home I loved headed the column, in boldface and large print.

There was a third column, too: my own guilt figured onto the ledger, though family and friends pounced if I mentioned that. But I did feel guilty—if I hadn't had the affair with Claire and flirted so overtly with my sexuality, perhaps he wouldn't have tried so desperately to win me back. Maybe he wouldn't have ratcheted up the drug use to cover his pain or felt the need to make the reckless choice to abandon his law practice and focus on his ill-defined finance schemes to garner big money, a so-called killing, so he could pay off his debt and we could live comfortably once again. I felt guilty for not knowing how bad his addiction had become. On the other hand, maybe this all needed to happen exactly as it had and we were exactly where we were supposed to be at exactly the right time.

I continued going to Al-Anon and DA meetings, injecting myself with spiritual sustenance from the twelve steps, participants' shares, and the sacredness of the rooms. People, with such broken lives, shared an endless depth of honesty and I felt inspired by their willingness to bare their pain. The American economy, in tatters, spared few and there was no shortage of men and women in truly tragic circumstances. Jobs lost, homes foreclosed on, marriages shattered, self-respect washed away like dishwater. I felt close to God in the rooms where my resentments faded and gratitude grew. I started going to a Buddhist center to listen to Dharma talks and learn about noticing, noticing, noticing, along with detachment and compassion.

✦

My jaw clenched tight and hot anger rose in my chest. *All these people here to see "loved ones."* Maybe they don't deserve us. Matthew, who had just arrived home from California for the holidays, and I were waiting inside the visitors' trailer, the first stop on our way to the men's jail at Nassau County Correctional. We were waiting for our number, 163-A, to be called. I felt sad for my son—that he would have to see his dad behind bars after having witnessed his father's DUI arrest four years earlier. But I sensed no enmity on Matthew's part. In fact, he lightened the situation, "No, we have to hum dad's new marching tune, the one he made up: Bars and Stripes Forever…"

We looked at each other, shook our heads, and chuckled. "Who else but your crazy father would make up a song like that?" I asked, trying to lighten our pain.

I had visited prison before when I accompanied Josh to Fort Dix, in southern New Jersey, to see his Filipino client, incarcerated in the federal penitentiary. I was afraid at the time—the barbed wire surrounding the facility looked menacing, and our admittance—as attorney and assistant—appeared to rest on the whim of a beefy, no-nonsense corrections officer who made us wait after we'd been metal-detected and everyone else had gone in. But when Josh and I drove away, at the end of the day, past the sentry booth, the experience was far behind. This night was different. I was no outsider—this was my own reality show.

The interior of the trailer had cocoa-tan paneling and it was warm and crowded. Toddlers in pastel-colored, stiff snowsuits wiggled from mothers' arms, shrieking at not being allowed to run free. It was noisy and the smell of cigarettes and lipstick hung in the air. Most of the people waiting were black and Hispanic. In the corner was an elderly white couple sitting close together, expressionless. I assumed they were visiting a son and since Nassau Correctional was the county jail, the first stop, whatever trouble he was in must've just occurred.

The previous evening Matthew and I had been at the Metropolitan Opera seeing *La Faniculla,* and tonight we were waiting to enter the gates of the county jail. Despite my irritation at having to spend even a minute of the holidays in a prison trailer, I was looking forward to seeing Josh. It had been ten days since I last saw him in the courtroom, and wanted to make sure he was okay.

I glanced up at the sign that stated: *All areas of this correctional facility and all persons entering this facility are subject to search by trained dogs and correction center personnel.* Next to it another sign read: *No cell phones permitted in building. No gum chewing.*

After an hour, the Sheriff Department officer, a wide man wearing a gray Smokey Bear hat with a yellow band, called our number. He sat behind a grated window with a slot for passing IDs and other papers. He was chatty, like a game show MC, announcing things like, "it won't be long now folks," when someone asked about the wait. Good job satisfaction, apparently, or maybe all this magnanimity was due to the holiday season.

I appreciated Smokey Bear's banter, however, and when he called our number, he looked at me and asked if it was my first time visiting. I wondered if he asked that because of my appearance, that of a well-dressed suburban woman, or if he asked that of everyone. I wanted to say, "You know, I don't belong here" because I longed for a crumb of acknowledgement, some understanding from the authorities that the prison trailer was not my usual hangout. Perhaps I was looking for exoneration, too. Later, I thought that feeling I am somehow different and not wanting to join the prison family is probably what everyone in this circumstance thinks. I would soon see I would be treated no differently than any other inmate's kin.

A corrections officer escorted a group of us through a chain-link fence area to the main building nearby where we then waited on another line in the lobby before advancing to the admittance windows. The jail was holding a toy drive in the lobby with cartons filled with wrapped gifts.

When we reached the window, I noticed more friendliness, as I heard a corrections officer asking kids their names, ages, and what they wanted from Santa Claus. I stiffened, however, when one of the officers, with a loud gravelly voice, got stern: "Look, we could do this the hard way or the easy way," when people didn't line up properly.

The corrections officer at our window asked our relationship to the inmate, then took our drivers' licenses. He asked Matthew where he lived in California and what he did there. When Matthew told him he was a recording engineer the officer went on and on about his own aspiring music career. He then stamped our hands and gave me a key for the locker to stash everything but the clothes we were wearing. I looked around and saw people familiar with the procedure. I felt nervous about doing something wrong, though I couldn't imagine what. Like the courtroom, the atmosphere was designed to intimidate, and it worked. My perfectionism was working overtime: I was gunning for best inmate visitor of the year.

We stashed everything quickly into the metal locker and were told we could use the restroom outside the next vestibule. As I got into the stall, I realized I was wearing my watch so dashed out, heart beating, to place it in the locker and re-fasten the elastic keyholder around my wrist.

Matthew and I then entered the dimly lit detection area where we were instructed by a corrections officer in a dark booth to take off our shoes and walk through a scanner. They gave us our shoes on the other side and we waited again as we stood before what looked to me a set of French doors with small window panes painted steel blue. When I looked through the doors I saw rows of long tables with plexiglass between prisoners and visitors. I got to see who from the waiting room was paired with whom.

We gained entry into a huge, sparse, high-ceilinged visiting area with cinder-block walls. Again that fluorescent lighting. Men of all ages, sizes, and colors were wearing the same short-sleeve orange, creamsicle color jump suit. A corrections officer, "COs" as they became known to me, directed us to two empty seats in a numbered section. The din of voices rose high as if we were in an old-fashioned dining automat.

Matthew and I waited what felt like a long time, but without a watch I couldn't tell exactly, both of us staring at the activity around us. I was incredulous we were there and with thoughts like "this is what life has become" seeping in, my eyes welled up. Matthew patted my back lightly. "It's okay, Mom."

We stared at the prisoner entry area, as inmates trickled through, coming and going. We could see a line of men waiting to enter.

"I see a bald head reflected," Matthew said. "See 'im?"

No, I didn't have twenty-three-year-old eyesight.

But then Josh emerged with a sprightly walk, a big smile, and a graying, stubbly beard. We hugged hard over the partition. There didn't seem to be any restriction on hugs and I wondered if it was always like this or just because of the holiday. In fact, I was surprised to see a Hispanic girl of about four years old with long, shiny hair and a flouncy dress sitting on the other side of the partition with her prisoner dad.

I sized Josh up. He'd lost weight but his eyes were warm and hopeful. No sign of the eczema that had rested on his eyelids.

"I haven't seen you this happy in five years!" I said.

He grinned.

"Getting the best sleep of my life."

My mouth opened in disbelief. He was supposed to be getting punished.

He must've picked up on my expression because he suddenly became withdrawn.

"I wasn't sure how to come out here," he confessed. "Whether I should look depressed or happy, not too happy though. Didn't want to piss you off."

He was no longer carrying the secret of his crime. He was facing his punishment head on and his peace of mind showed. It warmed me to see him relaxed but I had to admit to some jealousy. I wanted that serenity too.

In later visits, Matthew, Adam, and I became familiar with procedures at the county jail and learned things such as not to arrive too late in the visiting hours because you may not get in or to have Josh's DIN number at hand for quick processing.

During these visits, Josh told us about Milton, his bunkmate who gave him a contraband hamburger and fries and how he learned the phrase "three hots and a cot." He described the "business deals" inmates spoke about, "Yeah, one guy wants to start a 'poco loco hot dog stand' and stick little paper umbrellas in the hot dogs."

Matthew and I looked at each other.

"These young guys all have mad cars and hot bitches waiting for them but in the meantime they're borrowing a teaspoon of coffee from me," he said.

"Glad to see you're making friends," I said.

He spoke with affection of Red, a redheaded black inmate who he introduced us to as Red walked by after finishing a visit. Apparently, Josh was popular because he nodded or waved to a lot of orange jump-suited guys. He told us about how when playing ping pong one of his new friends said, "Hey Pop, you must've been pretty good back in the day."

"Ping pong? Wait a minute. I love ping pong." I said. Josh stopped talking about activities like ping pong, the Family Feud game, and instead grew animated describing how he learned to light cigarettes with a battery and steel wool, getting it to create a spark.

"Great new skills," I piped in.

Josh had always been good at reading his surroundings. If we had been dining at a posh restaurant he would watch and describe the pecking order of the staff to me: "You see, he's the captain and those guys over there are the head waiters…" I usually didn't care much about the hierarchy of wait staff but was impressed at his ability to get the lay of the land quickly. Those skills would hold him in good stead here.

He told us about running in the courtyard, estimating his distance as a mile, and how he'd gotten a reputation quickly as a lawyer since he still, at this moment, held his license.

"I really don't want to be giving any legal advice so I told 'em the office is closed, especially on Christmas," he said.

I was now in "prison world," a joke I shared with friends comparing my new milieu to people with new dogs, who say they were in "dog world." If you were a new dog owner, you noticed other dogs and how your dog compared to them. You made friends with neighbors who had dogs, were interested in TV shows or books about dogs. You were quite simply in "dog world." Also true of parents with children in nursery school because they were now in "pre-K world." When we had guinea pigs we were in "guinea pig" world, often slipping into the pet store to look at the baby guinea pigs while ours lazed around in their cages at home.

Now I welcomed myself into "prison world" where I started recognizing the same faces in the visiting trailer. On two occasions, Adam and I ran into friends visiting inmates. One visiting father of a friend of Adam's smacked him playfully in the arm he was so happy to see him. I even reached out to a friend of my sister Laura's whose husband, an ex-attorney, had been in federal prison, to get a sense of what she and her husband had experienced. And I wanted to know what life would be like for Josh once he got shipped to his permanent, medium security, facility. I read articles about wives whose husbands were serving time for white collar crimes. And some months later, a friend of my cousin's contacted me for support when her son was arrested. We were all in "prison world" together, not a club to which you ever want to belong.

Though Josh made light of his new home, I knew it was no field day.

Between 2010 and 2012, seven people had died in Nassau County Correctional, including five suicides and one homicide. A year after Josh served there, a thirty-two-year-old former Marine who'd served in Iraq hanged himself in his cell.

Nassau jail earned the distinction as one of the highest suicide jails in the state. The New York Civil Liberty Union's Nassau chapter received hundreds of complaints from inmates about being deprived of medication, not receiving mental health services, and being mistreated.

It was like Josh to always make a joke and while his minimization of our troubles irked me over the last few years, I realized he was shielding me and the boys with light-hearted stories of prison antics. My respect for him inched upward as I recognized the protection he was offering us in his small way and how he never complained, made any excuse for his criminal behavior, or uttered a word of self-pity.

"Yeah, it's like a sleepover for a bunch of twelve-year-olds," he told us. "After lights out, the COs come in and yell at us, like parents, 'If I have to come in there...'" He made it sound like summer camp.

✦

Journal entry from February 15, 2011:

Yesterday, Valentine's Day hit me hard. I saw a man buying flowers at Petal Pusher in Penn Station and it smarted. Always thought Valentine's Day was a trumped-up holiday but that was because I had someone to celebrate with. No one buying me flowers this year. Later, I picked the car up from the service station and drove home, tears spilling. It's the loss of Josh telling me, "it's all going to be okay." The comfort.

The next day, after spending two months at Nassau County jail, Josh moved to Ulster Correctional Facility in Napanoch, New York, about a two-hour drive from New York City. This was a stop-over between the county jail and a permanent facility, still to be determined.

I learned, and Josh learned all too well, that confinement meant not only counting time but being at the mercy of changes, moves, and procedures that were never communicated by prison staff. Josh could be shipped out at a moment's notice and if you're anxious to get to your next destination that was welcome, but the change could also happen when you were settled in, with a routine, a rapport, and friends. "It was hard leaving Nassau," he wrote me from Ulster. "It's funny how quickly you can make friends and get comfortable."

Once he got moved, it felt like he was far away, not a fifteen-minute run to the jail as if I were heading to the shopping mall. He was gone and I was truly on my own living in my sister's house. The loss of the life I had known felt even more real, bone-deep, particularly when he was officially disbarred from the New York State roll of attorneys, an event captured in the *New York Law Journal*.

Picking up his personal effects from Nassau County jail gave me pause as well. I tramped over there on a cold, rainy day, my umbrella leaving a puddle on the cement floor as I waited near the women's jail. I had carefully followed prison procedures of day, time, and ID requirements for retrieval of belongings. Inside the carton—which I stared at as I placed the box in the trunk of the car—were his shoes, hooded jacket he had bought at Jones Beach, and driver's license.

But when Josh moved to Ulster state facility, something shifted in me. The surrender to the pain gave way to an acceptance that what had happened had happened. There would be only moving forward, no retrieval of the past, and no certainty of the future. I would simply have to live within the ambiguity—about my marriage and the person I now had become after this traumatic event.

I had a session with Erica and recognized that when I was a girl, being the youngest in the family, I had always looked to my sisters and cousins to take me places. Whether they were going to a boyfriend's house, ice skating with their friends, or, when I was older, to hear their friends' rock band, I waited for their decisions to invite or dismiss me. But I never devised a plan to get there myself, and as I matured my plans were always made through other people. Al-Anon was tailor-made for me, a co-dependent, and I had learned so much. But now it was time to create my own path and Josh's imprisonment, in an unexpected way, gave me the space to break free.

One Saturday morning I paced in the kitchen of my sister's house, hanging around the wall phone, waiting for it to ring and hear the now-familiar voice on the other end announcing, "You have a call from a state correctional facility. Will you accept the charges?" I had a speech prepared. I was anxious to tell Josh about an image I'd had: we'd been in an empty well and how we had dragged each other down but I was climbing out, walking the rungs of the ladder step by step to the air and how I could either shake him off my leg or reach down and give him my hand and that's what I wanted to do.

When we spoke, however, he was very distracted. I heard background talking on his end and only a few minutes into the call he said he had to go because of the "count." I wasn't sure what the count was but I pictured it like a military call-to with everyone standing at attention at the foot of their bunks.

"No, you can't go. You need to listen to me," I said.

"Really. I gotta go. It's the count."

"Stop blowing me off! You just don't wanna listen!" I insisted.

"I promise. I'll call you back."

"No, please hear me."

"I'm in prison!" he screamed.

We got off the phone and he did call me back later that day but I further realized that I didn't need to explain to him anymore my intentions. I needed to trust myself and let my actions do the talking.

Bare, arthritic trees, cottonball clouds, and shiny curlicues of barbed wire against a clear, blue sky greeted Adam and me at the entrance to Watertown Correctional, the medium security facility, Josh's new home. It was nearly April and remnants of snow blanketed the rural landscape, a stone's throw from the Canadian border. The prison was a six-hour drive from Long Island and we did the trip in two days to be able to make the ten a.m. visiting hour, spend time with Josh, and get home before midnight. We'd spent the previous evening staying with a friend, a graduate student at Syracuse University.

Adam and I stashed our cell phones, watches, jewelry, and jackets in the car trunk: items we knew we couldn't bring into the prison. A grandmotherly woman, sitting at the gray, metal desk, looked up from reading her *Redbook* to ask for Josh's DIN number and our IDs. I waited anxiously for her to return because visitor entry could be unpredictable—an illness or shortage of COs or any number of circumstances could preclude the visit and we'd driven so far to get there. Little café curtains decorated the windows and Mega Blocks, which some child hadn't cleaned up, were strewn about. She returned and directed us to the door that led to an area with metal bars that opened and closed with a clang as we passed through the outside gate. Each chain-linked outdoor section we passed through, topped with a ceiling of barbed wire, opened and shut with a buzzer that told us to proceed. No people, just the chilling sound.

We finally entered the entry station and stood before an imposing, massive desk where a corrections officer sat, peered down, and took our information. Unlike at Nassau Correctional, there were no other visitors. Just me, Adam, and the COs. As the New York State Department of Corrections family guide says: *If you are a family member or friend of a person incarcerated in a **state prison**, your life has changed in many ways.*

I thought we'd be escorted in but we had to wait and when the CO returned he asked that Adam step into an adjoining room for a body scan. Having no idea what that meant, Adam and I nodded automatic yeses and they showed him in. I waited, heart pounding, imagining a strip search, glancing at the sign that warned that anyone caught with drugs on their person would be arrested. I didn't think Adam would have any contraband, but who knew? As Adam walked out seemingly undisturbed, the CO asked that I go into another small dressing room and remove my bra before going through the metal detector.

Josh was waiting for us at a bridge table as we entered. Sun sliced through the room. He had traded in the orange jumpsuit for a navy blue shirt and pants, his name and DIN number on the breast pocket near his heart.

"Hey, my baby's mama! How ya doin,' shorty?"

He was thrilled to see us and hugged us both, facing—and then sitting in one direction only—towards the three COs sitting at a high desk at the other side of the room. He had shaved the unkempt beard he'd worn in Nassau Correctional. He looked younger, better groomed, and not so skinny.

He told us about getting into the Alcohol Substance Abuse Treatment classes, which he was happy about, and leading the twelve-step programs—Narcotics Anonymous and Alcoholics Anonymous. I sensed his frustration that most prisoners didn't take their recovery seriously.

"I'm the only one guilty here!" he stated. "Everyone else, they didn't do anything."

Josh talked about his new friends, Harry and Bam-Bam, and whispered about the rudeness of the commissary manager telling us how he couldn't use the shower shoes his brother had sent because they were two-tone, black and brown. He pointed to the track outside telling us its distance—a third of a mile around—and how he used it to run even in the harshest weather.

"Why don't you wear a hat, stupid?" one of the COs had asked him when he was on the track. I later said to Adam, "if that's the worst thing that's happened, that a CO called him stupid, that's not too bad." Of course, I knew Josh wasn't telling us everything.

I saw families taking photos in front of a faux cityscape and wanted to take one but had to figure out how. Then I saw someone handing a man at a desk wooden blocks and realized you had to purchase them. I asked a woman visitor for change from her little, clear plastic case, like a make-up bag, where she had dollar bills. She must've been a regular because she was prepared with dollars. She wasn't too friendly but gave me the change without making eye contact. I inserted the dollar into an old cigarette machine, which dispensed small wooden kindergarten blocks, prison currency. I reserved a spot for picture taking and when it was our turn, the photographer-prisoner took a fine Polaroid family portrait.

In a letter, Josh reminded me of a story I'd told him from a book called *Everyday Zen* by Charlotte Joko Beck: You're in a rowboat on the ocean. You're alone. You see another boat coming toward you. At first you're elated, wishing for company. But as the boat gets closer, it looks like it's heading right towards you. It gets closer and closer, ready to crash into you. You scream and wave at it, getting angry as it gets closer. It brushes by you and keeps going. You look inside as it goes by and see there's no one in the rowboat.

There's never anyone in the rowboat. There's never anyone else to rescue us, make us angry, take away our joy. There's never anyone in the rowboat. It's always only about ourselves.

That spring, I drove to Chicago solo, a fifteen-hour drive, to attend a four-week writing residency. I brought almonds, bottles of water, books on CD, my GPS, and at mid-point I stayed with lovely friends of a friend who put me up in their home in Aurora, Ohio. I listened and sang Paul Simon's "You're the One, who Broke my Heart," to Phoenix's "Alphabetical." And on the return trip, when I had a tire blow out, doing sixty-five on Route 80 West, I pulled the car onto the shoulder and called AAA. The car repair involved driving to DuBois, Pennsylvania, to a Meineke, then discovering a broken rim, and spending the night in a hotel while the rim was shipped overnight. The next day, the mechanic inserted the rim onto the tire and I drove home comfortably. I thanked God to be alive and grateful to be on the road to a full recovery.

In 2011, Josh was released from prison and into the custody of his brother days before Thanksgiving, almost a year after they had handcuffed and led him through the gated door at Nassau Criminal Court. Adam and I visited him and took a long, meandering walk around the lake. It was a perfect autumn day, with a touch of spring in it.

By living at my sister's house, I kept Adam in college, paying most of his tuition out of pocket. I had divested the $483,000 sub-prime mortgage, the $40,000 Bank of America credit line, the $12,000 Hilton time share balance, and was close to paying off a $1,500 student loan of Matthew's and assorted bills. I hadn't touched my retirement savings, borrowed a cent from anyone, and apart from the Bank of America credit line, never paid a bill late.

Nearing bankruptcy, I learned to keep the most important thing—love—in the vault.

ABOUT THE AUTHOR

JANET LOMBARDI has written for salon.com, newsweek.com, *Newsday*, the *Daily News*, *Newsday's Parents & Children*, and many other publications. She has been featured as a "money matters" speaker on radio, and been interviewed for money blogs and print articles. Janet lives in Rockville Centre, New York, and is the mother of two grown sons.

Bankruptcy: A Love Story is her first book.

Printed in the USA
CPSIA information can be obtained
at www.ICGtesting.com
JSHW011138150923
48465JS00014B/210